Sustainable Place

FOR JONATHAN AND EMMA

Christine Phillips

Sustainable Place

A Place of Sustainable Development

Published in Great Britain in 2003 by
WILEY-ACADEMY
a division of
John Wiley & Sons Ltd, The Atrium, Southern Gate, Chichester,
West Sussex PO19 8SQ, England

Telephone   (+44) 1243 779777

Other Wiley Editorial Offices

John Wiley & Sons Inc., 111 River Street, Hoboken, NJ 07030, USA

Jossey-Bass, 989 Market Street, San Francisco, CA 94103-1741, USA

Wiley-VCH Verlag GmbH, Boschstr. 12, D-69469 Weinheim, Germany

John Wiley & Sons Australia Ltd, 33 Park Road, Milton, Queensland 4064, Australia

John Wiley & Sons (Asia) Pte Ltd, 2 Clementi Loop #02-01, Jin Xing Distripark,
Singapore 129809

John Wiley & Sons Canada Ltd, 22 Worcester Road, Etobicoke, Ontario, Canada
M9W 1L1

ISBN 0470847913

Cover: *Sustainable Place* by Christine Phillips (detail)

Designed and typeset by Florence Production Ltd, Stoodleigh, Devon

Printed and bound in Great Britain by TJ International Ltd, Padstow, Cornwall

This book is printed on acid-free paper responsibly manufactured from sustainable
forestry, in which at least three trees are planted for each one used for paper
production.

Contents

Preface

Given the growing imperative for sustainable development, *Sustainable Place* questions our assessment and evaluation of place and reviews the development of related aesthetic ideas; it defines an approach to aesthetic theory and practice that is relevant to sustainable design today.

'Sustainability' became a mantra after the Habitat I conference in Rio de Janeiro in 1992, but for many people the word still eludes definition. Its timely significance and common usage assume a common understanding dependent upon intuition rather than definition. The question frequently asked is 'What do you mean by sustainability?', and not 'What is sustainability?' In effect Habitat I, with its apparent universal agreement on the need for 'sustainable development', masked an ensuing fray over a definition of the concept. In 1987 the publication of the UN-sponsored Brundtland Commission report *Our Common Future* had defined the term 'sustainable development' as 'development which meets the needs of the present without sacrificing the ability of the future to meet its needs'. While this had the advantage of being sufficiently broad to allow for a wide consensus between nations, over time its all-encompassing character has led to vagueness about the concept of 'sustainable development', rendering it virtually ineffectual as its meaning grew to include almost everything. We talk of social sustainability, cultural sustainability, sustainable construction, sustainable materials and so on. However, Habitat I succeeded in establishing an empowering vision of man as both reflected and evoked by his activities in relation not only to his own environment, but to that of the natural world on a global scale.

The arguments expressed in this book particularly relate to issues influencing design strategies that may be used within the physical environment to achieve sustainable development. More specifically, they are about the intervention of the design disciplines of landscape architecture, architecture and master-planning.

Sustainability is the fundamental issue governing our relationship with the planet on which we live. The consumption of the earth's resources beyond its capacity of renewal is seen as the instigation of current crises in energy, economic theory, depletion of biodiversity and human-itarian considerations such as social deprivation. This consumption, related to industrialisation and urbanisation, has had such an impact that it may no longer be possible to maintain a balance for the a global ecosystem. The emerging evidence of climate change suggests that our energy use has tipped the balance detrimentally and that it may prove impossible to regain this balance; therefore, we may merely be able to prolong a certain qualitative existence even if future energy use becomes a benign consideration. Building development constitutes the single largest energy-consuming human requirement. Landscape – or more specifically areas of the planet, such as forests, oceans etc, where the ecosystem is able to work naturally – acts as a 'sink' for the emissions from this energy use, preventing them from destroying the layers of the stratosphere that give a constancy to the planet's climate. Thus the carbon dioxide and other harmful pollutants that are a consequence of all building development are absorbed and purified by landscape. This relationship is threatened, giving rise to our concern for sustainable development. This book therefore advocates that an assessment of place dependent upon the relationship of landscape, architecture and master-planning is essential to sustainable development. There is every reason to take stock and find ways not only of lessening energy use in the built environment through re-evaluation of design strategies for settlements, and passive and low-energy architecture, but also of equating the cost of all development with our capital assets in landscape.

In practice the set of principles that serve as a basis for making judgements and decisions regarding sustainable development are by no means clearly defined mandates. As may be deduced from the Bruntland definition of 'sustainable development' the concept is, like other important concepts – humanitarianism, equity and democracy – dialectical rather than analytical. This means that conflict over what is and what is not sustainable development is resolved through debate or discussion without necessarily disproving a particular theory. The conflicts often concern issues that involve the overlap of many disciplines. The best advice is to develop a philosophical and inquiring approach, starting with the whole and working through into the detail. Ponder these two quotations:

'The wisdom of the universe has but one science, the science of the whole and man's place in it.' (Tolstoy)

'Out of necessity we have to divide the world into parts and wholes, but there is no necessity in the way we do that.' (Bateson 1980)

In detail, any one indicator for sustainability is interdependent with, and subject to variation according to the qualities of, other indicators. This logic may seem contradictory to the bureaucratic mind. Phrases such as 'sustainable materials' are misleading: they imply that there is a list of materials and that only those materials on that list are sustainable. In reality a common-sense approach is called for. Purposeful development looks towards materials which will have passive or low-energy properties, either embodied or operational. Within this context a debate takes place. Some will say the right materials are those that occur naturally within a locality because they have little embodied energy, energy in transportation is low and they are likely to have an aesthetic harmony with their place. Others may say that to keep using natural materials for building inevitably depletes finite natural resources and that it is therefore justifiable to develop and use new materials although they may have a high embodied energy, and that with this may come architecture with minimal operational energy and the possibility of new and exciting forms expressive of our age.

From the above it is apparent that sustainability is a problem to be addressed by all who live on the planet, and that it demands a degree of selflessness if the earth is to be sustained for future generations. In response to this, issues of development are being redefined. This redefinition may only be achieved if there are ways of creating consensus, making decisions and monitoring effects at universal levels. At present the problem facing the developed world is how to maintain reasonable consumption and living standards while reducing carbon dioxide emissions. The developing nations need to meet basic needs, transcend conditions of marginality and improve levels of economic sustenance without generating the damaging pollution prevalent in industrial societies. United Nations conferences such as those on climate change (the Kyoto Treaty) have the potential to create a global consensus on the intent to reduce energy emissions. Action at local level by people concerned about the quality of life in their particular locality or place will obviously be vital to this process.

Global is not to be confused with globalisation, which is arguably a force counterproductive to the aims of sustainability (see Chapter Two). *Sustainable Place* does not advocate that the cultural identity of localities or nations, expressed through particular styles, should be superseded by a global corporate identity. In effect, the iconic presence of the multinational store within a locality may not only represent a usurpation of local cultural identity architecturally; it may also symbolise an overreliance on external dependents economically and a threat to the potential of that place to direct its own sustainable development. Aesthetics is the embodiment of a society's perception of what is beautiful, pleasing or benign and we give a physical identity to it by the creation of forms within our environment. The need to respond to the threat of environmental disaster is a universal need, but there is reason and potential for localities to express this within the diversification of their own cultures.

Two of the main case-study assessments are what may be termed 'very nice places', the inference being, 'Shouldn't you be concentrating on the city, isn't this where all the problems are?' Sustainability is of concern to all, whether we live in cities, towns or rural areas. Most would agree that Ludlow and San Gimignano epitomise both longevity and quality in settlement forms that are worthy of sustainment. Furthermore, the scale of urban configuration and its symbiotic relationship with landscape, albeit an extreme simplification of a large city and its relationship with natural landform, enable analysis that leads to a prototype form of assessment of sustainable development. The case studies, San Gimignano in Italy and Ludlow in England, are 10° latitude apart. Both are walled, medieval, hilltop towns with defined geographical boundaries and are surrounded by rural hinterlands. They allow the investigation of sustainable development where comprehensive modern redevelopment has not obliterated former historical stratification, and the evaluation of development that occurred without the high energy input associated with modern cities. Both have distinct regional characters not as yet taken subsumed under global anonymity. They are large enough to represent the complexities of urbanism yet essentially separated from a conglomeration of urban units with confused boundaries and functions, as may have been the case with a large city. Both places have traditional town kernels which have enjoyed constancy of site over a long time span; and receive sustenance from a wider rural locality and wider external situation.

The historicity of these two case studies should not be ignored for it exemplifies the inclusive and incremental processes in the development of place, of which the need for sustainability is the latest. The hypothesis is that in a place the quality and condition of landscape and architecture are indicative of the state of sustainability – humanity's coming to terms with, and responding to, the physical conditions, psychological and functional needs, cultural identity and institutional requirements in a particular environment. San Gimignano and Ludlow have been analysed using a wide-ranging set of sustainability indicators, by conducting detailed environmental, socioeconomic and spatial assessments. The whole gives an understanding of sustainability issues integrated with landscape, architecture and master-planning. Awareness of a design vocabulary for sustainable development is seen to emerge out of a purposeful interaction with place. In the plan and configuration of a place we are able to see the effects of design strategies devised to address such issues as land tenure, population changes, changes in economic activity and regulation of external dependencies as well as design methodologies of building with the specific microclimate and particular relief and geomorphology of the location. Through an understanding of the inclusive and incremental nature of these two simple structures, Ludlow and San Gimignano, we have, for example, some understanding of design strategies that save energy, whether these are physical or related to policy or behavioural patterns.

However, the problem of sustainability is arguably a causal effect of the processes of urbanisation and industrialisation over the last century. The form and structure of the city pose a most urgent and pressing problem of sustainability. The city is an extremely complex structure that has come into existence not through a once-for-all but through a process of growth that has met the needs of changing generations. At any one point in time city development is a flux of systemic interactions between the very different kinds of phenomena that make up urban life. A completely new city developed on a virgin site would be Utopia. Design strategies in response to the need for sustainable development are, however, being given material form in urban settings and these are reviewed together with a discussion of their contribution to aesthetics.

Paradoxically, while sustainability is seen as a problem created by the overconcentration of people living in cities, which is estimated to increase to three-quarters of the world's population by 2025, the problem is likely to be exacerbated by an overconcentration on the details of urban development to the neglect of natural landscape. *All built development* threatens the world's ecological balance and the impact of development has to be balanced, locally, nationally or globally, with natural resources, landscape and natural processes. Whereas urgency exists in the addressing of details such as greenhouse-gas emissions, greening, energy efficiency, urban regeneration, qualitative social housing, high-density high rises, etc, the first questions to be asked must be: Is this development absolutely necessary? Can its impact be accommodated by the natural world? And: How is this development related to an aesthetic of sustainability?

This book addresses the concept of sustainable place. The main themes throughout are: clarification of the term sustainable development; the interconnectedness of seemingly paradoxical issues – global-local, quantitative-qualitative and objective-subjective; and an aware-ness of the elements that could potentially form an aesthetic for sustainability. The introduction singles out climate change as the impetus for a shift in human awareness. Chapters One to Three use extensive, contemporary references to give a comprehensive current background to the interest in sustainability; and this enables a prototype framework for assessing sustain-able development for place to be posited in Chapter Four. This framework identifies the distinctive constituent features of place associated with man's interaction with landscape, archi-tecture and master-planning, and investigates and assesses their potential sustainability. This process includes assessing a locality's energy and environmental capabilities for sustainable development bearing in mind its social, economic, political and cultural prerequisites. It is a framework that may be applied to any place and which bears a direct relationship to national and international concerns for sustainable development.

In Chapters Five and Six the framework is applied to San Gimignano and Ludlow. If passionate urbanists can step aside from the problems of the 21st-century city environment they will find that in the incremental and inclusive development of these places there are parallels to be drawn with, and solutions to be found for, developmental issues and human need in settlements of all sizes, including megacities.

An awareness of aesthetics runs throughout the book. However, Chapter Seven specifically focuses on an exploration of potential aesthetic sources pertinent to sustainability. The question of aesthetics is inevitably of great significance to all who work in a design-related capacity, whose capabilities are directed towards bringing pleasure and quality of existence to the inhabitants of places through new development. Whereas this chapter looks to the more commonly appreciated design elements within environments, Chapter Eight appraises three contemporary master-planning projects in the light of sustainable development issues.

The conclusion to the book takes the form of an evaluation of the questions that it raises. In particular it asks how, if at all, the inquiry has clarified understanding of sustainability.

Introduction

What are the distinctive features of 'sustainable place'? Can the different constituents of these features be identified to form a framework of assessment? Is it possible to identify an emerging aesthetic relevant to sustainable design?

The term 'paradigm shift' used by the American historian of science Thomas Kuln (1962) seems to epitomise the state of knowledge and philosophy at the turn of the 20th century. Conceptual frameworks within which scientific or art theories have been constructed, although consistent within themselves, now need to be completely revised as evidence that challenges the factual accuracy of some of their aspects comes to light. This is reflected in the present state of architecture. The Japanese architect Kisho Kurokawa likens the present to 'The beginning of a major groundswell, of significant and wide-ranging changes in overall structure affecting all fields and areas world-wide. In such times, the only way to deduce the future is to search out overall changes in an integrated manner, transcending the process of modernisation. No amount of specialised understanding or knowledge in any individual field is of particular use in this endeavour. One must adroitly peruse all fields of endeavour, both vertically and horizontally, to discern the subtle signs of future orientation' (Kurokawa 1997a).

Is this sustainable development? This is a question that is being asked of activity in all fields from politics and economics to culture and technology, and not least within the professions of landscape, architecture and master-planning.

A most powerful reason for this shift in human attitude on a global scale is the emerging evidence of climate change. Global warming has given a new perspective on the permanence of landform and heightened consciousness of the ephemeral nature of life on earth. To what extent this warming is a natural part of the world's climate cycle and to what extent it may be attributed to human activity, or whether human activity can correct or control its effects, is equivocal. Common consensus is that our use of fossil fuels contributes to warming. In 1995 the Intergovernmental Panel on Climate Change (IPCC 1995), sponsored by the United Nations, concluded that 'The balance of evidence suggests that there is a discernible human influence on global climate.' This influence is not yet quantifiable. Climate change is a highly charged field of modern inquiry. Even with the most advanced computer simulations not enough is known about its natural cyclic effect. Human activity releases approximately 7 billion metric tons of carbon (in the form of CO_2) into the atmosphere every year, yet only half of this remains in the air. Oceans and terrestrial and marine plants act as a vast 'sink' for carbon dioxide. If noxious emissions from fossil fuels stopped immediately this would not prevent global warming, and it is not known whether the 'sinks' for carbon dioxide would over time correct human damage. However, it may be assumed that the rapidity of global warming would be lessened and the quality of the earth's environment would improve.

Critical issues are the magnitude and speed of climate change and man's impact on this change. Because there has been a relatively stable period of 10,000 years since the last glacial age we assume that alterations in climate are likely to be gradual enough for us to be able to adapt. However, there is evidence to suggest climate change may occur radically, in the span of decades or even years. The global average surface-air temperature has risen half a degree Centigrade since the late 1800s and 13 of the warmest years of the 20th century have occurred since 1980 (IPCC 1995). This would seem to imply that there is a connection between global warming and the impact of industrialisation. There have also been changes in world precipitation throughout the century. A slight change in physical conditions is able to affect weather patterns, sometimes with devastating consequences. One of the most feared of these changes is an abrupt collapse in what is known as the Atlantic 'conveyor belt' system that brings warm water north from the Equator, keeping the Atlantic coast of Europe several degrees warmer than it would otherwise be. However, other physical changes are already apparent. Mali in the Tuareg had a landscape and rainfall that until 25 years ago could sustain agriculture. The rains stopped in the 1970s and Mali is becoming an arid area unable to sustain human settlement. The periodicity and magnitude of natural occurrences such as El Niño have increased. Loss of precipitation, and consequently cooling, over the interiors of large landmasses poses the likelihood of more frequent 'killer' heat waves with temperature highs of above 120°F for cities such as Chicago.

That natural events such as volcanic eruptions have an effect on global temperature has been known for some time. In 1883 Krakatoa in the Indonesian islands caused emissions of volcanic ash and debris which, taken into the higher stratosphere, had a blanket effect upon solar radiation thereby causing the global cooling and frosts of 1895. A similar occurrence with the eruption of Mount Pinatubo in the Philippines in 1991 caused a global drop in temperature that lasted two years. The effects of human activity upon climate may be seen in a more localised way, in 'heat islands' or pollution domes above large cities. Here pollution forms a canopy above the city and creates the 'greenhouse' effect: solar radiation can get through but is then trapped and causes temperature highs over, around and within the city.

Inquiry into climate change is complex and integrated, and quantitative data for cause and effect are not yet available. On this equivocal basis, and possibly because of the uncertainty, we are developing a growing concern for environment and energy use while essential questions remain unanswered about the how, why and periodicity of climate change; how much is natural and how much is the impact of human activity? The permanence of climate-orientated problems must remain speculative.

Nevertheless, inquiry into the 'heat island' effect has found that the microclimate of the city is showing a direct relationship to human occupancy and activity, and building conurbations. In North America such correlation shows an estimated rural-urban temperature difference of from 2.5°K for a town of 1000 population to 12°K for a city of 1,000,000 (Barry & Chorley 1992). By comparison, European cities showed smaller differences in temperature. This could be a consequence of the master-plan types of the urban conurbation in these areas as most European cities have lower buildings and wider streets; or it may reflect attitudes and behaviour which have resulted in lower energy consumption per capita in these cities; or both.

Physical intervention in the city environment, through good interconnected design strategies, landscape, architecture and master-planning, may be able to influence the uncomfortable conditions of high urban temperatures. The following considerations (Yannas 1998) suggest how a beneficial change may be brought about in the microclimate of the city.

1. Built form: density and type to influence airflow, view of the sun and sky, and exposed surface area.
2. Street canyon: width-to-height ratio and orientation to influence warming up and cooling processes, thermal and visual comfort conditions, and pollution dispersal.
3. Building design: to influence building heat gains and losses, albedo and thermal capacity of external surfaces, use of transitional spaces.
4. Urban materials and surface finishes: to influence absorption, heat storage and emissivity.
5. Vegetation and evapotranspiration and evaporative cooling processes on building surfaces and/or on open spaces.
6. Traffic: reduction, diversion, rerouting to reduce air and noise pollution, and heat discharges.

This positive and holistic approach to correcting problems within the urban environment, plus the agreement of the industrialised nations to cut emissions of 'greenhouse gases' at the 1997 climate change conference in Kyoto, Japan, could mean that cities have considerably different microclimates in 20 years. However, given the equivocal nature of climate change, designers may approach the above with some uncertainty. Should we design for the present conditions? Should we design for conditions that are likely to occur? Can we design more adaptable buildings to accommodate change? While we may adopt a positive approach to design, which has been fully informed by climate, this indicator alone may be insufficient to assess the capabilities of a place to sustain development.

In assessing these capabilities we need to be informed by knowledge from many fields. Accurate though they may be, quantitative data that exclusively represent the interests of only one body may lead to misinformed design solutions. This suggests that any framework of assessment for sustainable place has to be flexible to accommodate changes in knowledge and the integration of that knowledge. The indicators used to ascertain sustainability must act as interdependent variables, able to identify varying stages of development. We need to identify the growth of sustainable development versus sustainability, which may mean prolonging life lived at a subsistence level.

The following chapters question our assessment process and evaluation of place given the need for sustainable development, and review the development of aesthetic ideas, as they arise in text and visually, to define an approach to aesthetic theory and practice that is relevant to sustainable design today. This is a three-stage process: defining the need for sustainable development and identifying the indicators in relation to this need; building a framework that can accommodate interconnectedness of issues, global-local, quantitative-qualitative, objective-subjective, which may be used to assess sustainable development; and simultaneously maintaining an awareness throughout of the potential elements of an aesthetic for sustainability.

The focus is upon man's interaction with landscape, architecture and master-planning. Landscape in its broadest sense, the physical conditions with which man has to coexist; architecture in its broadest sense, from building to facilitate this coexistence with landscape to architecture with a creative embodiment that reflects man's aspirations. For the purpose of this book 'place' is defined as a portion of the earth's surface, particularly one considered as a unit – an area, region, district or locality with recognised boundaries whether physical, functional, institutional or cultural.

The word 'sustainable' has many late 20th-century connotations that pertain particularly to limiting the extent of the damage caused to the environment by man. The implication is that consciousness of sustainability is leading to a global movement emphasising awareness of environment, energy use and humanitarian concerns, although the term 'sustainism' has not yet been coined. The adjective 'sustainable', as it is used throughout this book, is a derivation of the Latin *sustinere*, brought into the English language in the 13th century, and means capable of being sustained or maintained at a set level. The verb 'to sustain' means to keep going; to withstand, tolerate or endure.

Why the need for sustainable development? The most significant reason for a shift in human consciousness is the emerging evidence of climate change and the human influence upon this change. The two dominant constituents are environment and energy. For the foreseeable future all design solutions in architecture, landscape or master-planning will have an added overlay: to correct malign influences on the environment and create forms that have benign energy properties. The predominant aesthetic will reflect this concern for environment and energy, although its wide-ranging implications may not immediately be apparent or discernible.

Chapter One
Current Background

DIALECTICAL PROCESS

The last quarter of the 20th century and the start of the 21st have been characterised by a growing concern for sustainability as human activity has become life-negating, threatening the quality of life and the existence of life forms. This is a problem of great depth involving the interconnectedness of local and global concerns, subjective and objective responses, quantitative and qualitative assessment. The speed and advancement of knowledge in technical and scientific fields over the last few decades have given rise to optimism and a certain overconfidence in man's ability to provide scientific solutions to the problem of 'sustainable development'. However, these have not evoked sufficient moral or spiritual fervour to induce public acceptance. Lacking this connection, if decisions relating to sustainable development are to be effective they have to be made through debate, discussion, negotiation, and often compromise where the scientific is appropriately balanced by the human attitude.

In landscape and architecture questions are being asked about relationship and integration with the geophysical environment, with the current ecological infrastructure of the world and with the provision of climate control for human comfort without harmful excesses in energy use. Reducing the energy consumption of buildings and associated greenhouse gas emissions has become a priority for all concerned with the design, production and maintenance of buildings, in an attempt to curtail global warming. A responsible recognition of universal concerns, such as the need to preserve the biodiversity of this planet, must have action by people at local levels if it is to have effect. The world's insatiable demand for water, currently doubling every 21 years (Brown 1997), is reflected, or inevitably has to be reflected, in the specific attitude to a particular locality and place.

Sustainability is as much about the local as the universal; with the growing awareness of global issues there is a growing concern for national heritage, and the protection of local identity and the ecological capacity of local and national habitats. This duality poses one of the main problems in evolving any framework for sustainability. While accepting a multidisciplined, multicultural and universally communicative nature for sustainability, there must also be recognition of the individual subjective response to place.

To quote Clifford (1990): 'Much of what we do attempts to place cultural arguments and evidence beside the scientific, technical and economic rationales which so dominate and often debilitate our ways of thinking and doing.' Clifford goes on to explain that as our thoughts gravitate to the cultural arena they return to deep concerns about our ethical relations with nature: 'Our ancient understanding of the land, about symbolism and stories that place us actively but benignly within the world. It is our ordinary actions which will be our salvation or our downfall.' In a later article (1992), Clifford placed architecture strongly within a local context: 'Buildings are part of their place and rely on a subtle tension, not simply in terms of materials, craftsmanship and detail, but in the sense of place, the relationships to other buildings in space and time they crucially need to feed on and foster the things around them, they need to share enough of their meaning with other parts of the place they were made by, in and for, to stay alive.'

Sustainability is not just about conservation, heritage and protection of the environment, it is also about the spiritual vitality people need to feel to create buildings which are exuberant about their time and sensitive to their place; buildings which 'respect what we have learned over hundreds of years but with confidence to experiment and move us forward' (Clifford 1992).

The ultimate failure of sustainability would be at the point when man has so saturated the atmosphere with CO_2 and greenhouse gas emissions, and so adversely affected the climate, that there is no possibility of any renewal through the power of natural balance within the planet's ecosystem. The signs are that he is moving rapidly in this direction.

At present, the question is whether man is working positively towards generating good, life-enabling forces or carrying on with destructive, life-negating processes. He should recognise his unique position. He can cause change through sustainable rather than unsustainable activities. Yet, with some humility, he must accept that he is only a small part of the planet's ecosystem.

> Man did not weave the web of life,
> He is merely a strand in it.
> Whatever he does to the web,
> He does to himself.
> *American Chief Seattle*

Scientists may refute this humility and feel they have the right to be a little dictatorial and confident about man's ability to engineer, control and even create a future which ensures his existence. 'Science has got us into this situation, science will get us out of it.' 'The only way to proceed is through modern technology.' And this has a ring of credibility given recent advances in knowledge. For example, it is possible to predict the timing of natural disasters, such as when a volcano will erupt, thereby enabling the evacuation of settlements in its shadow. This has obvious advantages, in saving human life and reducing the risk factors for a development close to a volcano. However, risk factors in connection with property, health and danger to life tend not to prevent people wanting to return to their place in the aftermath of the eruption. Do they find such dangers stimulating? Is it a case of simply liking the place or that they feel their lives are purposeful in that place? Subjective response to place is a significant force to be recognised alongside the more quantifiable technical or scientific data.

Far from seeing himself as a victim caught within the web of the cosmos man may need to experience these tensions with nature to reaffirm a sense of purpose and worth. John F Haught (1993) expresses a spiritual connection: 'It is hard to imagine how any thorough transformation of the habits of humans will occur without the corporate human confidence in the ultimate worthwhileness of our moral endeavors. And without a deep trust in reality itself, ecological morality will, I am afraid, ultimately languish and die. Such trust . . . must be grounded in a conviction that the universe carries a meaning, or that it is the unfolding of a "promise". A commonly held sense that the cosmos is a significant process, that it unfolds something analogous to what we humans call "purpose", is, I think, an essential prerequisite of sustained global and intergenerational commitment to the earth's well-being.'

Stephen Gould (1991), known for his philosophy of scientific materialism, comes very near to an aesthetic viewpoint when discussing this connection of man to the natural world: 'We cannot win this battle to save species and environments without forging an emotional bond between ourselves and nature as well – for we will not fight to save what we do not love.'

Assessment of these qualitative issues has to be through dialectical processes. This is difficult because there are no clear boundaries, but failure to take these issues on board means there will be a lag in the advantages science can bring to the pursuit of sustainable development and human response.

VEHICLE OF CHANGE

A pivotal point for sustainability in terms of human awareness and international polity was the UN conference in Rio de Janeiro in 1992: The Earth Summit, Habitat I. Essentially this identified three critical areas affecting not only the survival of humanity but also the quality of that survival. The three conventions of the summit were: climate change, with the emphasis upon energy use and pollution; the unequal distribution of wealth and social inequality especially between the developed and developing countries, perceived as North and South; and biodiversity, with the risk of the extinction of many species through loss of habitat. Declarations were made stressing the urgent, radical need to readdress these issues in the light of evidence of socioeconomic imbalances and a dangerously deteriorating world environmental situation.

Much of the evidence for the propositions that were debated had been systematically collated over the 20 years preceding Habitat I. An important contribution to this was research findings from the Club of Rome. The club had been founded in 1968 and consisted at first of a group of 30 individuals from 10 countries, of varying professional and academic backgrounds, who were united in their concern for the present and future predicament of man. The over-riding and uniting conviction of the group was that the major problems facing mankind were of such a complexity and so integrated that traditional institutions and policies were no longer able to cope with them, or even able to come to grips with their full content. The research findings of the group were presented in a series of publications that culminated in *Beyond Limits to Growth* (Meadows et al 1992).

The group's first publication, in 1972, was *Limits to Growth* (Meadows et al) and focused, as the title suggests, on the concept that there is a limit to the growth ethic prevalent throughout the Western world – namely, that growth is determined by the numbers of people living on the planet and the carrying capacity of the planet. It predicted that if the trends in certain human activities continued, such as development and expansion, constantly increasing demands for products and the world's ever-growing population, the planet's limits would be reached. That there was no established methodology to address such a complex, global perspective inevitably suggested that any system introduced to cope with the interconnection of many variable parts would be open to criticism. The group used System Dynamics computer modelling to create a world model. Using this method of research enabled them to recognise that in the structure of any system 'the many circular, interlocking, sometimes time delayed relationships among its components – is often just as important in determining its behaviour as the individual components themselves'; the sum of the whole is greater than the sum of its individual components.

Five components identified as limiting growth were fed into this world model: population, agricultural production, natural resources, industrial production and pollution. And five major trends of concern were established: the acceleration of industrialisation; rapid population growth; widespread malnutrition; depletion of nonrenewable resources; and the deterioration of environment.

Criticisms of this work were that it produced an oversimplification of complex issues through a concentration on generalities which led to inaccuracy of detail. These criticisms are still relevant today and it is in their detail that we see the dissension and confusion that prevent an overall acceptance of the concept of sustainability. In particular: the time scales of some of the predictions proved to be false; the analysis was quantitative and could not take into account motivating qualitative aspects, such as changes in human attitude; it did not allow for man's ingenuity to buy time through advances in science and technology; it was not accurate about the extent of the world's unexplored stock of natural resources. However, if the essential truth of these findings is acknowledged it is apparent that our perception of reaching limits to growth will come through such indicators as detrimental and erratic changes in weather patterns, the extinction of increasing numbers of species and increasing numbers of human deaths through malnutrition. There is a more urgent and critical awareness of these indicators in today's world than there was in 1972 or 1992. By the time some of these processes are perceptible they may not be easily reversed. The delayed relationship of cause and effect in climatology could mean many years of remedial action before any improvement is experienced. Once a certain species is extinct it cannot come back.

LOCAL AGENDA 21

One of the main results of the 1992 Earth Summit was Agenda 21, a comprehensive programme of action throughout the world to achieve a more sustainable pattern of development. In Britain Local Agenda 21 emphasises the need for all sectors of society to participate in the formation of effective national, regional and local strategies for sustainable development. It states that in a sustainable community:

- Resources are used efficiently and waste is minimised by closing cycles;
- Pollution is limited to levels which natural systems can cope with without damage;
- The diversity of nature is valued and protected;
- Where possible local needs are met locally;
- Everyone has access to good food, water, shelter and fuel at a reasonable cost;
- Everyone has the opportunity to undertake satisfying work in a diverse economy. The value of unpaid work is recognised, whilst payments for work are fair and fairly distributed;
- People's good health is protected by creating safe, clean, pleasant environments and health services which emphasise prevention of illness as well as proper care for the sick;
- Access to facilities, services, goods and other people is not achieved at the expense of the environment or limited to those with cars;
- People live without fear of personal violence from crime or persecution because of their personal beliefs, race, gender or sexuality;
- Everyone has access to the skills, knowledge and information needed to enable them to play a full part in society;
- All sections of the community are empowered to participate in decision-making;
- Opportunities for culture, leisure and recreation are readily available to all; and
- Places, spaces and objects combine meaning and beauty with utility. Settlements are 'human' in scale and form. Diversity and local distinctiveness are valued and protected.

National and local government are being asked to take on a whole new way of addressing the inclusiveness and interconnectedness of issues affecting the environment. The term euphemistically given to this process is 'joined up thinking'. A problem experienced in one area is turned into an advantage when it is balanced by activities in another area. For example, possibly one of the first signs of climate change to come to the national consciousness in Britain is the frequent flooding of many of the country's rivers and the ensuing problems. Urban developments are acting as a series of bottlenecks along the courses of rivers, the established systems of drainage and protection are not coping with this problem and consequently property is being damaged with increasing frequency. Billions of pounds worth of damage to property is incurred yearly, and many people find their property is considered so high risk that they are unable sell it or obtain insurance cover. There is also an awareness of the necessity to protect the natural habitat of rare species, so there is a need to cultivate woodlands, water meadows and wetlands. River valleys converted to extensive wetlands, permanent water meadows and broad-leaved woodland canopy all have the potential to slow down the rate of run-off from surface rainfall water and retain water to be released through evaporation in dryer periods. Therefore suggesting how design strategies may be introduced into the land management of rural flood plains will, together with making surfaces within the urban development more porous, provide a sustainable solution to emerging local climate change. Looking at Local Agenda 21's list of conditions it is immediately apparent that there will be difficulty in devising appropriate and effective forms of measurement and monitoring for some of the more ethically orientated objectives: 'local needs are met locally', 'satisfying work', 'diversity and local distinctiveness are valued'. Pollution has a direct relationship with the physical conditions and quality of the surrounding hinterland. Some of the objectives, such as 'access to good food, water, shelter and fuel at a reasonable cost', suggest the need for defined boundaries and control over external dependencies. Many of them presuppose an enlightened civic consciousness of reciprocity between people and place: 'all sections of the community are empowered to participate in decision-making.'

As a consequence of the Earth Summit all local authorities in Britain had been asked to work towards the implementation of Agenda 21 or to provide their own similar local agenda. Questionnaires were sent to them towards the end of 1995 and the Local Agenda 21 survey results were produced in May 1996 (Hams 1997). Of 542 local authorities, 275 responded by the deadline for the questionnaires to be returned – just over 50 per cent. Positively, we may deduce that concerns about sustainable development are filtering through to local level. However, a response from only half the local authorities in Britain, together with the number of missed questions, suggests the attitude towards any assessment of Agenda 21's effectiveness in the United Kingdom should be cautious. As yet, local authorities may not have appropriately trained personnel or detailed policies to implement the agenda.

Habitat I had focused on sustainability equating to the carrying capacity of the planet, evaluated by the impact of population and development upon landscape or physical conditions. Habitat II, in 1996, focused upon the city. This in many ways encouraged the belief that sustainable development was synonymous with an urban renaissance. City sustainability emerged as being of critical importance over and above the needs of rural settlements, the reasoning being that the 20th century had produced a dominantly urban population. More people now live in cities than in all other forms of settlement combined. The consumption habits and functional requirements of this urban population are creating a great environmental deficit which threatens to bankrupt the natural balance of the world's resources. This problem is likely to be further exacerbated by a population explosion in many of the developing countries. If we think of the significance of natural landscape in balancing the environmental effects of energy emissions alone, an overconcentration on urban conurbations and the quality of life within cities, to the detriment of rural environments, would be harmful. Although there is an urgent need to equitably house a growing and diversified population and address the human misery of urban poverty, in terms of environmental sustainability it is important to maintain a balance between development and its impact upon natural landscape. Benign physical conditions and a reduction in energy emissions are crucial factors in sustainable development. Britain is a densely populated country and it is necessary to curtail further destructive encroachment of urban areas into healthy landscape. The relationship of rural hinterland to the city is of crucial importance.

In a press release on 16 April 1997 the Council for the Protection of Rural England (CPRE) stated: 'National and local government are still giving the go-ahead to housing, shopping centres and business parks in locations which can only be reached by car. National planning policies increasingly endorse the need to protect the countryside from over-development and reduce our reliance on the car. Out of town business-parks, cinemas, housing and shopping centres continue to get planning permission, while opportunities to regenerate the heart of our towns and to support public transport systems go begging.' This is supported by some interesting facts: an area the size of Bristol is urbanised each year in Britain; over 80 per cent of the distances people now travel are travelled by car; in 1986 there were 432 out-of-town superstores – in 1996 there were 1034.

In the press release the CPRE made certain recommendations that are listed below (with my comments in italic) and that have since been reflected in local policies towards development.

- As a 'smart growth initiative' they suggest that localities should build on the recognised benefits of energy efficiency, and show the financial gains to be made from development that is also efficient in using other natural resources (for example, land, water and minerals). *A problem here is that local government has been built upon the structure of small bureaucratic departments and may take time to adjust to interdepartmental negotiation in solving some of the problems.*
- After the 1996 summit on city sustainability, a focus was placed on providing sufficient and appropriate land for housing the increasing urban population. As a means of protecting the landscape against too much greenfield development and reducing energy emissions from transport, the CPRE suggested a target of 75 per cent of new housing to be built on previously developed land, and that a national target for reducing traffic growth be established.
- They advocated enforcing national planning policies to prevent local authorities giving the go-ahead to traffic-generating development without holding a full public inquiry. *The difficulty here is that public inquiries often become debilitated when faced with the economic strength of multinational organisations prepared to spend time and money going through one public inquiry after another.*
- They suggested the introduction of taxes on business and retail car-parking. These could be scaled to increase in relation to distance from the urban centre and so have most effect on out-of-town developments. *This would have to be carefully controlled to accommodate rural concerns. What about the population of the rural hinterlands who out of necessity have to use a car to travel to the outskirts of cities for provisions, trade or employment?*
- They advocated that urban capacity studies be undertaken to identify the opportunities to locate more development in urban areas. *The potential here is that this would also ensure the right kind of mixed development for encouraging meaningful urban communities.*
- In relation to the suburbs and their revitalisation they suggested planning policies to prevent further suburban sprawl and create focal points by encouraging jobs and businesses in focal points where people could walk to work and shop. *Does this suggest polycentred cities for the future?*
- They suggested a rigorous review of existing planning permission for out-of-town developments where construction had not yet started. The use of completion notices could help to reduce the lurking threat presented by such developments. It stated a disturbing trend which also reflects the inadequacy of Britain's cities to provide the appropriate qualitative environments in which to live: urban dwellers have sought relief from city pressures in out-of-town developments. However, in the interests of the countryside: 'Both the environment and quality of life is being put at risk. Decision makers at all levels need to get tough on the causes of traffic and sprawl before the countryside disappears beneath a sea of tarmac and traffic fumes' (CPRE 1997). *Development should enable the efficient management of a locality for the needs and pleasure of its community.*

ENERGY AND THE ENVIRONMENT AS A DRIVER FOR CHANGE

Against this background the visual appearance of Britain is changing. Increasingly over the last 10 years there has been a movement towards a greater concern for sources of energy and energy efficiency, as well as an awareness of how the needs of urban development can in part be fulfilled through the natural resources and physical conditions of landscape. In 1997 the British government spent more than £100 billion subsidising power stations that added to global warming and around £20 billion a year on subsidies to environmentally polluting industries (Brown 1997). However, in 2002 the signs are that renewable energies are on the verge of becoming a mainstream reality. By 2010 the government must meet global objectives by switching 10 per cent of electricity production to renewable resources and reducing greenhouse gasses by 12.5 per cent. The Performance and Innovation Unit (2001) issued surprising guidance as to how £100 million of government funds should be spent on subsidising renewable energies. Energy crops or biomass came off the best by far, receiving £33 million, offshore wind received £20 million and photovoltaics £10 million. In part this reflects sustainable governmental processes for addressing the interconnectedness of current problems – the devastating effects of BSE and foot-and-mouth disease on the rural economy – and global directives to reduce energy emissions.

While the national infrastructure and state of related technologies are by no means perfect, the long-term benefits look good. At present there is only one (very large and unsightly) generating plant in Yorkshire and another being built in Suffolk. As biomass is dependent on growing a bulky crop, such as coppiced willow or poplar, transportation requirements dictate that the source of the energy is within 20 miles of a generating plant. Therefore smaller and better visually designed models that are sympathetic to the regional landscapes they are to inhabit are called for that are acceptable to the public. Planners may then be able to insist that this form of energy generation is a built-in prerequisite for new development. Thermal processing technologies such as pyrolysis and gasification on a small scale are in a pioneering stage. However, one of the advantages is that they can be designed from the start to deal with a locality's waste management and achieve EU mandatory targets to reduce landfill sites and increase reuse, recycling and composting sites. These developments provide a purposeful, worthwhile employment strategy for a working rural environment that has of later years been frustrated by the 'you must diversify' camp.

Strategically placed willow plantations may help in the management of land prone to flooding and will most certainly attract a diversity of wildlife. This type of coppicing also acts as a filter for agricultural pollutants before they are able to reach rivers. In terms of public acceptance of this change, it is a question of aesthetics – 'What is this going to look like?' – and here design specialists in landscape, master-planning and architecture should unite to make benign change possible. Agencies like the Forestry Commission are already issuing guidelines for improving the visual impact of SRC plantations on landscape. It suggests that these are located in valleys and linked to existing features, and that care should be taken in both their siting and layout to reduce the unacceptable appearance of straight lines or large uniform blocks.

Much of the response to the sustainability objective of 1992 has been driven by the desire to reduce fossil-fuel energies and improve the quality of the environment, which relates directly to concern over climate change. Consequently, it is not surprising to find that this has been echoed in the debate that has directed the approach architects have taken towards sustainable development. In a 1995 survey of architectural practices and UK construction organisations who profess to use environmental initiatives it was found that 'Their actions are dominated by concern about energy consumption (and CO_2 emissions). Beyond this, while individuals are attempting a lot, there is very little agreement about what else needs to be done' (Eclipse Research Consultants, 1997). One of the first symposiums on sustainability, held at the Architectural Association, London, in February 1996, was predominantly concerned with energy conservation and renewable energy resources. A few exceptions were discussions focused on the city and questions of economic, political and social change, and ecosystems.

The panels of presenters explored many important questions: What is a sustainable environment? What is the political and theoretical basis of sustainable architecture? What is possible today? Where do we go now? However, presentations and debates were limited because of a preoccupation with energy. Reducing the energy consumption of buildings and the associated CO_2 emissions is an important global aim. Of the CO_2 emissions released in the UK, 50 per cent are a result of energy consumed in buildings (Taylor 1996).

Concentration on energy consumption and housing has shown significant progress over the last 30 years. Between 1970 and 1989 domestic energy consumption was contained, and even declined slightly if the fact that the average rate of increase of the domestic sector energy consumption was 0.5 per cent per year but the number of households increased at a rate of 1 per cent per year is taken into consideration. Also, the number of homes with central heating increased as did the number of appliances used in homes. Much of the credit for this must go to the use of improved technologies and materials, such as the provision of efficient insulation, in the design and building of houses (Domestic Energy Fact File, 1992).

With this background it is not surprising that architects have been quick to turn their attention to one of the most important issues of sustainability: designing buildings that have the minimum dependence on fossil fuel in either embodied energy or operational use. Many of the architects present at the symposium regarded this as a realistic goal, and possibly one of the areas of sustainability in which they could immediately begin to provide solutions. Hence the preoccupation with energy. Obviously, this is not all that architecture has to contribute towards sustainable development.

Discussion touched on the many renewable source energies and on passive techniques used in buildings. Possibly the most positive step towards sustainable development was to regard a building as a thermal organism, constructed with materials that have their own qualities of thermal inertia in combination with spaces that permit and generate the natural flow of air in and out, around and through, the building, providing for the modification of temperature and speed, ventilation and cooling, without mechanical assistance (Ford 1996–8).

Understandably, the symposium took on an exploratory and questioning character given the holistic quality of sustainability. Is the following definition of sustainability, already quoted in the preface to this book, an effective and all-encompassing one?

Meeting the needs of the present generation without compromising the ability of future generations to meet their own needs.

(Brundtland, 1992)

Is it acceptable or desirable to interpret this as follows?

Development that is at least as valuable to current and future generations as the value of environmental degradation that results . . . This interpretation permits for the extraction and use of even very large quantities of resources provided they are renewable or there are stupefyingly large quantities of reserves. It permits for waste and pollution levels that the planet is able to tolerate and accommodate. It does not require everything to stay the same and recognises that development implies trade-offs. It does not necessarily imply self-sufficiency and autonomy except within the boundaries of the planet.

(Howard, 1996)

Have words such as 'nature', 'environment' and 'sustainability' become so debased through misuse by manipulative systems that their effect is culturally impotent? Definition of these words varied at the symposium, and at times differences of opinion resulted in heated arguments. It would seem that even in a profession that takes aesthetic and qualitative aspects into account, the dialectical nature of sustainability strained both the panels' and audiences' capacities for communication, tolerance, negotiation and compromise. It was asked what effect small groups or individuals embracing such concepts as self-sufficiency, autonomy and communalism lend to the movement; and whether this is on the whole constructive or destructive. Although alternative technologies and renewable energies had been around for a long time they had become associated with a minority group of environmental enthusiasts seeking an alternative lifestyle; could sustainability itself be in danger of being seen as a marginal movement within architecture? How should we encourage the correct attitude towards such a global concern? Would it be useful to start concentrating on human civilisation as a dependent subsystem of the natural ecosystem of the planet, no more, no less? This question led to thoughts about the future direction of the city. Many modern industrial cities are less than 200 years old; are they creating the best answers for tomorrow's problems? Are our cities formed by political and economic systems that are out of harmony with environmental and social aspects of city life? And, are they steered by those who seek only financial gain? Is there an optimum size for the city? What factors control this? The needs of small settlements for timber and firewood can be met without annihilating local forests; the need for food need not overtax the soil; wastes can be absorbed by local ecosystems without degrading them; social require-ments can be satisfied when they are based on meaningful social units, extended family and community; automobile dependence is not necessary.

Over the last 10 years it has become obvious that it is not sufficient to say that sustain-ability is achieved by completely replacing fossil fuels with clean renewable technologies. However, while recognising the need for an aesthetic, the architectural profession has used processes of empirical experience, scientific and technological analysis, and intuition, as ways of developing an appropriate approach to a sustainable design methodology.

LANDSCAPE AND ARCHITECTURE: INDICATORS OF SUSTAINABILITY

Against this background changes in approach, attitude and methodology are evolving in land-scape, architecture and master-planning. Design strategies in these areas will have a direct influence on how 'sustainable development' relates visually. The acceptance of these design strategies will be governed by people's perception of 'what it is they like' and 'what it is they don't like' – or the aesthetic. The growing response is to work with the physical conditions and natural resources in both landscape and architecture to achieve favourable human thermal comfort and turn problems brought about by climate change to environmental advantage. Landscape, architecture and master-planning interact to intervene physically within the environment. They are concerned with physical conditions and societal needs and are required to respect political processes, exhibit sensitivity to cultural identity and generally support physiological and industrial activity. Taking this and the interconnectedness of sustainable development issues into consideration, both in identifying problems and providing solutions to those problems, it would seem reasonable to form the following hypothesis of 'place'. In a place, the quality and condition of landscape and architecture are indicative of the state of sustainability – humanity's coming to terms with, and responding to, the physical conditions, psychological and functional needs, cultural identity and institutional requirements in a particular environment.

Chapter Two
Problems and Resolutions

The concept of sustainability presents the urgent need for radical change in man's thinking and behaviour, so much so that it is termed the 'global revolution'. The 1992 Earth Summit in Rio de Janeiro began a series of international talks and negotiations in connection with the three conventions: climate change, unequal distribution of wealth and social inequality, and bio-diversity. In effect this summit had the potential elements of a deal between the developed or industrialised countries, termed the North, and the developing or Third World countries identified as the South. The South would sign up to agreements in connection with global policy on environment and development providing the North supplied the know-how and technical and financial expertise. A date was set for a further summit in 2002 to reassess the situation and evaluate progress. In 2002 the climate change convention is the only part of the deal to have reached a stage of global policy and resolution. Climate change has been perceived as the single greatest threat to the human race and therefore the most significant driver towards sustainable development. The other conventions are interconnected with climate change and are in need of urgent action if climate change agreements are to have full effect. This chapter discusses the terms, conditions and potential impact of the Kyoto climate treaty before looking at the problems and resolutions of other interconnected issues affecting global sustainability.

THE KYOTO CLIMATE TREATY AND BONN AGREEMENT

As part of the climate change convention, originally negotiated in Rio de Janeiro in 1992, industrialised countries agreed voluntarily to bring their greenhouse-gas emissions to 1990 levels by 2000. By the mid-1990s it became evident that this was not going to happen without global legal intervention. The legal protocol defining a course of action was negotiated in the Japanese city of Kyoto in 1997, and is known as the Kyoto Treaty. In July 2001 a world community of 189 nations met and adopted the Kyoto protocol in Bonn – the Bonn Agreement. This, the first significant global, legally binding environmental treaty in the history of mankind, is aimed at saving the planet from the worst effects of global warming, through the reduction of greenhouse-gas emissions. Its impact for those concerned with development and land management in landscape, architecture and master-planning will be far-reaching and will demand changes not only in how we design and build, and the materials and resources used in this process, but also in our attitude and philosophy towards the environment.

The Bonn Agreement was pre-empted by a consensus of scientific opinion in support of the argument that man's activities, energy use and the consequential greenhouse-gas emissions constituted the single largest threat to the future ecological balance of the planet. The reduction of greenhouse-gas emissions becomes imperative if the harmful effect of global warming is to be halted. Essentially, in the preindustrial world there were between 200 and 275 parts per million by volume (ppmv) of carbon dioxide in the atmosphere. With the industrialisation and population growth of the last century there are now approximately 370 ppmv and it is estimated that this, if unchecked, will reach 700 ppmv by 2100 while the global mean temperature will rise by 8°C. **(Figure 1)** The Bonn Agreement has already compromised the Kyoto Treaty. For example, whereas in the protocol scientists had asked for cuts of between 60 per cent and 80 per cent in greenhouse-gas emissions from 37 of the most developed nations, concessions in the agreement allowed for cuts of only 1 per cent to 3 per cent. The United States

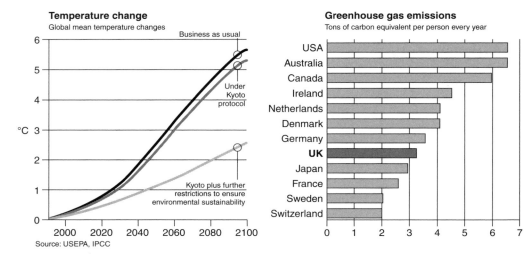

Temperature change
Global mean temperature changes

Greenhouse gas emissions
Tons of carbon equivalent per person every year

Source: USEPA, IPCC

Figure 1: Global mean temperature changes (left) based on three scenarios: no change in present-day energy emissions; reduction in energy emissions to meet the Kyoto protocol; and further reductions in energy emissions of the type needed to ensure environmental sustainability. Greenhouse gas emissions (right): the tons of carbon per person every year for 12 industrialised countries.

of America, with the highest concentration of greenhouse-gas emissions, did not even sign up to the agreement. Therefore, although this is a committed start, further resolve and deeper cuts are called for.

What are the terms and conditions of the Bonn Agreement? By law all 189 nations will commit to reducing their greenhouse-gas emissions by 8 per cent on 1990 levels by 2010. Industrial nations like Britain will commit to a higher percentage to allow poorer countries to develop. The protocol is expected to come into effect in 2002. Of new funds, £350 million are to be provided by the industrial nations each year to help the developing nations adapt to climate change and provide new clean technologies. Industrial nations will be able to claim credits by planting forests, managing existing ones and changing farming practices, thereby removing carbon dioxide from the atmosphere. Countries are being asked to submit their plans for reducing emissions and to monitor progress in order to give early warning if they are failing to reach targets. If countries fail to meet the targets set for 2010 they will have to add the shortfall, plus a 30 per cent penalty, to the next commitment period. As a financial incentive an international trade in carbon is to be initiated. Countries or businesses that save carbon by using clean technologies will gain credits that may be sold as tonnes of carbon on the international commodity markets. The estimated starting price is £10 per tonne. Countries that have difficulty meeting their targets will be able to buy in credits.

What does the agreement mean in terms of development and action? It is obviously a huge boost to all connected with renewable energies, clean technologies and energy efficiency systems. At present the most prominent renewable energy sources are: biomass, as discussed in Chapter One; wind energy, whereby turbines convert the force of air movement into power, dependent on sufficient natural wind-force; and solar energy, the harnessing of the strength of the sun for the generation of electricity whereby light is converted into power via a photo-voltaic cell. All these sources need further research and investment before efficient and cost-effective solutions can be provided for their use on a large scale. All raise questions about their visual impact and public acceptance. Climate change will inform energy policy and this will vary from country to country. In Britain it is envisaged that by switching to renewable energies emissions may be reduced by 60 per cent by 2050. (This is without further dependency on nuclear power.) Policy is also likely to dictate individual domestic and transport reductions of 40 per cent by 2020.

The agreement presents an incentive to global business in the birth of a new world trade in carbon. Basically, countries and companies that are both advanced and rich enough to invest immediately in new renewable energies, clean technologies and energy efficiency systems will be able to sell the carbon dioxide saved to a country or company unable or unwilling to do so. London is already being labelled the 'carbon capital' of the world. For the wealthiest companies in such global cities, with new economic incentives it will be possible to patronise innovative technology and architecture that encourage the growth of buildings able to generate not only enough clean energy for their own functions but also an excess that may be sold. Buildings that are energy producers rather than consumers are already a reality. However, most places that are unable to take advantage of this new lucrative financial market will look towards their own natural resources, in terms of physical conditions and climate, to maximise energy efficiency and maintain a state of equilibrium whereby growth may be justified not in quantitative terms – the expansion of built development or industry – but in qualitative terms, improvements that enhance the social or cultural wellbeing of communities within the terms of the climate treaty. Possibly a greater interest will be taken in places that were built in preindustrial periods, where passive- and low-energy architectural and development solutions had to be based on passive systems, making use of such considerations as site location, orientation, natural resources and climatic conditions to provide for human comfort and industry. The economist Herman Daly (1997) gives three conditions that a society should meet in relation to physical sustainability:

- Its rates of use of renewable resources do not exceed their rates of regeneration.
- Its rates of use of nonrenewable resources do not exceed the rate at which sustainable substitutes are developed.
- Its rates of pollution emission do not exceed the assimilative capacity of the environment.

Over the coming decades these will become considerations for societies in all places.

Financial incentives given to countries and industry raise questions about the nature and extent of global trade-offs in carbon. They could give rise to further exploitation of certain environments and unequal distribution of wealth may occur. It is important to bear in mind that the society in each place is responsible for taking control of its environmental impact and not shifting too much responsibility from one part of the countryside to another, or from city to country. Although the Bonn Agreement stipulates that developed countries may claim credits by planting forests, managing existing ones and changing farming practices, it does not legislate for biodiversity. Giving £350 million to developing countries to develop new clean technologies will hardly touch on the problem that two-thirds of the world's population live a marginal existence. Where human life depends on adequate supplies of water and food, and the opportunity for some material improvement, there is a great need for the other two conventions of the 1992 summit to be developed alongside the climate change convention or we are likely to have an irreversible fragmentation of the sustainable development objectives.

INITIATIVES TOWARDS ENERGY EFFICIENCY

Factor Four (Von Weizsacker et al 1997) puts forward ways of achieving sustainable development through efficiency strategies. It is a report to the Club of Rome, and follows the 1972 report *Limits to Growth* (Meadows et al), which drew attention to the rapid consumption and depletion of essential resources.

Factor Four offers a quantitative formula, dependent on efficiency incentives, which allows wealth to grow while resource use does not. It shows how, through resource productivity versus labour productivity, four times as much wealth can be extracted from the resources we use. It is a quantitative formula for revolutionising resource productivity in the use of energy, materials and transport. It explains how markets can be organised and taxes rebased to eliminate perverse incentives and reward efficiency.

Working on the assumption that gradual sustainable development is better than blind progress, *Factor Four*, if implemented, would not guarantee a solution to the world energy problem. Rather, it would prolong the time during which a solution may be found. Dependent on a new direction for technological progress, it advocates technologies that represent a quadrupling or more of productivity and that meet the criterion of sustainability set by the 1992 Earth Summit. It is essentially an efficiency revolution.

The Queen's Building, De Montfort University, Leicester, by the architects Alan Short and Brian Ford, is one of the examples cited in *Factor Four*. It exemplifies how significant energy savings of 25 per cent to 50 per cent in the operational use of a building are possible. This has been achieved through design, which maximises the potential for passive cooling and ventilation. A narrow floor plan allows daylight into the building from two sides, so most of the lighting is natural. The form also permits passive air movement through cross-ventilation, by the addition of eight large chimneys with louvred openings at various intervals, which allow warm air to rise and circulate throughout the building. To ensure acceptable temperatures, an automatic management system adjusts dampers, louvres and heating controls. However, the building is only 40 per cent automated; occupants can open or close windows to adjust comfort conditions. Externally, calculated overhangs and heavy masonry walls minimise cooling loads, and the whole design of the building minimises heating and air-conditioning demands. Heating is primarily by passive solar design and the internal gain from occupants and extensive engineering equipment – the building houses the School of Engineering and Manufacture. Any supplementary heating is provided by natural gas. The use of clean technologies and environmental design strategies to minimise electricity use by no means detract from aesthetic considerations, which define the building as architecture.

There are major obstacles to the success of the efficiency revolution: the need, if it is to be universally applied, for society to change qualitatively to embrace its concepts; the necessity for world consensus and agreement on economic and governmental strategies if it is to be successfully implemented; and the demands that an escalation in population growth may make on resources and energy. A philosophical change to the criteria, which will constitute progress, would be difficult to orchestrate. People do not change habits and patterns of behaviour unless they have good reasons for doing so. If their motivation is to be sustainability, this needs to be experienced as compelling and urgent by a critical mass of people in order to create sufficient momentum for global change.

THE ECOLOGICAL TAX REFORM (ETR)

The ecological tax reform goes some way towards the reconciliation of free trade and environmental protection. It is based on the principle of taxing things that are environmentally 'bad' and rewarding initiatives that act for the 'good' of the environment (Von Weiszacker et al 1997). Energy and resource prices would steadily go up by 5 per cent per annum over a very long period of time, and this would motivate such people as managers, architects, engineers and those concerned with design technology to work towards the least use of natural resources and greater energy efficiency. The assumption is that if prices begin to reflect ecological costs, products and firms that damage the environment would no longer have competitive advantages. The Scandinavian countries and the Netherlands have already initiated ecological tax reform. Notably, Denmark has established a carbon dioxide tax, which exempts industrial-process energy and is fully compatible with industry's needs. In Britain ETR is beginning to happen with steadily increasing petrol tax and city and road-traffic tolls to reduce energy use and eliminate congestion. However, there is a great need for standards and rules to be harmonised internationally. Developing countries with rapidly increasing populations and expanding industrialisation have the strongest need for ETR before they emulate the energy consumption patterns of the Western world.

UNEQUAL DISTRIBUTION OF WEALTH AND SOCIAL INEQUALITY

The world population is predicted to increase from 5.3 thousand million to 10 thousand million by 2050 (ICPD 1994). The authors of *Factor Four* estimate that 'the total Factor Four revolution, if it took place', from 1995 to 2050, 'would already be eaten up by this double dynamic of population increase and a very modest increase of per capita consumption'. According to this scenario, nothing of the efficiency revolution would be left to relieve the overstressed natural environment. **(Figure 2)** If efficiency gains of 4 per cent annually occurred in energy productivity during the same period, plus a decrease of 40 per cent in the birth rate from 2000 to 2100, the outlook for the future would be more optimistic. **(Figure 3)** However, a reduction in population is dependent on awareness and a more enlightened universal education, especially of women; a more equitable distribution of prosperity; and is interconnected with changes in governance and international trading and financial systems. From a comparison of the scenarios mentioned above, and the legislation for energy emissions already discussed, a modest ambition would be to buy time during the unavoidable phase of human overpopulation of the planet. This by no means addresses all the ecological problems such overpopulation may cause. However, what has been discussed in this chapter so far – the Kyoto Treaty, energy efficiency and ecological taxation – represent market-based, industry-based, technology-oriented solutions that assume the continuation of consumerism and commodification as progress.

Climate change has become the imperative that is informing energy policy. World leaders have set a target of a reduction of 60 per cent in energy emissions by 2050. They hope this will be achieved through efficiency savings, conversion to renewable sources and energy processes that involve a low carbon mix. It is unrealistic to expect that this will happen without a change in human attitudes towards patterns of consumption and perceptions of what constitutes growth. The most significant threat comes from the expected massive population increase in the developing countries. Climate change is occurring, in part, as a consequence of the numbers of people living on the planet and the stress that puts on the carrying capacity of the planet. It is unreasonable to expect to bring the entire populations of developing countries to the material living standards of developed nations; it is inhumane and a potential cause of war and revolution to ignore the needs of millions of people who subsist at marginal levels of existence.

Between now and 2050, 90 per cent of the increase in the world's population will take place in Third World countries. This is a massive increase in people who, unless solutions are found, will have to live in material poverty. In the Third World capital growth barely keeps pace with population growth for a number of reasons: investable surplus is extracted by foreign investors; feudal class structures allow local elites to take a more than equitable share of profits; a country's debt repayment may cripple attempts to provide education and health care; military regimes are kept in power at exorbitant prices; and there may be just too much poverty to entertain the idea of technical efficiency and good management systems that would generate an investable surplus in the first place. As Donella Meadows explains (Meadows et al 1992): 'It is much easier for rich populations to save, invest, and multiply their capital than for poor ones to do so not only because of the greater power of the rich to control market conditions, purchase new technologies, and command resources, but also because centuries of past growth have built up in rich countries a large stock of capital that can multiply itself yet more.' Certainly, lower population growth in rich countries permits individual personal wealth to be invested in speculative and usually profitable industrial markets, and is not totally taken up by essential welfare concerns such as health, education or adequate shelter.

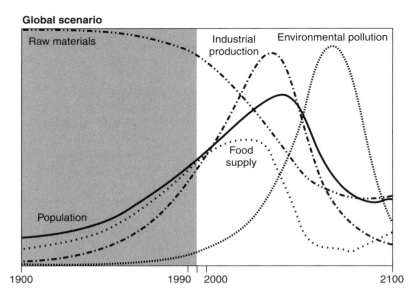

Figure 2: Global scenario 1. The relative growth and consumption pattern for raw materials, industrial production, population, food supply and environmental pollution, assuming a double stock of exploitable resources. On this assumption industrial output may grow a mere 20 years longer but then experience a sharp fall (Meadows 1992).

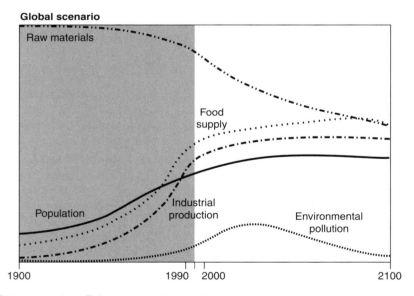

Figure 3: Global scenario 2. This more optimistic outlook presupposes that sustainability policies were introduced in 1975 (Meadows 1992).

The resolution and solution of the 1992 convention on unequal distribution of wealth and social inequality have not been addressed. This is an area where global polity is needed to bring about deliberate change. Solutions need to be sufficient and equitable to allow developmental progress, although this does not mean that everyone has to have the material living standards of the average person living in the West. That would not be realistic on an already ecologically stressed planet. Rather, it means reaching a state of equilibrium between quantitative and qualitative growth: 'The task of managing in the presence of ecological limits demands of the human mind greater subtlety, more careful classification. Poorer people desperately need food, shelter, and material goods. Wealthier people, in a different kind of desperation, try to use material growth to satisfy other needs, which are also very real but are in fact non-material – needs for acceptance, self-importance, community, identity. It makes no sense at this time of rapid growth on a finite planet to talk about growth with either unquestioning approval or unquestioning disapproval. Instead it is necessary to ask: Growth of what? For whom? For how long? At what cost? Paid by Whom? What is the real need here, and what is the most direct and efficient way for those who have the need to satisfy it?' (Meadows et al 1992). This advocates a radical change in human attitude. How stressed is the planet? How stressed are the people living on it? We all have a part to play but powerful man-made systems prohibit many people from ever having the opportunity to attempt to play their part. The consequence for all is environmental deterioration.

ENVIRONMENTAL ASSESSMENT

How may we approach this problem of environmental deterioration? Forms of assessment are needed at both global and local levels. An assessment formula used by environmentalists is known as IPAT:

Impact = Population × Affluence × Technology

Impact is the 'throughput' or flow of energy and resources from their original sources, through a system where they may be transformed into a product, and ultimately the pollution brought about in this process has to be carried out to various 'sinks'. This process causes energy emissions and therefore sustainable development looks at ways to reduce the impact of a place. The population of a place has a direct influence on resources drawn and emissions released, according to its size, how affluent it is and its consumption patterns, and the types of technologies it uses and the damage they may do. So human efficiency and economy in terms of Population, Affluence and Technology may limit the impact of a place and bring it closer to the earth's carrying capacity. If this could be done on a global scale harmful emissions would not destroy the stratosphere and climate change would be lessened. All built development, such as architecture, draws on resources, uses energy and causes emissions. Natural landscape acts as a 'sink' for these emissions. Thus design strategies, purposefully focused towards addressing the impact of a place, are of critical importance in architecture, landscape and master-planning. It is important to acknowledge the underlying theoretical principles of sustainable development – development that is holistic, incremental and inclusive. Only then can we begin to address such problems as 'the city' where many interactions occur simultaneously and therefore do not exist for a static one-factor-at-a-time analysis.

GLOBALISATION

Globalisation of the financial industry especially influences the flow of money from poor countries to rich ones. In 1993 the so-called developing countries spent three times more in servicing debts than they received in aid. They are unable to pay the interest on this debt so the crisis grows. Between 1983 and 1990, $673 billion was paid by developing countries to service a debt of $644 billion and $950 billion was still owed to the World Bank (Lean 1997). In Africa four times as much is spent on debt repayment as on health and education (Lean 1997). It is obvious that in this type of situation developing countries are forced to degrade the landscape by selling their natural resources. With poor health and education systems their people are vulnerable to exploitation whether that be by a multinational company or military dictatorship.

Global sustainability initially depends on writing off this debt and targeting aid properly. But more foresight is needed in economic thinking if we are to make the economics of sustainable development work. Herman Daly (1997) recognises the pivotal point for change. Up until now we have developed an economic system based on a world low in population and high in natural resources. The reality is that we now have a world high in population and low in natural resources. 'If factors are complements, then the one in shortest supply will be the limiting factor.' This conditions a radical new approach to economics which must be governed by the fact that 'the world is moving from an era in which man-made capital was the limiting factor into an era in which remaining natural capital is the limiting factor'.

Directly related to the globalisation of the financial industry is the theory of free trade. Free trade has become distorted by prices which do not reflect the full cost of production. For instance, the costs of resource depletion and of environmental degradation are not accounted for. The authors of *Factor Four* gave this example under the heading 'Development to Depletion': 'When the Ivory Coast in the two decades following independence sacrificed much of its natural treasures to the production of cash crops and other export commodities the young nation became a hero of the international banking community. Here was a country "taking off", enjoying a stable currency (linked to the French franc) and a stable political climate. Well, soon enough, the party was over, what has remained are skyscrapers, fancy hotels and an "elite" habituated to Western consumption styles, but otherwise widespread destitution, a devastated natural environment and political instability.'

The message seems to be that the prevalent philosophy of leaving trade development to the markets under the direction of entrepreneurs and financial consultants rewards those who overexploit the land. Profits are higher for unsustainable resource exploitation than for sustainable methods. The principles of free trade have somehow to be reconciled with the necessity for better global environmental protection.

Globally a most important factor is the debt crisis, and it is the inducement to developing countries to sell cash crops, ores, timbers and hydroelectricity to foreign countries and foreign companies at unsustainable rates and with the result that natural habitats are destroyed. **(Figure 4)** Many developments are export-oriented, carried out at the expense of virgin forests and other natural assets and thus contribute to this destruction. As developing countries expand their exports, so their resource exploitation increases. Since the mid-1970s world market commodity prices have fallen drastically. The result is that indebted countries have sold even more of their natural resources in order to maintain the servicing of their debts. Asian timber reserves, which provide an indicator, may only last 40 years (Brown 1997).

BIODIVERSITY

Biodiversity, the third convention of the 1992 Earth Summit, is often seen as a concern distinct from the problems of the other two conventions. Biodiversity, climate change and the depletion of natural resources are inextricably linked to human overpopulation of the planet. Herman Daly focuses on population expansion and the inherent nature of man to exploit for his own needs, and regards the problem of biodiversity as 'the ever-increasing takeover of total life space by one species, rather than in terms of the number of different species that can remain viable in the ever-shrinking total habitat left over for them as the human niche expands. Continued human expansion means that other species will disappear or become domesticated like cattle (or zoo specimens) for their instrumental value' (1997).

The destruction of biodiversity is the most emotive of sustainable issues, possibly because it is the most directly experienced and relates to something intrinsically beautiful disappearing. Endangered species are vanishing every day, providing a perceivable and malign indicator of the quality of the planet. In scientific terms, biodiversity acts as the ecological resilience against unpredictable climatic change or other alterations in the biosphere. It is irresponsible and

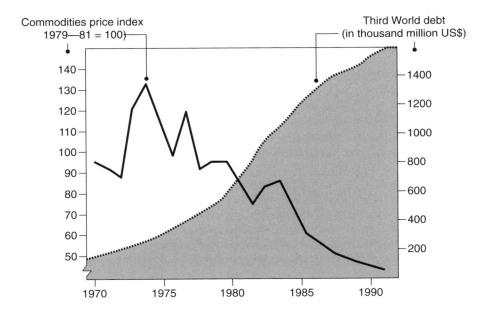

Figure 4: Rapidly increasing commodity sales by developing countries, and the ensuing collapse of commodity prices, may be the single most important cause of biodiversity destruction (Worldwatch Institute 1990).

unforgivable to sacrifice biological diversity to short-term advantages. Some 20 to 50 species may be lost daily (Von Weiszacker et al 1997). There are many and varied reasons for the acceleration of species extinction, which may be assessed more easily through a specific locality. However, one species less is like a link broken in a chain; the ecological balance of the universe is put at risk in a way that may not be easily rectified. As we engage in the master-planning of places, to meet human sustainable development objectives, this must be taken into consideration in both rural and urban land management. It is not sufficient to say we have put enough landscape into our cities to lessen the heat-island effect and thereby reduced the impact of energy emissions and brought greater human thermal comfort. This will have a benign effect on climate change in the long term, but we must also design habitats for different species into our places. If we allow the constant destruction of plant, bird and animal species through exploiting the environment to meet our own needs we only accelerate and exacerbate the problems of climate change for ourselves. The pace of this change is quick which means it is difficult for species to adapt, especially if they are not mobile or are dependent on other species for their mobility. So much of nature is interdependent and the collective impact of climate change is difficult to assess.

Organisations such as the Environment Agency and the Woodland Trust are showing a greater recognition of the need to link tracts of natural landscape over large areas so that there are wildlife links or paths. It is also necessary to design natural landscape paths through our cities in such a way that maximum indigenous landscaping is used, maintaining the possibility of conserving the biodiversity of that particular environment. Forests and rural landscapes must also be designed to act as effective habitats for the greatest number of species, not just regarded as businesses for profit or 'sinks' for polluting human activities. The extinction of a species means a link broken in a very complex chain. The bird that arrives in spring to eat the grubs on the grub-infested leaves of a tree saves the life of the tree.

URBAN MEGALOPOLIS – THE CITY

The increase in industrialisation and the concentration of urban living have escalated over the last century, bringing specific problems that cause us to identify many cities as areas of crisis. The 1992 Earth Summit dispelled the belief that the environment and development can be seen as separate entities. Their interconnectedness is vital to an understanding of sustainability. The following, taken from this summit's proceedings, exemplifies this: 'The right to development must be fulfilled so as to equitably meet developmental and environmental needs of present and future generations. In order to achieve sustainable development, environmental protection shall constitute an integral part of the development process and cannot be considered in isolation from it' (Weizsacker et al 1997). The 1996 summit, Habitat II, which focused specifically on 'the city', formulated the enormity of the task involved in the monitoring and assessment of various types of cities. It advocated 10 policies for better cities (Local Government Management Board 1997). Certain reservations about these policies are shown in italic.

1. Welcome the opportunities provided by the growth of cities, but combat inequality and environmental degradation. Otherwise the cost of cities will outweigh their benefits. *Emphasis is placed on the 'growth of cities' and there is no mention that in certain urban areas physical growth may have reached an optimum level because of demographic, geophysical or economic reasons. It therefore may be beneficial to set limits to growth.*

2. Release the energies and tap the resources of people and businesses, but don't leave everything to markets. Governments must coordinate the actions of others, monitor, and correct abuses. Freedom to build must be balanced by a duty to protect the interests of others. *This stresses the importance of institutional infrastructure in guiding, coordinating and regulating sustainable development objectives. What strategies are there for replacing the market forces of capitalism?*

3. The best way to protect the interests of the vulnerable and disadvantaged people where government resources are scarce is to attack supply constraints, especially in the supply of land and finance, on a very large scale. Use positive measures, such as guided investments, rather than negative ones. *Are existing forms of land tenure and property speculation in need of urgent reform?*

4. Strengthen the economic, political and civic institutions of the city. Establish open, transparent and accountable government. Create an enabling framework for civic action and respect non-governmental and community-based organisations as independent expressions of civic society. Always involve women. *This demands an educated and enlightened civic society. How do we create a state of reciprocity so that money earned through the city is relevant to development that works for the common good of all citizens?*

5. Maximise the use of public-private partnerships to draw in additional resources and capacities, but don't confuse 'private' with 'commercial'. All partners must receive benefits from their participation. The public sector holds a fiduciary interest in the future for all citizens.

6. Concentrate on scaling up successful ideas, attitudes and approaches, not just projects and programmes. Use scarce public funds to lever additional resources from larger structures and institutions on a sustained basis. Strengthen links between formal and informal structures. *As with many of these issues, an emphasis is placed on creative change, adaptability and flexibility in city politics.*

7. Increase local control over resources with accountable structures and transparent performance monitoring. Public policy can make a difference, even when resources are scarce. Strengthen government capacity, but don't see urban management as a panacea. *This goes some way towards the containment and self-reliance of specific urban units.*

8. Don't take on too much: focus on a few key cross-sectoral issues such as urban poverty, the 'brown agenda' and supply constraints. Lay down time-bound goals and strategies to address them. Maximise the flow of information and learning. *This stresses the importance*

of a step-by-step approach in each locality according to the priority of need. *Progress and development will vary from one locality to another.*

9. Don't divorce shelter and human settlements from wider economic, political and social policies. Adopt a holistic approach. *In a system where knowledge has been divided into highly specialised parts, such as economics, is it reasonable to expect we adopt a holistic approach?*

10. Make policy according to the local situation, not imported models or ideologies. Global market economics does not supply all the answers to problems of equitable and sustainable human settlements development. *Again this emphasises the necessity of individual and particular local solutions to the objectives of global sustainability.*

The urban megalopolis trend directly concerns those people working in the design of cities: urban designers, town planners, architects and landscape architects. Today half the world's population lives in cities and it is likely that this figure will grow to three-quarters by the year 2025. The city will present the most demanding of challenges if environmental sustainability is to be achieved. It will have to meet the prerequisites of the conventions on climate change, unequal distribution of wealth and social inequality, and biodiversity. Greenhouse gases, greening, energy efficiency, transport systems, information technology systems, recycling not just of waste but of all sorts of products, plus the need to cultivate an environment that is conducive to the expression of cultural identity and the psychological wellbeing of all humanity, become major factors of consideration. These are factors that the 20th-century industrial cities have not addressed adequately. Conceptions of what constitutes good city design and form are in urgent need of radical critical reform, especially if 20th-century urban design problems are not to be repeated in newly developing cities, particularly in Southeast Asia.

Dean Hawkes (1996a) sees the problem of sustainability as the problem of the city: 'The processes of urbanisation have destroyed the symbiotic relationship between humanity and nature. Modern cities are supported by extensive hinterlands from which they extravagantly draw resources. This has resulted in the consumption of non-renewable resources and the destruction of nature both in the city's immediate surroundings and globally'. This expresses a conflict between the objectives of urbanism through industrialisation and the processes of nature. Sustainability demands that a more inclusive relationship is developed between natural environment and city form. Climate change agreements have provided the motivation for research on environmental and energy concerns in relation to landscape, architecture and master-planning within urban design. Dean Hawkes (1996b) identifies the next challenge: 'The city that produces all of the energy it needs for its buildings and the urban infrastructure is, of course, a vision. To take the first steps towards its realisation would transform the agenda for research and practice in architecture more radically than any idea since the advent of the modern movement.'

In asking the question 'Will we learn to make cities work?' Sheena McDonald gives a pessimistic invocation of the so-called 'Blade Runner City' – 'a nightmare vision of high rise, high tech, impersonal ghettos for the rich, while the poorer struggle at street level amidst rotting infrastructure, car gridlock, pollution and chronic crime' (Murray and McDonald 1997).

Kevin Murray (Murray and McDonald 1997), an urban planner, foresees the future of the city with optimism. He recognises the emergence of a new urban agenda, particularly across Europe, as we go through the postindustrial period and enter the 21st century. The city will become a major central focus: of culture and activity, and a safer and much more environmentally enjoyable place. He foresees radical alteration in the built form as a result of technological evolution, especially as regards the office. There will be less need for the typical office as people work more from home and move around to work in various locations. Workspace will need to be flexible and adaptable. Spaces will be completely different, designs more innovative, there will be more glazing and structures will be 'wacky'. 'Structures that we're not even working with at the moment, which technology will help allow.' The city will become decentralised and polycentred. The traditional form of the city, with fringes of industrial and employment areas, suburbs and then countryside, will disappear. This does not mean that the old fabric of the city will have to go. Indeed, it may be a major asset, not only for tourism and maintaining an interesting, characterful place, but also functionally. The implications of cable-free technology make, for example, the Georgian terrace useful for a range of activities either as homes or workstations. By comparison the 1970s office building with raised floors, dropped ceilings, and a certain kind of heating and ventilation, will become outmoded and inflexible. Over the next 15 years system-built concrete warehouses and concrete offices will become the main casualties of change.

Our conception of what epitomises a sustainable city will not be driven by architectural configurations, no matter how innovative. A society must feel that both individual identity and community aspirations are reflected and affirmed in the physical presence of place. The issue of community is of crucial importance. Therefore the operation, management and planning of the city must be focused around the community. If a large part of the city population is of a transient character, or the configuration is too large and sprawling without defined boundaries, the individual's sense of belonging to a place or community will be lost.

The way cities have developed says more about the energy-consuming activities of power and expansion than about the more purposeful activities of collective humanity. Kenneth Frampton (1983) stresses the importance of maintained urban form and the necessity of defined boundary or 'bounded domain' as a form of resistance against the megalopolis. He cites the example of the master plan of Rotterdam which, until 1975 was revised and upgraded every decade because of changes in function. This procedure changed in 1975 in favour of a nonphysical, infrastructure plan conceived at a regional scale and concerned with the administrative allocation of land use and the logistics of distribution. In the process, through the disintegration of boundary, structure that balances a state of 'being', 'cultivating' and 'dwelling' is lost. Frampton considers 'the absolute precondition of a bounded domain in order to create an architecture of resistance. Only such a defined boundary will permit the built form to stand against, and hence literally to withstand in an institutional sense, the endless processal flux of Megalopolis.'

Kevin Murray envisages the city as a series of 'urban villages', each with a strong sense of area. He considers that the major forces for change in the shaping of future cities are: globalisation of the world economy; rapid pace of change in information technology; and the issue of environmental sustainability and strong pressure in terms of tax on private transport which will influence the technology and development of public systems (Murray and McDonald 1997). In contrast to Kenneth Frampton, who stresses the importance of the bounded physical conurbation, Kevin Murray sees the major forces of change as institutional or technological.

In Britain London is the only truly global city (Phillips 1995). However, many other cities and towns have formed, and are forming, economic and social relationships with similar European and international cities while maintaining varying degrees of autonomy for the protection of their own environment. This is exemplified in the popularity of the 'twinning' system. This has led to healthy competition and beneficial exchanges as regards civic development, economy and employment, culture and the quality of life, and pride in city form. The developing economies of Southeast Asia, Africa and South America are likely to provide an even larger competitive arena in which the city will have to operate. So we are bound to ask the question: how much control and responsibility are to be held by the nation for the city? As a global city, one of London's problems is that it is perceived in the provinces as belonging to the world and is thus losing its cultural identity as a national capital (Phillips 1995).

In the United Kingdom there is a movement towards a new regime of devolved parliaments and this may both liberate and strengthen provincial cities, especially if it is supported by an efficient taxing and economic policy. Kevin Murray foresees radical change: 'If the cities feel that their functions and the way that they're funded are not adequately supported by government, it's quite conceivable they could link up with other cities in Europe, and form a sort of new Hanseatic League and actually push in a different direction from national governments' (Murray and McDonald 1997).

Murray regards Britain's cities as major repositories of the skills, the talent, the education, the wealth and the civic government of the country. So a major issue will be how they are funded and administered as a function of that perception, and how they will be managed in such a way that they operate efficiently in a competitive international financial environment. He envisages cities having elected mayors, paid councillors and a key cabinet of senior executives. These people will lead the civic direction and be judged on performance by the citizens of the place. The lifestyles of the inhabitants of cities will benefit from changes in information technology and developments in modes of transport. People will enjoy flexible work patterns and communication systems will enable them to work from home. Homes may be operated from a distance through 'smart cards' and 'mobile phones'. The need for environmental sustainability is likely to make the city a less polluted and 'greener' place to be. The car industry will produce silent and pollution-free cars. Action to reduce congested urban road spaces mean more streets will be pedestrianised, more bicycles used. Good public transport will become a priority civic consideration. However, Britain is a long way from this reality with pressure for low-cost social housing within the city, and public transport systems that are inefficient, costly and inadequate for the numbers of people they aim to serve.

The times call for innovation in major city planning. The last couple of decades have seen an increase in multilateral communication and the growth of global information technology, both of which are necessary to foster an inclusive perspective of sustainability at a world level. However this period has also witnessed the power and expansion of a global financial industry and certain dominant cities, termed 'global cities'. Arguably, this development may be considered a counterforce to sustainable development upon the planet.

In the late 1980s cities such as London, New York and Tokyo began to function as transterritorial marketplaces for top-level management and coordination services which concentrated on international transactions and flows of finance and investment worldwide. With this came the imposition of specific forms on the spatial organisation in these cities, brought about by changes in social and economic structure and the consequent growth of a new urban hierarchy and of city politics oriented to world concerns. This caused further division between the rich and the poor within these cities. It has also given these cities elite status within their host countries. Traditional city plans have not coped adequately with this transition vertically or horizontally, functionally or aesthetically. Grid and concentric plans have focused development in a particular area of the city – agglomerations of high density – and high-rise buildings have been built rapidly to facilitate the vast, complex and specialised operations of the global financial industry as well as to provide expensive housing for its high-earning employees. These places tend to stand apart from the common community activities of the rest of the city and, on a global scale, interact more with similar areas in other major world cities. However, they do depend on, and have a certain detrimental effect on, their host cities. The volume of people, and their patterns of movement and consumption, stress the transport infrastructure and property market. In terms of social structure, these places have seen an increase in social and economic polarisation (Sassen 1991). Inequalities in the bidding power for land space within these cities mean it is difficult for lower income groups and public sector workers to find affordable housing and thus live near work locations. These recent developments may hardly be described as sustainable – little regard has been paid to environmental protection and they draw extravagantly on natural resources. But questions are being asked, not only about the durability of the spatial form associated with this expansion but also whether this type of economic expansion is justified and viable in the long term.

Innovation is needed in the philosophy of city planning and in the type of physical form the city should adopt. Questions have to be asked. How can the desire for consumption be tempered by the necessity for ecological sustainability? Have we reached a point where expansion and power are less purposeful than equity and equilibrium? Does the potential of sustainability hinge upon how selfish and avaricious the city is? How near are we to Lewis Mumford's vision, described nearly 50 years ago?

> An age of expansion is giving place to an age of equilibrium. The achievement of this equilibrium is the task of the next few centuries . . . The theme for the new period will be neither arms and the man nor machines and the man; its theme will be the resurgence of life, the displacement of the mechanical by the organic, and the re-establishment of the person as the ultimate term of all human effort. Cultivation, humanisation, co-operation, symbiosis: these are the watchwords of the new world-enveloping culture. Every department of life will record this change: it will affect the task of education and the procedures of science no less than the organisation of industrial enterprises, the planning of cities, the development of regions, the interchange of world resources.
>
> (Mumford 1961)

A prototype of a self-sustainable city of the future is given by the Japanese architect Kisho Kurokawa in relationship to his philosophy of symbiosis. The potential of this philosophy will be realised in what he terms an 'eco-media city'(Kurokawa 1997b). His plan and urban design strategies for Eco-Media City 2020, Malaysia, address a new urban agenda for sustainable development. Globalisation and the takeover of major cities as centres of international business and finance are not inevitable. The eco-media city has differing essential concepts of cultural identity, 'oneness with nature' and the built-in ability for a region to determine its own level and speed of development. A crucial element in this development strategy is the abundance of natural resources within a region, for a city is to be predetermined by the environmental strategy of incorporating forests and animal life into its design.

Eco-Media City 2020 is, as suggested, due for completion in 2020 and is intended for a population of 250,000 to 500,000. It will preserve the natural environment with the objective of forming a symbiosis between nature and the city, preservation and development, and nature and advanced technology through the dynamic creation of more forests and the effective use of natural resources. In part the purpose of the city is to decentralise key functions from Malaysia's capital, Kuala Lumpur, and its success will be heavily dependent on the cultivation and growth of eco- and multimedia technologies.

The proposed development will start approximately 50 kilometres south of Kuala Lumpur. The concept is based on a series of nodal points, or a network of small cities, which coexist with the natural environment and constitute a symbiotic cluster of cities, each complementing the other. Each of the five small cities will have a key activity such as government, research, university, airport or financial. The plan has greater flexibility and adaptability than the more conventional grid or concentric plans. It spreads the impact of highly concentrated city functions over five geographically dispersed nodal points, thereby avoiding the focus of high-density development in one prime location. This lessens the likelihood of traffic congestion and eases the competition for prime location premises, thus allowing for a greater socioeconomic diversity. The spatial arrangement – nodal points within landscape – allows for the possibility of future expansion as and when required; and the environmental impact of each nodal point is both taken up by surrounding landscape and easily monitored. The infrastructure is based on a multi-level network that combines three types of services for traffic and communication: a transportation network of high-speed, silent monorailways and highways linking core centres with an international airport that acts as a hub; a goods distribution network based on a system of containerisation modules, whereby goods are matched to appropriate container sizes and have access to transport infrastructure; and an advanced information network of a high-speed, large volume, digital information infrastructure for satellite and wireless. **(Figures 5a and 5b)**

Kisho Kurokawa's philosophy adds a new dimension to the concept of cultural symbiosis. His hypothesis is that if new city form becomes a process of imitating the likeness of European models, as some sort of equivalent of modernisation and progress, then the world will become abnormally homogeneous. 'Extreme "Eurocentricism" would have ended in the global adoption of European norms everywhere, with only minor differences among the races.' His thesis of symbiosis among different cultures advocates that the world would be far richer were these cultures helped to survive, resisting the drift towards homogeneity. It may be said that at present we are experiencing a fundamental breakdown in human attitude towards the city, and benign qualitative lifestyles, societies and institutions have become dysfunctional, inadequate to cope with the demands of sustainable development. In Kisho Kurokawa's words: 'Western society in the past has considered nature as opposed to humanity. Humans have constructed buildings and cities, while nature has remained outside and in opposition. However in Asia, including Japan, people have long considered themselves part of nature. This has given rise to a strong sense of gratitude for

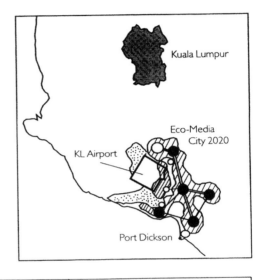

Figures 5a and 5b: Eco-Media City 2020, Malaysia: Architect Kisho Kurakawa. Figure 5a (above) shows the position of five nodal points within the proposed rainforest (diagonal shading). Figure 5b (right) shows the linear relationship of the development to Kuala Lumpur.

the benefits of nature and recognition of nature as a precious gift. Moreover Asians have traditionally protected such resources . . . The many ethnic groups of Asia have continued to live in ways that value human sensibilities in the abstract, while actively cultivating a sensibility towards nature.'

A vital part of the life of a city is expressed through cultural identity and cultural exchanges with other places. Kurokawa envisages that in the 21st century cultural exchange will take place through multimedia channels such as those represented in Eco-Media City. The small villages and farms already present on the site of the new city are to be included in its design. He sees multilateral progress for a global population as not merely economic or environmental but also cultural, and consequently supports the ability of a region to determine its own speed and type of development.

Where Kisho Kurokawa's philosophy relates to the symbiosis of nature and the city it is significant to environmental sustainability in a 21st-century context. Eco-Media City is in part an experimental exploration of the relationship of ecotechnologies and multimedia technologies and city sustainability. As previously noted, this experiment is dependent on the locality's potential for the cultivation of abundant natural resources – the imperative in his design strategy is the incorporation of forests and animal life in city design. It could be called 'the city in the forest'. An enormous man-made tropical rainforest is to be created, within which the small cities and any indigenous farms and villages will be located. **(Figure 5a)** The place is suited to forestry with long sunlight hours, high humidity and high rainfall. The climate is conducive to rapid tree growth so it is expected that the tree canopy may reach a height of 30 metres in 20 years.

One of the beautiful qualities of this plan is its inclusiveness. Small-scale highly advanced cities, traditional villages and farmsteads, silent monorail, international airport and information highways are all united within the dominance of the forest. Possibly it is asking for Utopia to expect this city will withstand global pressures of tourism and mass consumerism. However, the message for environmental sustainability is clear. The trees will shade a large part of the built city environment, therefore buildings will have less need for air-conditioning equipment, and the consequential lower ambient temperature of the city environment will mean considerable energy savings. Little or no thought has been given to the combination of cities and afforestation in modern urban planning, but it is the most influential design strategy for both lessening ambient city temperature and reducing the heat-island effect. Tree canopy not only reduces the need for summer air conditioning and winter heating but it also reduces the effects of heat radiation off concrete, automobile exhaust fumes and other sources that keep the ambient temperatures of cities high.

In Eco-Media City design strategies are focused on working with the physical conditions of the locality to make ecological and energy savings. All types of hybrid ecotechnologies, such as bioelectronics, biosensors, bioreactors and biomass, will be used to address some major city problems such as waste and rainwater run-off. Water will be controlled and purified through soil filtration and supply systems developed to use and recirculate water.

At present, it is the cities in the developed world that create the most global environmental damage by their extravagant consumption of natural resources, and an excessive use of energy in both buildings and transport. If developing countries emulate this city pattern, with the added dynamic of their projected population expansion, it would be impossible to achieve sustainability. Therefore, there is an urgent need for a more relevant and purposeful approach to the city.

The problem for the city is how to identify and address good practice and sustainable development in terms of landscape and built form. British cities that are acting positively – Manchester and Edinburgh, for example – are monitoring what is happening in other European cities. However, concepts of good practice and sustainable development are not the monopoly of the Western world. Evaluation of cultures and knowledge of development on a global scale would help to clarify and define the term sustainable development.

MAKING SENSE OF SUSTAINABILITY

If sustainability is to make sense certain recognised facts have to be realised or comprehended. Only then may it be possible to assess or monitor its progress, align human behaviour and expect to engage human consciousness on a global level. The first two chapters describe some specific problems, especially that of interconnectedness between seemingly contradictory tensions – global-local, objective-subjective, qualitative-quantitative. To give an internal consistency to the whole concept of sutainability, indicators are likely to come from general principles that are universally recognised but still have meaning when they are applied to all the variations involved in differing localities. In this way global consciousness is not confused by the magnitude or variety of local issues and the necessity to provide for local identity and particular solutions to local peculiarities is not compromised.

To occur, a 'global revolution' would require a massive transformation of world consciousness, ethically, morally, economically and politically. At present there is not a master plan for such a transformation. Hopefully, change will occur through evolutionary, and not revolutionary, processes as equilibrium, consistency and stability are preferable to violence, erratic development and insecurity.

Climate change is informing development towards environmental sustainability. The reduction of greenhouse-gas emissions has become a global imperative. However, the implementation of climate change policy is unlikely to be successful unless it addresses the implications of interconnected problems, especially inequality, biodiversity and the city. Sustainability demands the ability to foresee in order to forestall. Even with the positive environmental strategies put forward in Eco-Media City, of planting an enormous rainforest to bear the impact of future city development, if we look at the whole pattern of development for Southeast Asia the prospect of sustainable development without radical reform is slim. Slash-and-burn agriculture has long been practised in Indonesia and is a necessary part of existence for people living at marginal levels. Men and women who are preoccupied with the business of survival are not worried about the effects of fire on biodiversity or carbon emissions. However, burning for agribusinesses has become an industrialised process over the last 20 years, carried out by global companies and ignored by national governments. Financial profits from the oil palm plantations that replace rainforest are considerable. The world's demand for consumer products such as soaps, salad dressings and biscuits comes at the expense of tropical rainforest which is now one of the planet's environmental disasters. Burning, together with the changes in weather patterns associated with El Niño, delayed monsoons, and longer dry seasons before extreme storms that cause damage and soil erosion, have destabilised the balance of nature and rainforests (Simons 1998). The remains of a dead, rotting rainforest release carbon emissions and do not neutralise them. Development has to do more than keep up with damage by replacing it with a few benign examples of design strategies for the city. It must eradicate the problems that cause the damage in the first place.

Certain factors stand out as preventing the functioning of sustainable development. The massive population increase poses problems of sufficiency and equity; the globalisation of the economy has become an exclusive element which fractionalises itself from the interests of the whole of humanity and is not held accountable for its impact; and various types of city form, whose infrastructures are neither effective nor efficient in terms of the consumption of natural resources and energy, and whose institutional, social and cultural structures are inadequate, fail to provide stable, consistent, qualitative environments for their citizens.

Before concentrating on the material development of a place it is necessary to define what is required of its society. Meadows et al (1972) define a sustainable society as one that would be interested in the quality rather than the extent of development; it would differentiate between types of growth and their purposes; and it would explore the costs of growth, both to human beings and in terms of the planet, before deciding on any proposal.

Chapter Three
Four Premises for Sustainable Development

Sustainability is a dialectical and syllogistic process where the scientific needs to be appropriately balanced by the human attitude. However, in approaching a formula for assessing the sustainable development of a place, and in our need to identify a common aesthetic for sustainability, the acceptance of essential logical truths is necessary as the basis for further analysis, even if the analysis is to be the analysis of variance. This chapter presents four premises which, taken at their most essential, are the common denominators of a framework of assessment and an aesthetic. They have the potential to be applied locally and globally, and their focus on man's interaction with the environment is not compromised by simple or sophisticated technologies. Three of the premises are drawn directly from the professions of landscape or architecture and the fourth is concerned with the economics of sustainable development.

THE INTERCONNECTEDNESS OF SUSTAINABILITY
The architect and mathematician Christopher Alexander puts forward a structured way of thinking capable of coping with the complexities of sustainability issues (1965). He recognises the city as a vast and complex system, which in turn is part of an even bigger system of social organisation whose values and goals are being questioned, and provides two ways of viewing its infrastructure. He likens these to abstract mathematical terms: 'the tree' and the 'semi-lattice'. Both are ways of thinking about how a large collection of many small systems makes up a large and complex system. He defines sets, in relation to the city, as 'collections of material elements like people, blades of grass, cars, bricks, molecules, houses, gardens, water, pipes, the water molecules that run in them etc.' He defines a system thus: 'When the elements of a set belong together because they co-operate or work together somehow, we call the set of elements a system.' A semi-lattice is formed of subsets which have far more permeations and greater flexibility of integration and interaction than tree structures, which have more restrictive conditions. **(Figure 6)**

Alexander's axiom for the semi-lattice is: 'A collection of sets forms a semi-lattice if, and only if, when two overlapping sets belong to the collection then the set of elements common to both also belongs to the collection.' The importance is in the difference between structures in which no overlap occurs and those in which overlap does occur. The semi-lattice is potentially a much more complex and subtle structure than a tree. So, for any practical form of assessment that is to encompass the interconnectedness and complexity of the concerns involved in a study of sustainable place the methodological structure should be that of a semi-lattice. Alexander's diagrammatic reasoning provides both an analytical tool and a universal metaphor for the holistic nature of sustainability.

Alexander makes a comparison with bureaucratically organised cities of a tree-like structure, and suggests the possibility of greater adaptability and variety through adopting the semi-lattice: 'As long as we conceive of the city as a collection of segregated units, having no relationship with one another, such as the separations made between residential communities, commercial and industrial zones and shopping and recreational areas, we are denying meaningful growth. The largeness of the city only emphasises the isolation of its parts.' Whenever there is a tree structure it means that, within the structure, no piece of any unit is ever connected to other units except through the medium of the unit as a whole. 'It is a little as though the

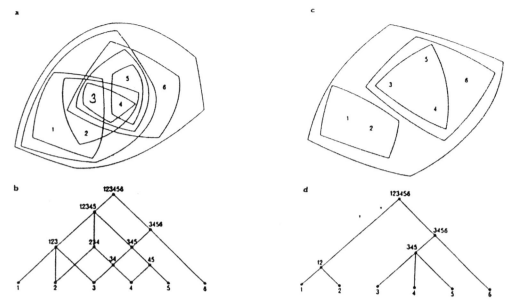

Figure 6: Two ways of viewing the city's infrastructure: subsets forming a 'semi-lattice' (a) and (b); and 'tree structures' (c) and (d). (Alexander 1965)

members of a family were not free to make friends outside the family, except when the family as a whole made a friendship.' A system which allows for interconnection between physical conditions, functional needs, institutional requirements and cultural identity, not just within the city but also within a wider world context, is a fundamental part of sustainability. For example, in the United Kingdom the factors that cause acid rainfall to be a problem in the Midlands and Wales cannot be isolated to locality, but are relative to factors such as pollution put into the atmosphere in places as far afield as Russia and cosmic forces that cause the rain to fall on the high land.

Habits in ways of thinking are difficult to change. Alexander reassures bureaucratic thinkers who fear disorder as a result of change: 'The ideas of overlap, ambiguity, multiplicity of aspect, and the "semi-lattice" are not less orderly than the rigid "tree" structure, but more so. They represent a thicker, tougher, more subtle and more complex view of structure.'

LIMITS TO GROWTH

Economics, too, needs to be seen and addressed as part of this structure. In *Beyond Growth* (1997) Herman Daly regards the economy as a subsystem of the larger system of sustainable development. 'Unless one has the preanalytic vision of the economy as subsystem, the whole idea of sustainable development, of a subsystem being sustained by a larger system whose limits and capacities it must respect . . . makes no sense whatsoever.' Governments, world-banking institutions and businesses, including the business of architecture, while embracing the ethos of sustainable development, reverently perceive of the economy as being apart and not subject to the same terms of contract. Governments base their policies for national prosperity on fast growth, to be achieved by speeding up the flow of energy and materials through the economy.

The consumption of the earth's resources beyond its sustainable capacities of renewal is seen as the instigation of the current crisis in economic theory. This has brought into conflict the needs and requirements of the North and the South. Herman Daly writes: 'While all countries must worry about both population and per capita resources consumption, it is evident that the South needs to focus more on population, and the North more on per capita resource consumption. Why should the South control their populations if the resources saved thereby are merely gobbled up by the North's over consumption? Why should the North control its over consumption if the saved resources will merely allow a larger number of people to subsist at the same level of misery?'

Consumption is the crucial factor in economic change and a 'yardstick' of sustainable development. Daly discusses it under the headings 'Value Added', 'Physical Transformation' and 'Welfare'. All three are dependent on land and natural resources, a relationship that is often overlooked when we regard the economic characteristics of the late 20th century with its 'global financial industry' and the 'credit/debt society'.

Value Added is clarified through example. The entire extractive sector (mines, wells, quarries, etc) account for a mere 5 per cent or 6 per cent of GNP, a seemingly insignificant figure in comparison with the 95 per cent input from the efforts of human beings through labour or investment. However, Daly argues: 'If the 95 per cent of value added is not independent of the 5 per cent in the extractive sector, but rather depends upon it – is based on it – then the impression of relative unimportance is false. That 5 per cent is the base upon which the other 95 per cent rests, that to which its value is added. Value cannot be added to nothing.'

Most world economies have worked on the principle that the larger the supply of a natural resource, the lower its price and, consequently, the faster it is used up. 'We tend to treat natural value added as a subsidy, a free gift of nature. The greater the natural subsidy, the less the cost of labour and capital (value added) needed for further arrangement. The less the humanly added value the lower the price, and the more rapid the use.'

Physical Transformation applies in particular to energy. It is based on the first and second laws of thermodynamics (Georgescu-Roegen 1971; Soddy 1922): that matter/energy is not produced or consumed, only transformed, thus matter/energy is arranged in production, disarranged in consumption, rearranged in production, etc; and that this rearranging and recycling of material building blocks takes energy, that energy itself is not recycled, and that on each cycle some of the material building blocks are dissipated beyond recall.

Daly elaborates on the qualitative effects of recycling. 'We not only consume the value we add to matter, but also the value that was added by nature before we imported it into the economic subsystem and that was necessary for it to be considered a resource in the first place.' Recycling does not return natural value into the environment. 'Taking matter/energy from the larger system, adding value to it, using up the added value, and returning the waste clearly alters the environment. The matter/energy we return is not the same as the matter/energy we take in. If it were, we could simply use it again and again in a closed circular flow. Common observation tells us, and the law of entropy confirms, that waste matter/energy is qualitatively different from raw materials.'

Growth economies continually increase the physical scale of matter/energy throughput to accommodate the economic activities of production and consumption of commodities: they are quantitative. Throughput begins with depletion and ends with pollution. Daly advocates qualitative improvement in the use made of a given scale of throughput, as a result of either improved technical knowledge or a deeper understanding of purpose. This development he identifies as 'steady-state economy' (SSE), and he says of it: 'A SSE therefore, can develop but cannot grow, just as the planet earth, of which it is a subsystem, can develop without growing.' This is by no means a static state. 'There is continuous renewal by death and birth, depreciation and production, as well as qualitative improvement in the stocks of both people and artefacts.'

Are not growth, increased production and increased consumption necessary for human welfare? Governments base industrial relationships with national labour forces on this principle; developing countries borrow capital from creditors in more prosperous economies on the strength of increased production of consumable commodities for the export trade. Daly's argument under the heading Welfare is that this is not the way towards sustainable development. 'Welfare is the service of want satisfaction rendered by stocks of capital, both man-made and natural. The proper economic object is to transform natural into man-made capital to the optimal extent, to the point where total service (the sum of services from natural and man-made capital) is a maximum.' Optimal scale occurs where 'the marginal benefit of services of more man-made capital is just equal to the marginal cost of natural services sacrificed when the natural capital that had been yielding those services is transformed into man-made capital.' He reasons that the world, as a whole, has overshot the optimal scale. Further, human welfare is not a function of consumption but of capital stocks: 'We cannot ride to town on the maintenance costs, the depletion and replacement flow of an automobile, but only in the complete automobile, a member of the current stock of automobiles.'

Given that natural capital stocks are in short supply, what are the implications for economic development? Daly states the physical situation: 'Our dowry of natural capital is more or less given, and is not the product of human labour and capital. Parts of that dowry are highly systemic and indivisible among nations. And the part that is divisible was divided by geologic, not economic, processes.' His argument continues: 'If we accept that natural and man-made capital are complements rather than substitutes, then what follows? If factors are complements, then the one in shortest supply will be the limiting factor.' This proposition gives rise to the following thesis: the world is moving from an era in which man-made capital was the limiting factor into an era in which remaining natural capital is the limiting factor. Daly gives these examples: 'Barrels of pumped crude oil is limited by petroleum deposits (or more stringently by the capacity of the atmosphere to absorb CO_2), not by pumping capacity; and agricultural production is frequently limited by water availability, not by tractors, harvesters or even land area.' To summarise, he is saying we have moved from a world relatively full of natural capital and empty of man-made capital and people, to a world relatively full of the latter and empty of the former.

Economic logic requires that we maximise the productivity of the limiting factor in the short run, and invest in increasing its supply in the long run. This is a pivotal point where new patterns of scarcity dictate that changes in behaviour are needed if we are to remain economic: 'Instead of maximising returns to and investing in man-made capital (as was appropriate in an empty world), we must now maximise returns to and invest in natural capital (as is appropriate in a full world).' Of course, there are major problems to be resolved within this change – political inconvenience and confusion over an equitable solution to the credit versus debt divide, to name two. Inevitably, limits would mean less building, including development connected with human welfare such as schools and hospitals.

Daly, referring to Soddy (1933), acknowledges that the ruling passion of the age has been to convert wealth that perishes into debt that endures and brings in perennial interest. Hence a global financial industry exists like some sort of religious icon. What hope of convincing those who like a flutter on the stock exchange that there are comparable forms of excitement? Much of the money circulating as investment ends up in the commissioning of large architectural projects. To what extent is architecture subject to market forces? Is it, therefore, incompatible with the ethics of sustainable development? The economics of sustainable development pose ethical questions that the architectural profession needs to address; not the least important is the question of moral responsibility for its part in the fast flow of natural resources through the economy.

Soddy (1926) gives an explanation for the misguided economic reasoning of the first half of the 20th century: 'Because formerly ownership of land, which, with the sunshine that falls on it, provides a revenue of wealth secured, in the form of rent, a share in the annual harvest without labour or service, upon which a cultured and leisured class could permanently establish itself, the age seems to have conceived the preposterous notion that money, which can buy land, must have the same revenue producing power.' He says of the banking system that banks create and destroy money with no understanding of the 'laws that correlate its quantity with the national income'. And that, by continually changing the value of money as they create and destroy it, the banking system converts the pound sterling into an inconsistent and constantly variable form of measurement.

Revenue-producing power has become the basis for the growth ethic. Daly regards the fact that growth has been and still is our central organising principle as the major problem: 'We are in need of a fundamental ethic that will guide our actions in a way more in harmony with both basic religious insight and the scientifically verifiable limits of the natural world.' He suggests this ethic is to be found in the terms 'sustainability', 'sufficiency', 'equity' and 'efficiency'. 'We should strive for sufficient per capita wealth, efficiently maintained and allocated, and equitably distributed, for the maximum number of people that can be sustained over time under these conditions. It may not be possible to sustain all human life.' The technical and economic problems involved in achieving sustainability are not that difficult. The hard problem is in overcoming our addiction to growth as the favoured way to assert our creative power, and the idolatrous belief, whether we think in religious terms or not, that our derived creative power is autonomous and unlimited. Such idolatry cannot admit that the elimination of poverty requires recognition of limits, not faster growth, limits to growth in per capita resource use, limits to population growth, limits to growth of inequality. This suggests a need for local control over the availability of resources balanced by the extent of external dependencies, whether or not growth, in quantitative terms, is justifiable given local circumstances. In this way we may attempt to measure and control the environmental impact of a place. Refusal to recognise these material limits results in growth beyond the carrying capacity of the earth, with its consequent destruction, followed by a reduction in the cumulative number of lives to be lived in conditions of material sufficiency, as well as in the premature deaths of many people now living below sufficiency.

The framework of assessment should take into consideration the factors that limit economic growth in real terms: measurement of local and global natural resources; giving these resources appropriate economic value; adjusting to reasonable levels of production and consumption. Accordingly the wealth of a place may be judged on its stock of natural resources and its potential for their regeneration versus its dependence on external resources. Whereas quantitative growth may not be possible in all places, qualitative change, which addresses sustainability, sufficiency, equity and efficiency, is.

ENERGY-INTERACTION OF ARCHITECTURE AND THE ENVIRONMENT

Simos Yannas (1996) establishes a premise that gives form and meaning to the evolving interaction of architecture and the environment in the pursuit of sustainable development. He posits the potential of the architect to 'design buildings which have a minimum dependence on fossil fuel, whether in the form of embodied energy or for operational use. The form and elements of a building can be made to respond to natural cycles both daily and seasonal and to exploit ambient energy sources and sinks.'

This is to be achieved through what Yannas calls the evolution of a 'shared science', in operation with 'spatial and temporal interactions in natural and man-made environments'. This shared science is to combine with the interactions of space dimensions, the size and shape of an open or enclosed space, to produce an effect. It will also work through the limitations of varying conditions over a period of time. The determining design factors become 'climate', 'site', 'building type' and 'design brief'. His concept of 'appropriate' stresses the localisation of this process: 'Appropriateness involves questions of where, for whom, for what purpose, when and for how long and why.' So, although we have a goal that is of global concern – the reduction in fossil-fuel use, we have a design concept that addresses the peculiarities of specific place.

A key to understanding is the term 'shared science' and how this is to operate with the above. The shared science seems to relate what is known about the geophysical environment, climate, ecological infrastructure and building technique to accomplishing a desired and purposeful effect in the creation of human habitat. Yannas goes on to determine the type of human experience required: 'A cognitive feel for innate qualities of different architectural forms and materials as these manifest themselves in different building types and in different climate – empirical knowledge which is derived not only from measurement but from experience of buildings – modelling and simulation, which are means of informing design and assessing buildings in practice.'

The interaction of environmental conditions, exactness of technique and appropriateness of design is stressed, together with the quality of intuition. This would suggest that the internal consistency of an architectural aesthetic for both global and local concerns for sustainability may be satisfied through the recognition of the general principles of the shared science of appropriateness. Thus it is possible for all architects to share a common objective, knowledge and skills, without devaluing specific local or national styles yet allowing for these to coexist appropriately as they occur as part of a particular cultural identity. The methodological implication within a framework of assessment is that indicators are likely to encompass universal principles such as passive systems, landscaping and resource efficiency in interaction with such ambient forces as movement of the sun, winds, light and shade.

Dean Hawkes (1996c) discusses how environmental concerns influence the design of the building envelope. He differentiates environmental design strategies between two architectural forms: the 'exclusive' mode and the 'selective' mode. The effectiveness of the exclusive mode is dependent on the isolation of the internal envelope of the building fabric from exterior ambient forces. The effectiveness of the selective mode is dependent on benign interaction between the interior of a building and exterior ambient forces.

With the exclusive mode the building envelope, usually square and deep plan, is used to exclude the effects of the external environment on the internal conditions. Thermal comfort of the occupants, lighting, heating, cooling and ventilation are controlled artificially through energy-using mechanical plant. The internal environment is protected from the fluctuating demands of the exterior environment. This type of building is usually automated and its performance is usually compromised by user interference, such as the opening and closing of windows.

In comparison the selective-mode building usually has greater transparency and complexity because it admits and controls ambient energy sources. Its development is dependent on the cost-effective exploitation of ambient energy sources without incurring any penalties in terms of environmental discomfort. Therefore such design strategies as use of solar gain for winter warmth, natural lighting and ventilation are major components of this type of building. The aim is to create as natural an environment as possible, and users are able to exercise effective control over their environment for their thermal comfort through such processes as the opening of windows or drawing of blinds.

To put this into a time context, the historical approach to building was, of necessity, to control extreme discomfort caused by the natural environment or climate by adapting the form and fabric of the building envelope – the selective mode. Occupants and building design and form worked with the natural environment through site and orientation, such as windows placed to take advantage of solar gains, achieved thermal comfort through adjustments to seasonal energy demand or manual adjustments. With the advances in science and technology throughout the 20th century it became possible to replace all elements of the natural environment in automated buildings with mechanical and electrical service systems. This involved high energy consumption. The energy crisis of the 1970s and the present-day crisis in energy emissions have forced a redress of the balance between the relative roles to be played by the fabric of the building and mechanical systems. We require buildings of low energy in either embodied or operational use. This focuses attention again on 'bioclimatic architecture', 'environmental design', 'passive and low-energy architecture' and 'selective' mode buildings – or simply architecture that works with rather than against climate. Since the 1970s science has played an important role in developing new technologies of environmental control, and processes of testing, monitoring and simulating environments, so that problems of heat, light, sound, ventilation and pollution may be quantified. Through the monitoring and directing of the sources, flows and destinations of the energy used in buildings it may be possible to control energy use and emissions.

Environment at the threshold is the essential of a new approach to architecture, and this, as Dean Hawkes explains, 'revolves around the transition that occurred from the technologically dominated attitudes of the 1960s and1970s – as represented in built form by the deep-plan, air-conditioned office building stereotype, and in theoretical terms by the "exclusive" mode – to the humanistic, environmentally responsible approach of the bioclimatic, "selective" mode. Central to this is the idea of environmental diversity, realised and experienced spatially and temporally. This envisages spaces in which environmental uniformity, in all its dimensions of heat, light and sound, is replaced by variations, within limits, which maintain, in the occupants, a sense of the dynamics of the proper condition of humankind.'

The logical progression of this reasoning is to extend this type of environmental work on architecture to master-planning within cities, so that form, orientation and spaces have the beneficial effect of reducing the energy needs and energy emissions of the city. Again, it is in effect like sculpting with physical conditions, overshadowing and natural light, solar radiation, and winter heat or summer overheating. However, here we must go back to the significance of Yannas's point about the design brief. Places develop incrementally and will demand particular and appropriate, unique design solutions not easily discussed within the realms of stereotypes. In many cities there are many times more ambient energy sources impacting on buildings in the form of sun or wind than they use in their functioning. However, only a small proportion of these are used constructively in the design of our environments (Anderson 1990).

The argument presented here is taken up in the two case studies in Chapters Five and Six. Both relate to urban forms which have longevity of development. Towards the end of the book, in contemporary examples of emerging master plans that meet the needs of today's problems, the argument is readdressed. This gives historical precedence and contemporary adaptations to this premise.

AN ENVIRONMENTAL AESTHETIC

Jay Appleton posited his Habitat Theory after considerable reference and research (1975). It was concerned with landscape but is equally applicable to architecture or environments of habitation. The theory postulates that 'aesthetic satisfaction, experienced in the contemplation of landscape, stems from the spontaneous perception of landscape features which, in their shapes, colours, spatial arrangements and other visible attributes, act as sign-stimuli indicative of environmental conditions favourable to survival, whether they really are favourable or not.' This expresses the precept that, in part, suggestion and association connect with aesthetic experience, and that this originally derived from a place which afforded the opportunity for the satisfaction of basic biological needs. Man may once have needed to get to the walled, hilltop city to ensure his survival and safety in a threatening landscape; although this is no longer a necessity, comfort and aesthetic satisfaction are associated with the landmark of the walled, hilltop city. This implies that man's relationship with the environment satisfies functional biological needs and provides psychological comfort.

Appleton further develops the argument with another characteristic of man in his environment: 'Outstandingly important, however, in this elementary relationship between man and his perceived environment is the extent to which he is able to exploit it in securing an advantage in his relations with his fellow humans, with other creatures of the animal world, and with those inorganic forces of nature which used to be poetically called the elements.'

Concisely, Habitat Theory is about the ability of a place to satisfy human biological and psychological needs. This is further reduced in scope in Appleton's Prospect-Refuge Theory (1975). Here aesthetic satisfaction, as experienced in landscape and architecture, is reduced to one phrase: 'To see without being seen.' Appleton explains: 'It provides a kind of shorthand reaction to environment by latching on to a facet of behaviour which automatically exploits the advantages latent in a creature's surroundings.' This implies that an environment or building which affords both an opportunity to see and a good opportunity to hide is aesthetically more satisfying than one which affords neither. These theories have been applied by Grant Hildebrand (1994) to the architecture of Frank Lloyd-Wright and show very positive results in terms of human psychological comfort in relation to prospect and refuge spaces. This argument is explored further in Chapter Seven.

With industrialisation and large numbers of people living almost exclusively in built-up urban environments instinctual interaction with landscape has deteriorated. Landscape is indiscriminately exploited to provide energy and consumer products to facilitate the lifestyles of a city population. Sustainability forces the reassessment of our attitude towards landscape. Appleton's premise is that man is descended from ancestors who, being at risk as soon as they were born into the world, reduced the danger of premature extinction proportionately in the only way they could by using the environment to further their chances of biological existence. Brenda Colvin expresses the significance of this interrelationship not only for our biological survival but also for our spiritual wellbeing: 'Humanity cannot exist independently and must cherish the relationships binding us to the rest of life. That relationship is expressed usually by the landscape in which we live' (Colvin 1948). Both of these concepts are instrumental in the shaping of new attitudes towards sustainable development. We are now faced with so many destructive forces on the environment that it becomes a necessity to regain a cognitive feel for the benign qualities of landscape and to positively design them into man-made environments. Landscape design strategies are possibly the most creative area of sustainable development. In the landscape of the planet there is the potential to overcome humanity's problems of energy and energy emissions; and it is likely that the reality of this would be greater than the sum of its parts for it could give a new spiritual depth to man's existence. The aesthetic of sustainability.

Science helps the process of analysis and quantification; historical hindsight provides experience of how man has made use of landscape for his own biological existence. Michael Hough (1995) gives an example of how the contribution of landscape to city problems such as energy emissions can be quantified: 'A Douglas fir with a diameter of 38cm. Can remove 19.7kg. of sulphur dioxide per year without injury from an atmospheric concentration of 0.25 parts per million . . . it shows that to take up the 462,000 tones of sulphur dioxide released annually in St. Louis, Missouri it would require 50 million trees. These would occupy about 5 per cent of the city's land area.' Johann Heinrich von Thunen's 'The Isolated State' (Hawkes 1996b) symbolises the historical relationship of the city and landscape. **(Figure 7)** Landscape and city have a purposeful relationship. Landscape provides the sustenance for the thriving of an urban nucleus. The potential of the city is proportional to the availability in its immediate surrounding landscape of natural resources to facilitate its functioning in terms of energy, production and food. In relationship to the present-day concern about energy and energy emissions, the impact of the city is accounted for within a given radius of the city centre. The significance of forest close to the city is symbolic of the importance of a low-cost, available energy source as an essential to the economy of the city. Things have changed, however, and the forest may now be significant as an essential energy-emission 'sink' for the city. The geographical area of modern cities is expansive and may be formed by a number of nuclei. The city may be dependent on vast quantities of varying external geographical sources – an unspecific environment

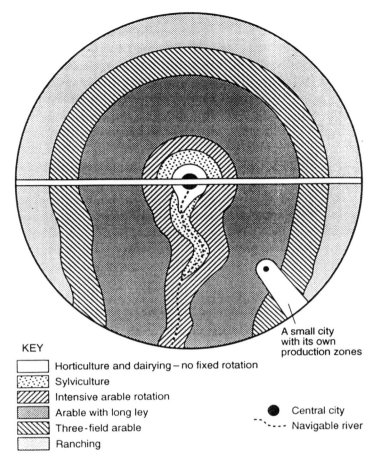

KEY

Horticulture and dairying – no fixed rotation

Sylviculture

Intensive arable rotation

Arable with long ley

Three-field arable

Ranching

A small city
with its own
production zones

● Central city

- - - - - Navigable river

Figure 7: Johann Heinrich von Thunen's 'The Isolated State'.

not related to a landscape hinterland. Whereas a certain reliance on external dependents can be stimulatingly competitive, overreliance is an indicator of vulnerability and weakness. It brings a greater risk of inconsistency of energy supply, and an inability to control the quantity and quality of food and other natural resources.

World sustainability requires man to acknowledge his destructive activities and to change those activities through self-regulation. Is it reasonable or realistic to expect this innately benign awareness from human beings? Is it not more likely that changing physical conditions, laws, economic restraints and social requirements will provide the corrective to man's instinctive desire to exploit? On a more positive note, in architecture we are beginning to experience a rebirth of building with climate, and such things as 'passive cooling' and 'natural ventilation' are again being used in building design showing that natural forces may be exploited to have a benign influence. Essential to sustainability is the equation between man and nature. If man chooses to dominate and exploit, such natural 'sinks' for carbon dioxide emissions as the tropical rainforests will be destroyed. Nature, being absolute, will not react with a compassionate response, and ultimately a change in atmosphere and climate will prohibit human life form. Therefore, paradoxically, if man now wishes to exploit his environment to his own advantage and survive he will take stock of the impact of his development and consumption habits which debilitate the functioning and regeneration of the natural environment, especially as it may be perceived in landscape. The refuge landscape offers is safety from exposure to the extremes of climate change; the prospect is of sunsets instead of heat islands, a view from the window of a tree canopy instead of traffic gridlock and, from the city, the prospect of forests, rivers and land which are benignly associated with human sustenance. The aesthetic is about valuing, and wanting to sustain, the benign qualities of nature because they act as sign-stimuli indicative of environmental conditions favourable to survival.

CONSISTENCY AND LOGIC

The four premises in this chapter give an internal consistency and logic to sustainability. They encompass universal principles which are also pertinent to particular places. The diagrammatic reasoning of the semi-lattice becomes a useful methodological tool for any framework of assessment that is to encompass the interconnectedness of interdependent variables in order to identify varying stages of development in particular localities. The equating of economic power with its limiting factor, natural resources, and making use of the naturally occurring climate in daylighting, ventilation and space heating to control energy and energy emissions within our places, are common denominators in sustainable development. Man's territorial behaviour and consequent relationship with place is both biological and psychological, but what is important is that humanity regains this inclusive connection. Many complexities exist in the particulars of the vast array of places. Design strategies are about finding new creative ways of exploiting ambient forces to make sustainability work for us in providing energy, 'sinks', sufficiency, equity and a sense of human worth and wealth which connects with a quality of life.

Chapter Four
A Framework of Assessment

What are the distinctive features of 'sustainable place'? Can the different constituents of these features be identified to form a framework of assessment? This chapter posits a framework in answer to these questions. Its design, construction and methodology arise out of a need for a system that takes aesthetic qualities and human response into account alongside, and appropriately balanced with, the more tangible and quantifiable characteristics of sustainable development. Although this framework is intended to aid those working within the fields of landscape, architecture and master-planning, the inclusive nature of sustainability has been accommodated within the range of cross-disciplinary sustainability indicators. In the context of place value, the significance of incremental development is acknowledged throughout. Each place has a past and present that give potential in a projected future.

The introduction to this book and Chapters One and Two explored the character of sustainability, the nature and diversity of problems, and the tensions created by the interconnectedness of seemingly paradoxical issues – global-local, quantitative-qualitative, objective-subjective. An awareness of the potential elements of an aesthetic for sustainability is emerging out of a response to these concerns. The whole is significant in the conceptual building of a prototype framework of assessment for sustainable place. Sustainability is not a 'static state' of development but a wide and diverse range of issues held together through a symbiotic relationship, rather like the billions of cells functioning together to maintain correct body temperature, constantly having to adapt to infection and changes in external conditions. Failure of a certain part to function correctly can cause stress in other areas. The analogy of a body can be taken as representative both of the global environment and of particular place. Indicators of sustainable development have therefore to be relevant to global objectives yet pertinent to a framework that has application at a local level.

The certain logical truths drawn from the premises for sustainable development in Chapter Three form the a priori reasoning for the framework. The framework has a methodology capable of dealing with the interconnectedness of the issues under assessment. Environmental considerations and the availability and use of natural resources need to be equated, in real terms, to economic potential. Designing and building with climate to maximise the ambient energy sources of a place is important in minimising fossil-fuel energy production and energy needs and emissions. Sustainable development involves a partnership between man and the physical conditions of the planet that sustain his existence. This is essentially an inclusive relationship with landscape, both biological and psychological. Industrialisation and urbanisation have weakened this relationship to the point that it becomes a necessity to positively design benign qualities into environments. Man needs to regain a cognitive feel and perception for features which act as sign-stimuli indicative of environmental conditions favourable to survival.

The framework adopts a number of definitions and terms in its conceptualisation and these are listed below.

Sustainable place: A place which, through natural or man-made attributes, is able to foster conditions physically, functionally, culturally and institutionally that prolong and nurture life-generating forces for man.

Sustainable society: 'A sustainable society would be interested in qualitative development, not physical expansion. It would use material growth as a considered tool, not a perpetual mandate. It would be neither for nor against growth. Rather, it would begin to discriminate kinds of growth and purposes for growth. Before this society decided on any specific growth proposal it would ask what the growth is for, and who would benefit, and what it would cost, and how long it would last, and whether it could be accommodated by the sources and sinks of the planet' (Meadows et al 1992).

This dispels the attitude that development is growth in quantitative terms, which has led to the global trebling of population over the last 50 years and put increasing pressure on the planet's ecosystems through the depletion of natural resources and excessive and harmful energy use. It wisely advocates that a society should carry out a form of 'stock taking' to justify the impact of its presence on the globe.

Boundary: Defined boundary is a prerequisite of any form of impact assessment. With sustainable development come new concepts of what boundary should do. How can boundary assist with changes being made environmentally, in particular in addressing problems associated with climate change? In relation to the seasonal flooding of many of the rivers in Britain, focusing attention on flood-defence systems within county or regional boundaries may no longer be appropriate; it may even exacerbate the problem. Flood-defence systems put in place to protect development in the upper region of a river may cause a greater volume of water for towns in the lower region. This suggests that a sensible boundary would define the whole course of the river and its related tributaries. And within this boundary urban and rural landscape could be addressed to provide effective solutions. Defined boundaries are also necessary to calculate the true impact of urban development and the environmental wealth of a place in relation to the need for sustainable development. Expansion and growth may not be justified in a place of poor environmental or physical conditions, especially if the place is heavily reliant on external dependencies for energy, natural resources, pollution clearance and food sustenance. 'The Isolated State' presents a stereotype master plan that establishes a simplistic interrelationship of an urban nucleus supported by a rural hinterland. **(Figure 7)** Where such a relationship of landscape and town exists, the impact of a place may be taken up within its own boundary. However, many modern cities are vast conglomerations of numerous urban nuclei and their impact is not taken up within their defined boundaries. With sustainability comes the need for accountability for such concerns as the reduction of greenhouse-gas emissions and renewable energy sources, and defined boundary assists the process of proportioning accountability in terms of measurement, control and quality. Defined boundary, through containment, strengthens the cultural identity and autonomy of place in both a cultural and aesthetic sense, making it easier for a society to identify and withstand powerful global influences that threaten the form and character of a place. Boundary is also a precondition in determining architectural form, not only in terms of the aesthetic but also in relation to appropriate form and arrangements to maximise efficient ambient energy resources.

THE MASTER PLAN

The master plan gives the features of a place assessment that have direct bearing on landscape, architecture and master-planning. It has a central hypothesis that leads out to four constituent parts. **(Figure 8)** The central hypothesis has visual implications. The quality and condition of the landscape and architecture of a place are indicative of the state of sustainability: humanity's coming to terms with, and responding to, the physical conditions, psychological and functional needs, cultural identity and institutional requirements in a particular environment. This suggests a first stage of becoming familiar with, or getting to know, the physical attributes and ambient forces inherent in an environment that is to be assessed in terms of sustainable

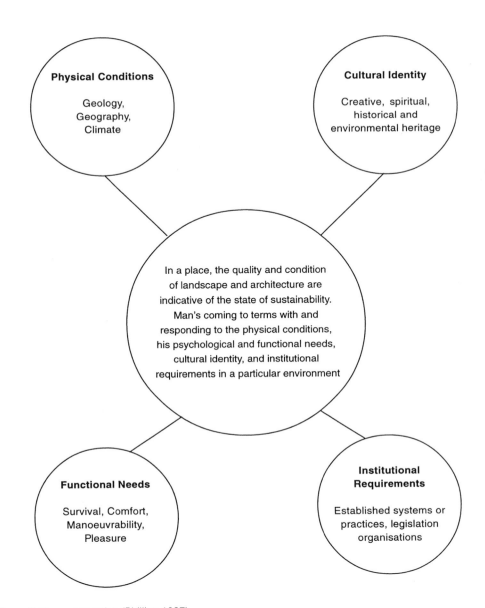

Physical Conditions

Geology,
Geography,
Climate

Cultural Identity

Creative, spiritual,
historical and
environmental heritage

In a place, the quality and condition
of landscape and architecture are
indicative of the state of sustainability.
Man's coming to terms with and
responding to the physical conditions,
his psychological and functional needs,
cultural identity, and institutional
requirements in a particular environment

Functional Needs

Survival, Comfort,
Manoeuvrability,
Pleasure

**Institutional
Requirements**

Established systems or
practices, legislation
organisations

Figure 8: The master plan (Phillips 1997).

development—observation that is in part dependent on a cognitive feel for the environmental effects resulting from different architectural form and materials in various climates, landscapes and spatial arrangements. Empirical knowledge is derived not only from intelligence based on measurement and processes such as modelling and simulation for testing the effects of certain collective arrangements, but also from experience of assessing the interaction of such collective arrangements in practice. The constituent parts of the methodology used for this assessment are physical conditions, functional needs, institutional requirements and cultural identity. Emphasis has been placed on the interaction of man, landscape and architecture. This system takes aesthetic qualities and human response into account alongside, and appropriately balanced with, the more tangible and quantifiable characteristics of sustainable development.

INDICATORS

The central hypothesis for the master plan indicates that the assessment process is to be accomplished through the use of sustainability indicators. **(Table 1)** These are listed in their constituent parts which, in turn collectively, are used to assess the environmental impact of the place. The indicators arise out of the considered evaluation of the current concern for sustainability and were modified during empirical research on the San Gimignano case study (Chapter Five). One difficulty that is immediately apparent is the relative qualities of such indicators as 'geographical convenience', 'human misery' and 'private spaces'. While these are important considerations in sustainable development, they are not easily measured or obviously visually apparent. In the absence of a jury to give consensus, the rating of positive or negative is dependent on the experience and expertise of the assessors.

THE INTERCONNECTEDNESS OF CONSTITUENT PARTS

The identified constituent parts of a place act in an integrated manner. They are interconnected and constantly flexible, holding and pulling each other into a state of balance that is part of the holistic nature of sustainable development. A place is made up of an infinite number of subsets in relation to, and interdependent on, each other. **(Figure 9)** These are the analytical elements of this multicriteria assessment method. Nationally, most places seek a solution to current problems of sufficient and equitable housing. Government initiative has identified the need for a specific number of new homes over a period of time. (An institutional requirement related to a functional need.) Traditionally local authorities have allocated land for housing development. However, the growing fear is that this allocation will consume even more of one of Britain's highly controversial natural resources: countryside. (Past institutional requirements must change to accommodate protection of scarce physical conditions.) Many 'brown sites' and derelict buildings within cities have been suggested for housing development. Two problems arise: people generally wish to move away from unhealthy and unattractive urban environments to the country; these sites provide insufficient incentives for this type of building speculation and builders do not want the extra technical, legislative and speculative risks that may be involved. (Growing awareness of the malign effects of urban physical conditions is causing a negative cultural attitude towards the city. Functionally, it is not cost-effective to develop these places unless there is a significant increase in the potential value of the properties, which may only be guaranteed by the displacement of one income group by a higher income group.) Incentive structures and an assurance of environmental and cultural quality are called for. This suspicion and dislike of the urban environment will only be overcome through institutional policy that protects cultural identity, facilitates the functioning of the civic place and improves the physical conditions of the environment. A sustainability assessment should inform decisions in all constituent parts. Factors susceptible to changes beyond a society's control – geological faults, climate changes, alterations in political boundaries or policies, problems of ethnicity – also affect sustainable development capability. These must also be identified in the assessment process.

Physical conditions

In effect these are a locality's natural wealth and stock of resource assets, which should determine the type and extent of development. We are critically aware that the earth's natural resources are not infinite and that the physical processes and 'sinks' of the planet will not always continue to balance out the harmful effects of greenhouse-gas emissions and other toxic waste. Man's ability to control natural processes such as climate change is equivocal. Therefore, in each locality knowledge and perception of the physical conditions become vital considerations. They are the energy base on which all other constituent parts are dependent. The recording of a low quality or quantity here limits the potential of sustainable development. Most of the indicators in this section respond to quantitative and qualitative measurement.

Table 1: Sustainability indicators listed under the four constitutent parts: physical conditions, functional needs, institutional requirements and cultural identity.

Physical	Functional	Institutional	Cultural
The countryside	Resource efficiency	Economic base	Equilibrium
The climate	Passive systems	Integration or reductionism	Human scale
Geological formation	The town and its plan		Humane housing
Topography	Boundary	Systems that reward efficiency and saving resources	Individuality
Geographical convenience	Efficiency technologies	Incentive structures	Enlightened behaviour and attitudes
Agricultural and fishing (ecologically acceptable sufficiency): locally; for export	Relief, climate and buildings	Professional government: local; national; international	Heritage: environmental; historical
Vegetation and forestry: indigenous; cultivated	Mixed use development Polycentred development	Communication and infrastructure: local; national; international	Cultural stimulation
Resources (materials, minerals, water, soil, air): regeneration; depletion; unexploited	Reduced need for public transport		Permanence of population
Renewable energy (hydro, wind, wave, solar, biomass)	Spaces: prospect/enclave; private/public; transitional	Legislation: taxes; building regulations; conservation	Regional character
Biodiversity	Landscaping and amenities	Pattern of conservation	Sense of community
Degeneration of the environment: erosion; pollution; heat island; acid rain; exploitation	Place gives pleasure Recycling: materials; resources; waste	Welfare services: health; education; social services Land tenure	Religious and ethnic toleration
External dependencies (oil, gas, electricity, other)	Reuse of buildings Information technologies	Opportunities Public transport	Creativity: 'Creativity, if it has any meaningful boundary, lies within the moment when potential begins to emerge into reality'.
	Footprint	Property speculation Population changes	
			Human misery
			Local particularity

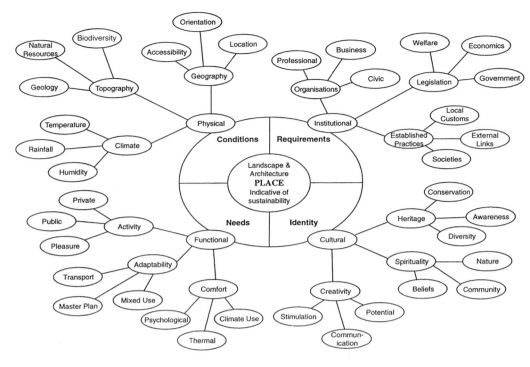

Figure 9: The interconnectedness of constituent parts (Phillips 1997).

Functional needs

Functional needs indicators reflect how, through the use of design strategies, landscape, architecture and master-planning facilitate man's comfort, activities and pleasure in a particular place. Bearing in mind the physical conditions, it is important to assess need and not greed. At what temperature and degree of humidity does mechanical air-conditioning become a need? Have all forms of passive control been investigated? Is the expectancy threshold of human tolerance too high or too low? These are essential considerations in energy use and efficiency. This section looks towards sufficient and efficient use of local resource, design strategies to accommodate the functional activities and thermal comfort of a society, and development that meets the necessity of environmental sustainability without recourse to large amounts of external dependencies. Most of the indicators in this section are both quantifiable and qualifiable.

Institutional requirements

Institutions, organisations and societies – locally, nationally and globally – have to be held accountable for the guidance and protection of equitable rights of individuals, communities and nations, and for the protection of, and guidance towards, environmentally sustainable practices. If we are to have healthy, pleasant and creative urban environments where collective civic responsiveness is practised, professional government is needed to guide investment, coordinate communication infrastructures and provide incentive structures that reward sustainable development. Within the city, forms of land and property tenure, open to ruthless speculation, create new classes of 'haves' and 'have nots' and reduce the urban conurbation to areas of exclusivity and affluence contrasted with areas of extreme poverty and ugliness. Large superstores sell produce from sources thousands of miles away in another country while the same type of produce rots in local orchards because it is uneconomic to harvest it or a local market has not been created. Competitive global market forces may not work in the interests of sustainable place, hence the requirement for accountable institutional infrastructure to guide sustainable development. Most of the indicators in this section are both quantifiable and qualifiable.

Cultural identity
This is the most difficult of the constituent parts to bring into quantifiable analysis, yet the most influential in the formation of an individual sense of belonging, community awareness and a healthy confident attitude towards change. Individuals who feel their cultural identity is valued and respected project this back into their environment encouraging qualities of equilibrium, tolerance and enlightenment, all necessary in the fostering of the positive attitude on which sustainable development depends, both locally and globally. When describing aesthetic attributes the distinction is made between two kinds of sign-stimuli: 'natural' deriving from landscape or nature; and 'cultural' deriving from forms and arrangements employed by man as symbolic of cultural identity. Sustainable development is destroyed through wars, exploitation of people or landscapes, inefficient or wasteful resource consumption, excessive and harmful energy use and energy emissions, and excessive population increase. Responsible attitudes and behaviour, at local level, become essential prerequisites for global sustainability and this is reflected back to a society through the qualities of the environment in which it lives. In this section a case may be made for certain indicators through advocacy.

THE WORKING METHOD PROCESS
There are four defined stages to the assessment of sustainable development.

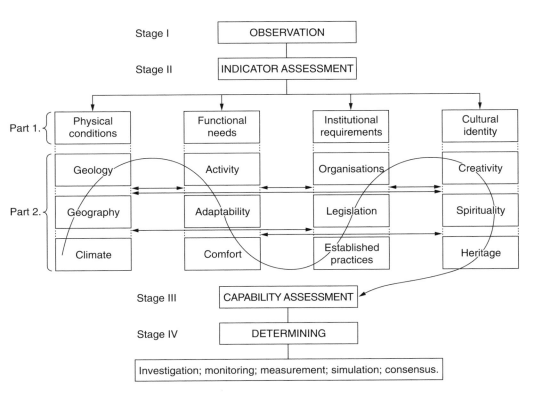

Figure 10: Sustainable development assessment: the working method process (Phillips).

Stage 1: Observation
Aim: Identification of sign-stimuli indicative, or not indicative, of sustainable development.

Method: Cognitive experience in exploration and evaluation of place within determined boundary.

Presentation: Visual, informational drawings, sketches or photographs; written account; verbal recording of observational study.

Stage 2: Indicator assessment
This stage consists of two parts: filling in the indicator matrices and, in each case, following this with a statement of assessment.

Part 1: The indicator matrices

Aim: To record a positive, negative or not applicable rating for the indicators in each of the four constituent parts of the framework; the evidence for the rating to have been verified scientifically, technically, statistically or, in the case of qualitatitive indicators, supported by reasonable argument; to comment on each of the indicators.

Method: According to the level of expertise required, a specialist in each of the constituent parts investigates the available source material to complete the indicator matrix. Where source material is unavailable it may be necessary to carry out research or a survey, or set up an experiment. A plan showing the interconnectedness of constituent parts is made for the area within the boundary of assessment, so that strong and weak links between indicators can be established. **(Figure 9)**

Part 2: Statement of assessment

Aim: To produce an analytical informed statement of assessment of the main indicators of concern, taking into consideration the interconnectedness of indicators from each of the four constituent parts and, where appropriate, directed by the assignment brief. This will serve to highlight initiatives or risks.

Method: This stage to be directed, co-coordinated and supervised by an interdisciplinary specialist with knowledge of the interconnectedness of sustainability indicators. Specialists in each of the four constituent parts to provide thorough and detailed investigation and evaluation of indicators of concern and produce statements of assessment of these indicators, listing the most innovative initiatives or problematic risks in each of the constitutent parts: physical conditions, functional needs, institutional requirements and cultural identity.

Presentation (Parts 1 and 2): Completed indicator matrices and completed interconnected-ness plan where appropriate; statements of assessment for significant indicators.

Stage 3: Capability assessment
Assessing a place's capability for sustainable development.

Aim: To take the most significant initiative and risk in each of the four constituent parts, together with the findings of the indicator matrixes quantifying positive and negative indicators,

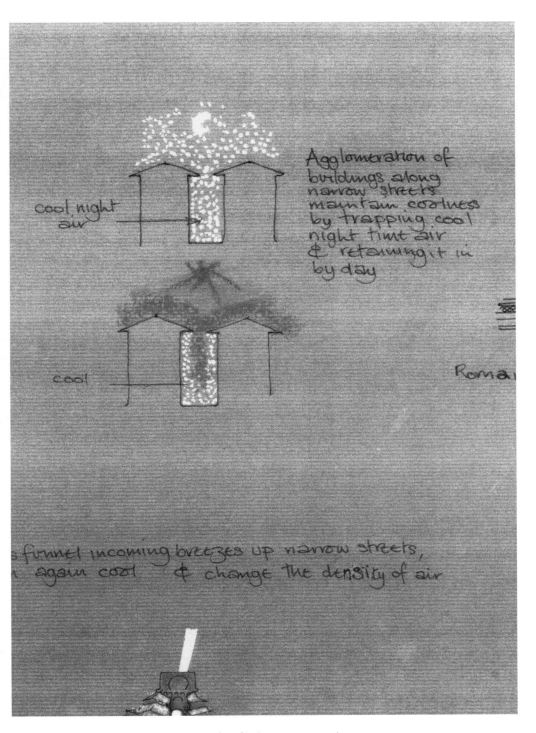

cool night air

Agglomeration of buildings along narrow streets maintain coolness by trapping cool night time air & retaining it in by day

cool

Roma

s funnel incoming breezes up narrow streets,
n again cool & change the density of air

Detail from observational sketches for the San Gimignano case study.

and compile the capability matrix to give a high, moderate or low assessment of the place's sustainable development capability. Completed capability matrices – sustainable place assessments – are shown at the ends of Chapters Five and Six.

Presentation: A report on Stages 1, 2 and 3 – observation, indicator assessment (including the indicator matrices and statement of assessment) and capability assessment. This may be used to assess the place's sustainable development potential or to determine whether further specialist action or inquiry is needed. It is an advisory report which may form the end product or be used as a guide to Stage 4, directing attention to, and determining solutions for, problems of sustainable development in landscape, architecture and master-planning.

Stage 4: Determining
Aim: To direct concerns that result from the advisory report indicating that further inquiry is necessary before a solution can be determined with appropriate expertise – for example, investigation, monitoring, measurement, simulation, consensus. To determine action or nonaction on the basis of evidence that there is, or is not, a solution to the problem.

Method: The capability matrix presents the totals of positive and negative indicators from the indicator matrices. It highlights the most important initiatives and risks and, supported by the advisory report as a whole, forms the basis for recommendations for further inquiry. The client may make a decision to engage the relevant expertise so that a solution may be found to a specific problem, and determined action may consequently be taken to address that problem.

Presentation: Creative discussion; advocacy for initiatives and further inquiry; guidance; direction; knowledge of appropriate research sources for specialist or technical expertise.

METHODOLOGY
At the outset of the methodology it must be acknowledged that this framework, based on current investigation of sustainable development, can only give an approximation of an assessment of sustainable place. It bows to the pressure of accepted ways of measurement in fields of combined qualitative and quantitative analysis. It recognises that the presence of an indicator in one part, 'x', may have no relevant meaning without interaction with an indicator in another part, 'y'. For example, consistent daily sunshine figures in the climate indicator for physical conditions become paramount if the resource efficiency indicator in functional needs points to the use of solar energy generation. Not all the indicators are equally weighted. One may be more critical than another – if the place happens to be in the shadow of an active volcano, even though all other indicators in physical conditions may register as positive, the importance of that one negative indicator outweighs them. At this point in time, scales that would qualify or quantify indicators have not been determined. The methodology recognises the presence of positive and negative indicators and comments on their character and impact; for example, the character of agricultural practices may be positive or negative, the impact of external dependence on energy sources may make future development unsustainable. Value judgements, presented through advocacy in the statement of assessment, give an approximation of the capability of sustainable development in a particular locality.

THE ASSESSMENT AND ITS USE
The assessment works at three levels. The initial matrix of indicators, presented before each of the constituent parts, records the presence of positive and negative indicators, and their character and impact, to give an indication of potential strengths and weaknesses within the place. It might be of use to all organisations or concerns that wish to have an overview of a

particular locality. At a second level it acts as a diagnosis, through the combination of obser-vational studies, indicator matrix and statement of assessment, whereby considered evaluation and judgmental advocacy put forward matters of concern that may effect change – either to prevent unsustainable development or to cure malign agents acting within that environment. In this capacity, its use would be fundamental in areas of the world where crisis or disaster recovery is necessary, such as cities, war zones and areas affected by natural disasters. Finally, it works at a more universal level giving a further framework to our knowledge of sustainable development globally. All parts of this assessment work towards the identification of initiatives and areas that should be further investigated in the advancement of human knowledge of sustainability. This will eventually lead to more quantifiable and qualifiable scales, and the estab-lishment of thresholds to the indicators that will have universal application.

THE APPLICATION OF THE ASSESSMENT

The framework of assessment is a tool that may be applied at many levels of environmental assessment. Similarly, it may be applied by an individual, as a case study over a considerable time span, or form the system of an environmental agency and be applied by a group of profes-sionals. It may be applied by local concerns in the formulation of such policies as Agenda 21, or by governmental and global environmental agencies to provide solutions to more far-ranging global issues of sustainability. Similarly, the skills and professional expertise of those applying the framework will vary. Even in the study of San Gimignano (Chapter Five), the first experi-mental case study, considerable communication was involved with professionals local to the area. Ideally, the framework should be executed by a group of five or six people with diverse skills and expertise in sustainable assessment concerns so that all the constituent parts may be competently addressed.

THE CASE STUDIES

The prototypical testing of the framework of assessment has been carried out on two walled, medieval hilltop towns and their surrounding rural areas: San Gimignano in Italy and Ludlow in England. Although the framework of assessment was designed for any place with well-defined boundaries, whether they are geographical, functional, cultural or institutional, the choice of case studies is pertinent. In particular, these two relatively simple town structures, surrounded by a rural hinterland, enabled the investigation of the inclusive and incremental nature of sustain-able development in settings where comprehensive modern redevelopment has not obliterated historical stratification. Further, in specific relation to environmental design strategies within landscape, architecture and master-planning, these places allow an evaluation of development that was designed to function through the use of ambient energy sources, without the high-energy input associated with modern cities.

Both San Gimignano and Ludlow are large enough to represent the complexities of urbanism, but neither has been absorbed into an agglomeration of urban units with indistinct boundaries. Both places have traditional town kernels which have enjoyed constancy of site over a long time span; a hierarchy of townscape regions; and receive sustenance from a wider rural locality and wider external situation. Culturally, they have unique regional characters not as yet taken over by global anonymity, which may bear testimony to the idea that cultural and aesthetic qualities grow out of regional self-reliance.

The assessment, in both studies, covers an area within an approximately 10 miles radius of the town centres, making it possible to equate the impact of each town – in terms of its environmental cost in such areas as pollution, energy requirements and food production – with the natural environmental capital of the region. The case studies trace changes indicative of sustainable development. Urban and rural communities express a settled or general course or direction and quality of their past and present life in the external appearance of their habitat. Change is actuated by society's response to successive changes in physical conditions, functional needs and institutional requirements, and in the redefining of cultural identity.

Such an approach promotes an understanding of issues of sustainability that is integrated with landscape, architecture and master-planning. Awareness of a design vocabulary for sustainable development is seen to emerge out of a purposeful interaction with place. In the plan and configuration of a place we are able to observe the effects of design strategies which address such issues as land tenure, changes in population and economic activity, and the regulation of external dependencies, as well as design methodologies of building with specific microclimates and the particular topography and geomorphology of a terrain. Defined boundaries, and the homogeneous relationship of local materials and local units of measurement, lead to a language of spatial arrangements particular to place.

A reciprocity exists between urban and rural, landscape and architecture, which is reflected in the harmonious appearance of both places – the siting, orientation and type of development plus the use of local building materials – suggesting that the strong sense of cultural identity in both towns is related to the degree of regional self-reliance. This also tells us about the carrying capacity of both places, and therefore the nature of sustainable development at the time of their development and in the present time. In both places a strong purpose existed politically and commercially for development, the potential of which could not have been realised without the institutions, marketplaces and collective services of an urban environment. Ludlow was to become the capital of the Welsh Marches, San Gimignano a strategic banking and commercial centre for trade between northern and southeastern Europe. This development was possible because of the favourable natural resources that were available locally – food, building materials, and materials for industry and energy sources. The prosperity and productivity of an urban population depended on this and, vice versa, the quality of existence of the rural population was given potential through interaction with urban activity.

The approach to these case studies follows the methodology outlined in the framework of assessment. Each study begins with a set of six visual observational studies and moves through indicator matrices and statements of assessment in connection with significant indicators for each of the four constituent parts. Both studies conclude at the end of Stage 3 with a capability assessment, drawn from an evaluation of incentives and risks analysed in the statements, that estimates the potential for sustainable development. The purpose of this is to form an advisory report to direct towards further expert investigation (Stage 4: Determining). Neither case study is taken into Stage 4. Both studies were undertaken as part of the research to test the prototype framework of assessment. The objective was not to provide a solution to a specific brief dictated by market forces, as may be seen in the examples in Chapter 8, but rather to aid the process of human enlightenment through research. Concerns surfaced naturally out of a broad investigation and the final stage, if carried out, would have been to determine solutions not only to specific local problems but also to aid understanding of sustainable development at a more universal level. Where it was considered of interest, historical or empirical detail which is not part of the assessment has been included.

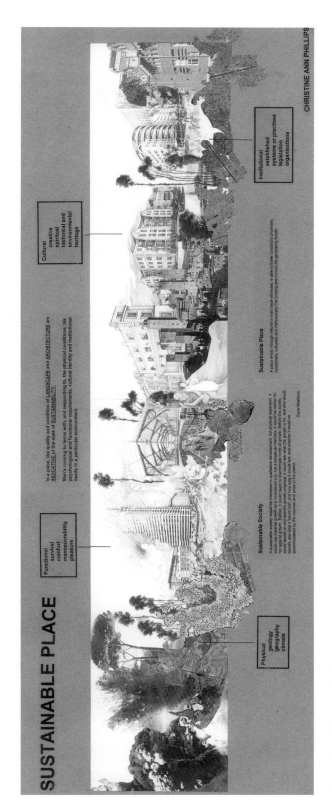

Colour Plate 1 Sustainable Place

Colour Plate 2 San Gimignano from the southeast

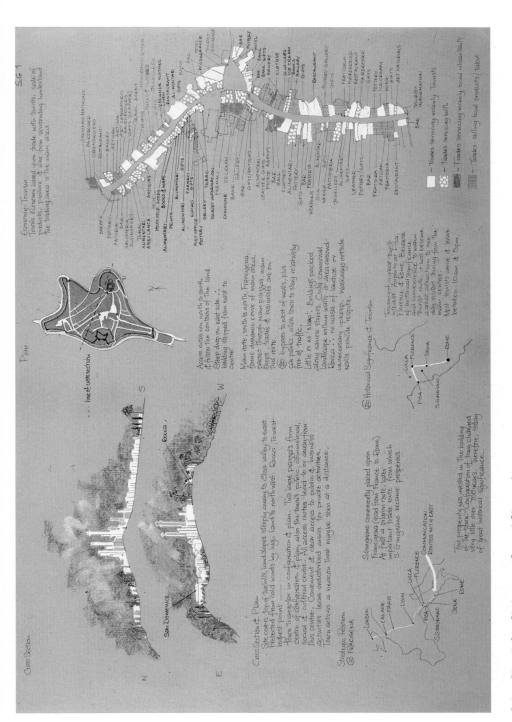

Colour Plate 3 San Gimignano – General Observation

Growth of Town

Colour Plate 4 San Gimignano – Growth of Town

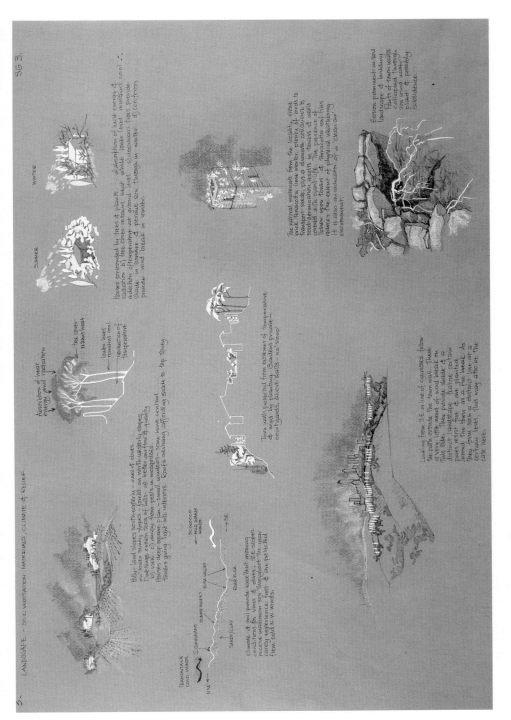

Colour Plate 5 San Gimignano – Landscape

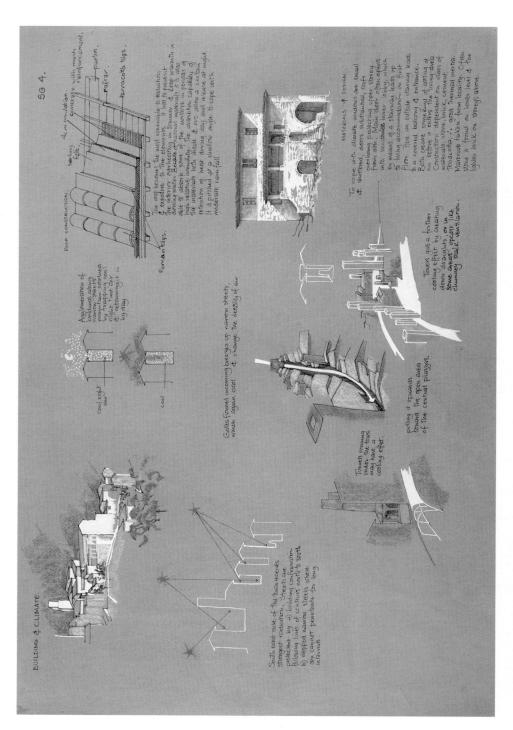

Colour Plate 6 San Gimignano – Building and Climate

SG 5.

SPACE

PUBLIC / PRIVATE

Town plan.
Very clear demarcation of public & private areas. The central piazzas & axis over divide town in two. All trade business & communal activities take place in the central axe with the exception of library, hospital & youth hostel.

ST AUGUSTIN'S PIAZZA
LIBRARY
HOSPITAL
YOUTH HOSTEL
ROCCA GARDENS

The rest of the town is mainly restrict private areas. The private leading to residence, piazza provides a pleasant communal area. The Rocca Gardens is the only communal landscape within the town.

Trees help form windows between walls & surrounding landscape.

HOUSING
Housing is enclosed. Often the ground floor is a warehouse lobby accommodation, various above ground level. Houses to grow vines. There is very little space within the town walls.

GARDENS
Gardens are enclosed private either in courtyards or behind walls.

CORRIDORS

Outside of buildings the whole town acts as a transitional space between the sanctuation of urban circulation & the landscape or world outside the walls.

Prospect Refuge satisfaction

enclosure prospect poor

enclave refuge poor

Good opportunity for both the satisfaction & comfort afforded by enclosed refuge spaces & the satisfaction afforded by panoramic views or prospects.

Narrow entrance into large communal space of Collegiata Piazza

Some narrow alleys lead to view of open landscape about city walls

Area leading to Duomo Piazza

Creating a series of windows & doorways into the landscape or communal or more peaceful surroundings.

Colour Plate 7 San Gimignano – Spaces

Proposed Territorial University

The Convent of St. Dominica was built in
the 13 on the site of the earliest castle
at San Gimignano. Until recently it was
used as a penitentiary. In response to
proposals to turn the building into a
hotel, a citizen's association was
formed advocating a more sustainable
form of development as a Territorial
University

The architects Pietro Guicciardini and
Marco Magni have drawn up plans
for redevelopment.

Colour Plate 9 Ludlow looking North/East from Whitcliff. Centre of town built upon the ridge of a spur of land which runs along the line from castle past St. Lawrence's Church

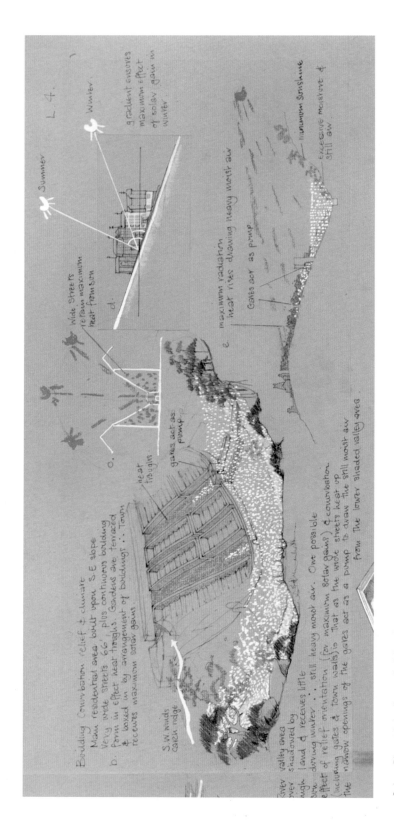

Colour Plate 10 Ludlow – Building Conurbation Relief & Climate

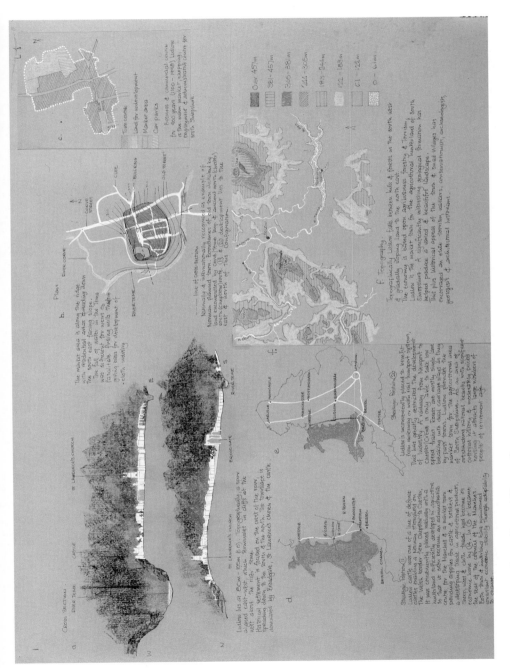

Colour Plate 11 Ludlow – General Observation

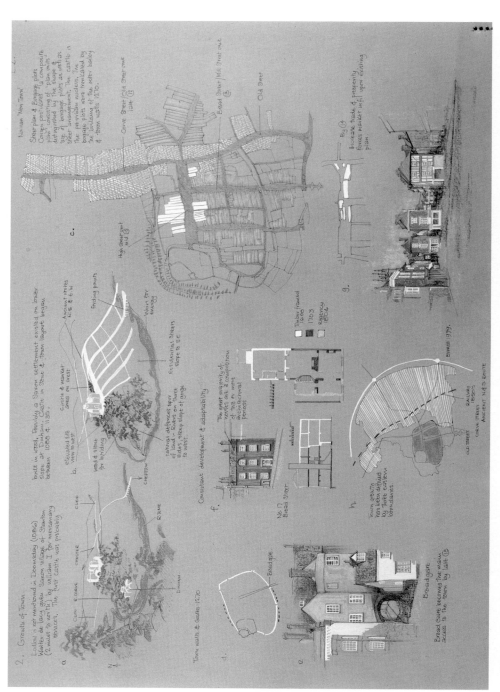

Colour Plate 12 Ludlow – Growth of Town

Colour Plate 13 Ludlow – Landscape

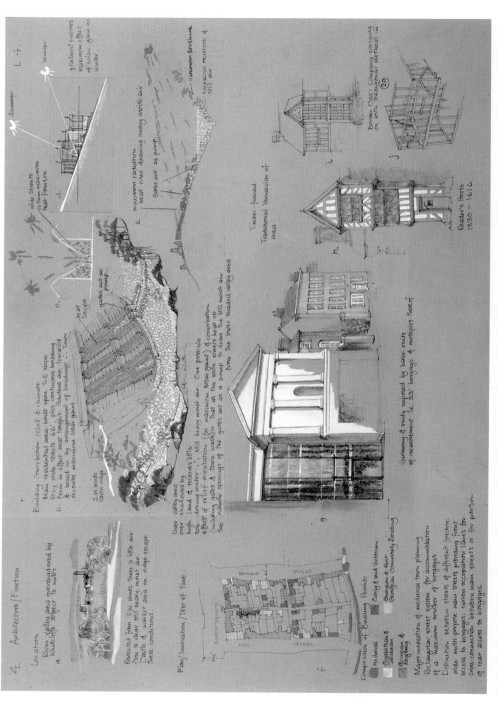

Colour Plate 14 Ludlow – Architecture and Function

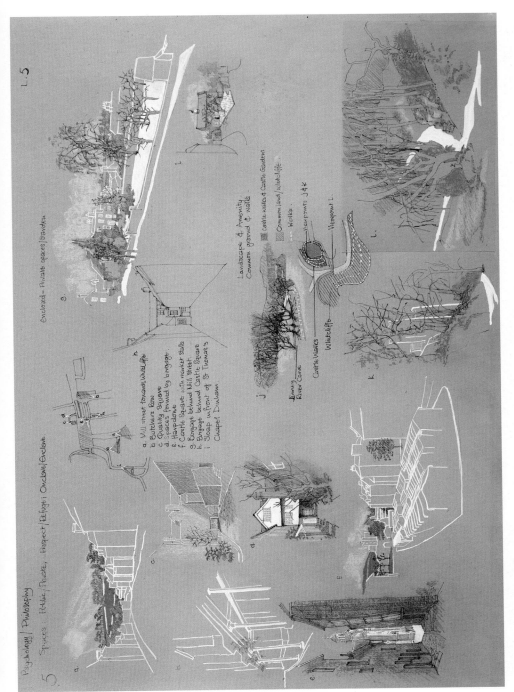

Psychology / Philosophy

5 Spaces: Public/Private; Prospect/Refuge; Onclose/Enclose.

Enclosed - Private spaces/Bravado

L.5

a. Mill street towards Whitcliffe
b. Butchers Row
c. Quality Square
d. Spaces framed by burgages
e. Hanaplane
f. Castle Square with market stalls
g. Burgage behind Mill Street
h. Burgage behind Castle Square
i. Sloap in front of St Thomas's
   Chapel Dinham.

Landscape & Amenity
Common ground & walks

▨ Castle walks & Castle Garden
▩ Common land/Whitcliffe
···· Walks
— Viewpoints J & K
— Viewpoint L.

j. Jimmy
   River Corve

Castle Walks
Whitcliffe

k.

l.

Colour Plate 15 Ludlow – Spaces

6.

Town Plan to 2006

L.6.

Town Council initiative for Market Square enhancement

Bringing trees, handstand & seating into the town centre giving more public amenity & providing potential community meeting area.

Proposed Maritn Building provision for young people facilities & accommodation.

Market Space Enhancement

Cattle market taken to new site (small site outside the town. Building modernised intervention into landscape.

Sites identified for housing development

Sites allocated for redevelopment

Open space to be rebuilt

Town centre

Built-up town development

Conservation area

Old town

Active conservation

Site allocated for industrial / business development

N

Chapter Five
Case Study 1: San Gimignano, Italy

INTRODUCTION

This assessment of sustainable place concentrates on San Gimignano and district in Tuscany, central Italy.

San Gimignano and district fall between latitudes 43° 20' and 43° 30' north. This is an internal area of Italy, within the continental zone of Europe, a region of many small hills, sloping towards the Elsa valley in the east, which establish a sense of geographical definition. San Gimignano is on the top of one of the hills at a maximum height of 343.9 metres, the site of the Rocca. The towns of the district are: Pencole, Ulignano, Castel San Gimignano and San Donato. To the north is Certaldo and the Apennines, to the west the hills of Poggio del Comune and Volterra, to the east the Elsa valley and the hills of the Chianti, and to the south the Montagnola Senese and Siena. The highest point within the district of San Gimignano is on the Poggio del Comune, at 624 metres. The lowest point is near Ulignano: Crocetta at 196 metres.

The surrounding landscape is agricultural and rural, and the land is extensively cultivated, mostly with vines and olives and the occasional sunflower field. Fields are precise and square, small and around 3 acres. The land is hilly and bulldozers are used to work the fields. About 57 per cent of the district is composed of small farms. Of the land that remains much is inaccessible hilly and rocky woodland of hardwood – ilex, cypress and pine.

The villages and towns are small in population. The 1996 figures for the walled town of San Gimignano are 1750, for San Lucia 327, Ulignano 651 and Castel San Gimignano 150. (This does not take into consideration farms within the areas.) In an attempt to hang on to a visual identity the region has resisted motorways and large industry.

The image of San Gimignano acts as a beacon, a landmark, which can be seen for about 15 kilometres radius. The vertical lines of the towers form a triangular shape immersed in the crown of a hill. From first sighting to arrival, a journey towards San Gimignano builds up a sense of expectation, purpose and direction. This image is fairly precise. The vertical towers emphasise the horizontal roof line of the buildings that follow the shape of the top of the hill, the dividing line softened by trees, mostly pines and olives. This is echoed in the relationship of villas and farmhouses within the surrounding countryside, the precise vertical shapes of the cypresses replacing the towers but nevertheless defining the place of habitation. A state of reciprocity exists between landscape and architecture, town and country. No two places or buildings are the same, yet there is a striking harmony and unity to the whole. An order exists, even down to the small square fields of lines of vines or olives.

Roads are not good. They are narrow, often in ill repair, liable to subsidence and full of bends. The exception is the relatively new road from Poggibonsi which brings the tourist off the main Rome-Florence motorway up to San Gimignano. However, most roads wind up towards the town, which may be viewed from prospect points at varying intervals. This sets a certain order of mind and approach, positive and direct. Going to San Gimignano is not a disorderly, casual perambulation through sprawling suburbs.

The boundary of the place of study falls short of large towns. San Gimignano has no large industrial units. But approximately 10 miles to the east and north are the new industrial towns of

Poggibonsi and Certaldo. These too have old walled, medieval hilltop conurbations, but new industry and its servicing residential areas have spread over the lowland surrounding the old towns. The new buildings are unsympathetic to the area and typical of industrial areas all over Europe that were put up very quickly after the Second World War. Materials are universal components of precast concrete, corrugated sheeting, plastic coatings. On leaving these towns large boards line the verges advertising supermarkets, trattorias and banks. Tourists shun these areas.

The economy of San Gimignano relies on agriculture and tourism; there are no large industries within the area. This is in contrast to the general Italian economic situation which has moved away from agriculture towards industry. In Italy, in 1950, agriculture represented 25 per cent of the economy, in 1990 just 4 per cent (Ufficio Agricoltura, 1996). San Gimignano and district has the look of prosperity – rich crops of vines and olives, traditional buildings sensitively renovated, good places to eat, drink and stay. Luxury art and craft products and food delicacies are sold in the shops.

The Growth of the Town

The completeness of San Gimignano's medieval configuration provides a historical indicator which gives an insight into a specific approach to urban lifestyle, synonymous with the small medieval hilltop cities of Italy. However, other similar cities did not develop such a rich or extensive urban conurbation and do not command the level of popularity and interest that San Gimignano does today. Sustainable development is about identifying benign approaches to urban lifestyle.

It is important not to regard San Gimignano narrowly, as the growth of a market town in feudal times. At the height of its prosperity, in the 13th century, its significance was greater than that of a fortified medieval market town. Similar to other hill towns, it had a rural community that produced for, and serviced, the needs of town dwellers such as the craftsmen, artists, clergy and militia. In return the latter provided trade, spirituality and protection within the town walls. However, this urban conurbation is a reflection of more worldly and commercial influences. From the 11th to the 13th centuries, because of its strategic geographical position, San Gimignano's commercial and economic possibilities were considerable and not just local. The area was famous, as it is now, for its Vernaccia wine.

San Gimignano was significantly, strategically positioned at a convenient time in history to take advantage of business and commercial opportunities. Placed on the Via Francigena, the road that linked Rome with France, and consequently the Middle East with Europe, and with a natural harbour at Pisa, the town was in a good position for taking part in the commercial activities and transportation arrangements for much of the then known world. Similar to the global cities of London, New York and Tokyo, which are strategically placed to benefit from the world financial industry, San Gimignano was conveniently placed for commerce in the 13th century. It was also a convenient stopping point for pilgrims. In 990 Archbishop Segerre of Canterbury stayed there on his way to receive benediction from the pope in Rome. The town had both reason and purpose for growth. It attracted the kind of creative, intellectual and business minds needed to make it a successful and prosperous place. This is reflected in its physical configuration. Purposeful growth is an indicator for sustainable place.

In the 13th century San Gimignano had a population of 10,000 which thrived on international commerce. Seventy lawyers, with local practices, were needed to service transactions. Banking and moneylending agencies from Rome and Florence had set up houses there, mostly in the Piazza Cisterna. The business of making usurious loans at 20 per cent to 30 per cent flourished. The monarchs of England and France borrowed from banks at San Gimignano. To build one of its towers, of which there were between 72 and 75, a person had either to be of noble birth or own a merchant ship at Pisa. The town was able to draw in affluent people both as permanent residents and as visitors who wished to make business transactions. In 1262

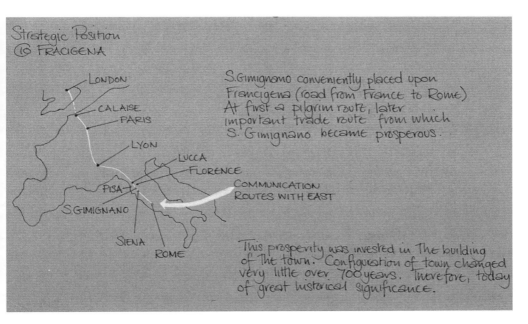

San Gimignano's strategic position in the 10th century.

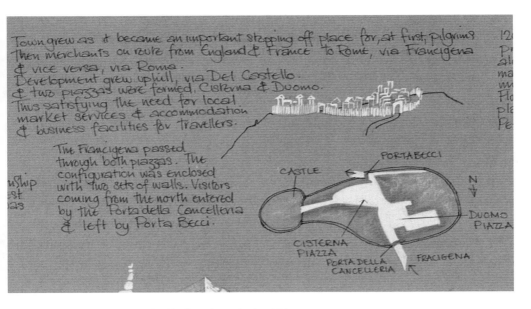

San Gimignano's position on the Via Francigena in the 10th century.

there were nine inns that could be called hotels. San Gimignano's artisans and craftsmen were able to make a living in luxury goods: gold valuables sold in the street called Gold Lane; cloth was dyed, especially silk, with a colour derived from saffron; and honey and Vernaccia were produced.

The coming together of all these positive influences, local and foreign, caused an explosion of urban citizenry. Against this background the physical configuration of San Gimignano grew. One of the main characteristics of this culture was its public state. The town functioned as a large house or household. Divisions between private and public were not as clear-cut as they are now. There were regulations on architecture and buildings, but basically San Gimignano grew out of functional needs and citizenship (Pietro Toeska, private communication 1996).

The origin of the town's name is still a matter for conjecture. On the site now occupied by San Domenico there was originally a fortress for fugitive Romans – a place that was possibly protected from attacks by Attila the Hun by St Gimignano, bishop of Modena. It became a bishopric in the 9th century when the first market was instituted by the bishop of Volterra. In 929, Hugo of Provenza gave land to that bishopric and in 949 San Gimignano was cited as a village. The configuration of the town that we experience today is the result of 200 years of building, from 1100 to 1300. How has San Gimignano been able to sustain a predominantly medieval architectural image throughout 700 years?

The early years were times of constant feuds within Tuscany with frequent skirmishes between rival states and no central authority – Italy was not unified until the act of union in the middle of the 19th century. The walls of San Gimignano were demolished in 1259 by order of the Florentines. However, in 1261 they were rebuilt under the more liberal Sienese supremacy. The great powers were Siena, Pisa and Florence, and of these Florence was the most aggressive, conquering many small towns in the area. Within San Gimignano, the rivalries and fighting between two powerful families (the Guelphs, looking to Florence for support, and the Ghibellines, looking to Siena) weakened the unity of the town. This contributed to the eventual subjection of San Gimignano to Florentine authority in 1353. The Florentines built the Rocca as a symbol of the town's subjugation on the highest point, the hill of Montestaffoli, but, of more consequence for San Gimignano's economic growth, they redirected the Via Francigena to the valley area between Rome and Florence. This took away the town's strategic importance. Contributing to this rapid and definitive decline was an outbreak of plague in 1348, which reduced the population from 13,000 to 4000 and meant the town was unable to regain its independence from Florence. The redirection of the Via Francigena, in the lower Elsa valley to the east, removed all pilgrim and trade traffic. A sudden halt was placed on progress, expansion and economic growth. Poverty, the end of passionate politics and dependence all impeded change, amplification, rebuilding and sustained growth.

San Gimignano regressed into being a peasant market town although conservation action has occasionally been taken to protect its architectural heritage. Although a law was enacted in 1288 that forbade the demolition of houses, palazzi and towers unless it was in order to rebuild them, by 1580 the number of towers was reduced from 72 to 25. Today there are 13. These owe their existence to a law of 1674 that ordered the restoration and preservation of the ruined towers, in respect of the town's former greatness. During the 19th century the Romantic interest in medievalism brought a mild tourist revival and interest in restoration and conservation but nothing that revived economic growth. In 1902, San Gimignano was described as miserably poor and had three hotels; it was not exactly of worldly significance (Gardner 1913). Economic revival has come over the last thirty years with tourism, improved methods of transportation, increased wine production and the immigration of people from more affluent parts of Europe and America. However, having remained so perfectly frozen in time, San Gimignano now enables the evaluation of a medieval urban configuration.

SUSTAINABLE DEVELOPMENT ASSESSMENT

STAGE 1: OBSERVATION STUDIES

The Observation Studies are illustrated in the six colour plates 3–8. The series as a whole aims at establishing a comprehensive record of sustainable development as it is embodied in the landscape, architecture and planning of this place. This record includes the plan and cross section of the town, the location, geophysical infrastructure and topography of the boundary area; an account of growth and change within the town; the characteristics of surrounding landscape; the functionality of plan and architecture, including building with space syntax, climate and natural resources and proposals for future development.

Aerial perspective, San Gimignano.

San Gimignano from the southeast.

STAGE 2: INDICATOR ASSESSMENTS
Physical Conditions: Indicator Matrix

Indicator	Positive	Negative	Comments
The countryside	/		Visual appeal – harmony of landscape and development. South slopes of hills intensively cultivated – prosperity – north slopes craggy uncultivated woodland. Very appealing, hence tourists.
The climate	/	/	Type of landscape in this latitude subject to adiabatic weather conditions – 20°C swing in temperature and relative humidity between night-time cooling and midday heat. Humidity uncomfortable, especially during hottest months (June to September). Rainfall 672mm; wettest months March and April. Prevailing winds northwest (cold) and south (warm).
Geological formation		/	Recent formation Pliocene; marine sediment. Outcrops of sedimentary rock and soil – claustic to north and east, nonclaustic to west and south; landform and building materials subject to erosion.
Topography		/	Hilly landscape – narrow winding roads subject to subsidence. One wide good-quality road leading from the Rome-Florence motorway at Poggibonsi to San Gimignano. One river – the Elsa – to east; few and poor bridges.
Geographical convenience		/	Poor roads – railway and motorway to the eastern lowland boundary. Connected to the tourist route only by detour from Pisa-Florence-Rome motorway.
Agriculture and fishing (ecologically acceptable sufficiency): locally; for export	/ / /	/	57% of area composed of small arable farms. Methods of farming cause erosion, ie machine damage, monoculture, direction of ploughing and removal of natural vegetation. Population dependent on consumption of local food products. Products from outside the area tend to be expensive and not easily accessible even in supermarkets. Good local and tourist markets for products grown and processed locally – wines, olives, oils, cheeses, processed meat products, local delicacies, eg nougat, ice cream, wild boar products.
Vegetation and forestry: indigenous; cultivated		/	Remaining indigenous landscape on northwesterly slopes of hills. Inaccessible hilly and rocky woodland of hardwood, ilex, cypress and pine. Cultivated crops suitable for soil and climate – vines, olives and occasionally sunflowers.
Resources (materials, minerals, water, soil, air): regeneration; depletion; unexploited	/	/	Abundant natural resources. Building materials – stone, wood, clay for bricks. Large mineral deposits, eg oxides – iron, copper, manganese. Good air quality (no large industrial town – plenty of woodland). Water supply within town, dependent on natural springs, excellent (five of the seven original town wells pass as drinkable water). Water table low in summer months in many rural areas and cessation of water supply a problem. Soil – sandy clay – plus climate suitable for vines and olives. No attempt at ecological regeneration: attitude that land is to be exploited for man's needs. However, climate, constant states of erosion and areas of inaccessible forest with abundant wildlife mean constant natural regeneration. Serious states of erosion through overcultivation and agricultural mismanagement.
Renewable energy (hydro, wind, wave, solar, biomass)		/	Great potential for solar energy on southeasterly slopes – presently not utilised.
Biodiversity	/		Very good – cultivated small fields balanced by areas of woodland wilderness plus conducive climate – therefore interaction of wildlife: birds, animals, plants. Hunting threatens wild boar.
Degeneration of the environment: erosion; pollution; acid rain; heat island; exploitation		/ / /	Many forms of erosion unmonitored and not corrected may lead to unsustainable development. Stagnant pools of water, used for irrigation, are breeding grounds for pests such as mosquitoes. N/A N/A Benign physical conditions of this area are endangered through financial exploitation.
External dependencies (oil, gas, electricity, other)		/	Italy, generally, is dependent on external sources for energy supply.
Totals	7	12	

Physical Conditions: Statement of assessment

The Countryside

The southeasterly slopes of the many small hills provide a good situation for the growing of vines and olives. They receive maximum sun throughout the year, rarely experiencing frost, and are protected from cold north-westerly winds in winter. Craggy woodland covers the northwesterly slopes. The general appearance is one of visual appeal, harmony and prosperity.

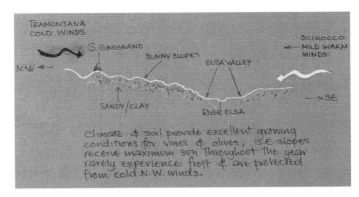

Vines and olives are cultivated on southeasterly slopes.

Contrasts of colour, light and shade provide an unusually stimulating environment which goes through subtle changes according to the season. Dark evergreens of the cypresses and pines, soft sage green of the olives and pale yellow ochre of outcrops of sandstone, sharp bright green of the vines and poplar groves, are highlighted against the red brown of the soil. The farms and villas, usually occupying the crest of a hill, are built of materials harmonious with the landscape. The materials come from the area: terracotta tiles often covered with golden coloured lichen indicating the pureness of air quality; buff stone, terracotta bricks or warm coloured stucco, yellow ochre, iron red, pale lime wash. The verges have a great variety of brightly coloured flowers, reflecting an absence of the use of pesticides. Very few farm animals are to be seen, indicating that this is not an area of animal farming. Wild boar inhabit the forest areas, and the hunting of them provides a local delicacy found in the produce of local delicatessens or on restaurant menus. The indication is that this environment is extensively cultivated where it is farmed or left to wilderness on the craggy forested slopes.

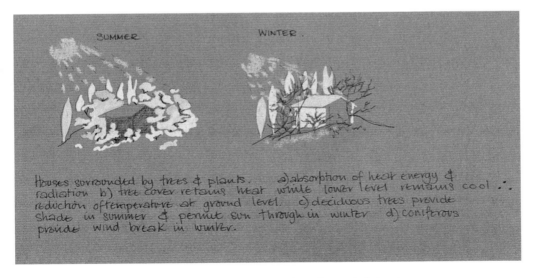

Trees help to keep buildings cool in summer and protect them from winds in winter.

An avenue of trees circles the walls of the town of San Gimignano.

The characteristic appearance of both farms and villas implies that some thought has been given to providing protection from extreme weather conditions and pests such as mosquitoes. Farms are seen emerging from tree areas, which provide protection from winds in winter and a natural form of cooling for the walls in summer. The placing of a building on a hill ensures better airflow and gives more protection from mosquitoes which tend to dwell around the stagnant water, used for crop irrigation, in valley areas. Cypresses usually line the north side of buildings or driveways and act as a windbreak. An avenue of trees circles the walls of San Gimignano providing a cool, comfortable walking area.

The Climate

Winters are mild and wet, summers hot with high relative humidity. The topography of Tuscany is variable, and consequently climate is susceptible to considerable change from one area to the next and both temperature and humidity vary considerably over the region. **(Figures 11 and 12)** The wettest months are March and April, the driest June and September. The most prevailing winds are, from the northwest, the tramontana, which is a cold wind, and from the south the sirocco, a warm wind.

The landscape in this area is subject to an adiabatic climate during the summer months. The valley areas and southeasterly slopes receive the intense rays of the sun early in the day and as the cool night air expands through heat it moves up the slopes taking with it moisture from plants and night-time condensation. By midday the air may become uncomfortably hot and humid. The higher the dwellings, on top of a hill, for example, the better the opportunities for airflow which may relieve the situation. As the sun goes down the air is cooled. Occasionally, the constant compression and expansion of air will build up convection and localised thunder storms are experienced.

The intensity of heat from the sun and the relative humidity are at their most uncomfortable during the middle of the day, mid-morning (10.00 am) to mid-afternoon (4.00 pm). The

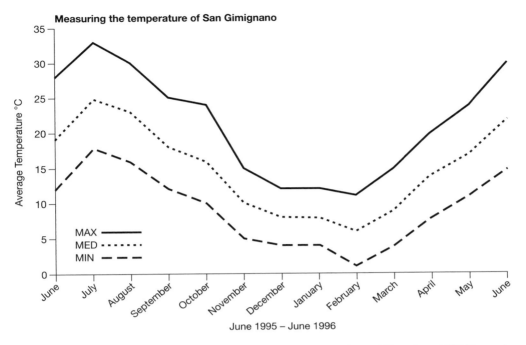

Figure 11: The average monthly temperatures for San Gimignano for June 1995 to June 1996 (Convento Cappuccini, Siena).

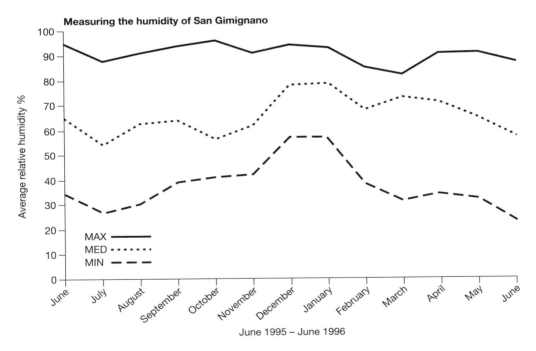

Figure 12: The average relative humidity for the same period. The rainfall for the year June 1995 to May 1996 was 672.2 millimetres, the wettest months being March and April, the driest June and September (Convento Cappuccini, Siena).

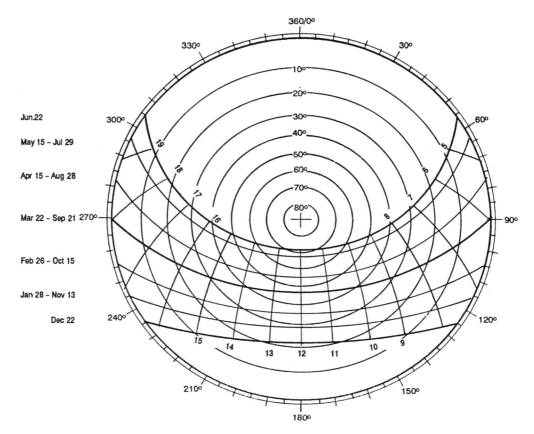

Figure 13: The sun path for latitude 43° north (Szokolay 1996).

sun path for latitude 43° north indicates moderately high yearly sunshine. **(Figure 13)** Solar energy could form an alternative future source of energy and would be especially viable on the extensive southeasterly slopes. Energy sources have always presented a problem as Italy has no natural deposits of coal, oil or gas and is reliant on external dependencies.

Geological Formation

In terms of cultural or architectural history, this area encompasses a considerable time span. The indications that the landscape is part of this 'age value' aesthetic are everywhere visible in the presence of weathering and erosion, yet in geological terms it is of recent formation: Pliocene, marine sediment. The materials of buildings within the area indicate that geologically the region surrounding San Gimignano is rich with potential building materials. Sedimentary compositions of both clastic, unconsolidated, and nonclastic, consolidated, occur throughout the area – clastic to the north and east, nonclastic to the west and south.

No durable building stone can come from the clastic variety. However, in the past peasant farms were built out of a type of unconsolidated sandstone from this region for which the local name is *tufo*. Clastic stone, *tufo* or sandstone, siltstone/mudstone, shale/claystone is used in bricks or crushed for roads or cement. The town of San Gimignano is on a hill of clastic stone. The architecture of the town is built with nonclastic stone mined in the area to the west and south. This includes consolidated sandstone; travertine, a form of limestone and an excellent building stone, compact and durable; *calcare cavernoso*, a grey hardstone with a cellular appearance from decomposed marine sediment, which is used extensively for building in San Gimignano. Serpentine, an igneous rock found to the west of San Gimignano, is also used in the town. It is green or red in colouring and gives a smooth mottled effect when polished. Varying compositions of sandstone, sand and sandy clay make up the land which falls away from San Gimignano to the Elsa valley which runs from southeast to northwest. Because of outcrops of clay, bricks are more common towards Certaldo. Place names such as Mattone, which means 'bricks', give a connection with a place that made bricks in the past.

The sandy clay soil around San Gimignano is beneficial for the production of wine and olives, as is indicated by the proliferation of small vineyards and olive groves. San Gimignano is famous for Vernaccia wine which was probably introduced to the region around AD 1200. In 1276 an official document – *Ordinamenti della Gabella* – states that a duty tax of 'three coins' was established for each export transaction of Vernaccia sent outside San Gimignano's jurisdiction.

Considerable uncultivated woodland exists, predominantly on northwesterly slopes. Place names such as Il Castello della Salva (castle of the wood, as San Gimignano was originally known), indicate that woodland was probably more extensive and has been cleared in the past centuries for building or energy purposes. Large areas of woodland remain, especially to the west.

The indication is that physical conditions have played a beneficial part in the habitation and early settlement of this area with building materials, soil for cultivation and wood for fuel. However the general appearance of the landscape and architecture indicates that the climate and geological formation are conducive to erosion. Observation reveals many examples of erosion in the town of San Gimignano and surrounding district.

Degeneration of the Environment

Erosion of the land
Geologically the landscape is still in formation and is undergoing changes in composition and states of consolidation. Over time, there are consequent movement and changes of level.

Mass wasting Mass wasting is common throughout the landscape because of recent sedimentary formation. Soil and many forms of sedimentary rock are poorly held together and are susceptible to movement through gravitational force. There is abundant visual evidence of downhill movement. This constitutes an important process in the denudation of surfaces and occasionally threatens property.

Wind and water Sandstone and limestone are particularly susceptible to weathering through the action of wind and water. During long dry periods water deep within the sandstone is drawn to the surface by capillary force. This water carries dissolved mineral salts. As evaporation takes place, minute crystals remain behind. The growth force of these crystals is capable of causing granular disintegration of the outer rock layer.

This applies to sandstone used in building and outcrops of sandstone. The pressure of growing crystals disrupts the sandstone into scales and flakes. Sandstone grains thus released are swept away by wind or rains causing aeolian erosion, which is especially prevalent in poorly cemented sandstone.

Soil In some areas the equilibrium between the rate at which soil forms and that at which it is eroded or degraded has been upset, either by natural weathering or human mismanagement. A major cause of soil erosion is the removal of natural vegetation, leaving the ground exposed to the elements. Although deforestation does not take place at a serious level, olive groves are frequently taken up. More common is the removal of vegetation from between olive trees or vines. Constant ploughing and clearing, together with the direction of planting – down the slope

Mass wasting is evident on the east bank beneath the town walls: the downhill gravitational pull has removed soil from the roots of the tree and if this continues the tree will fall, bringing more of the bank away and denuding the surface for further erosion by wind or water.

Below: Near Certaldo landslip on the hillside has formed a sandstone cliff and a house is threatened with subsidence.

Wind and water are causing granular disintegration of the outer rock layer.

Aeolian erosion in the foundations of the town wall, east side; cement is being dissolved out.

In the stone foundations of the town wall, east side, recession of the sandstone face eventually produces a niche or shallow cave.

Caves resulting from erosion form sheds on the lower east side of the town.

Below: Erosion as a result of the removal of vegetation.

into the valley rather than terracing – subjects the soil to all forms of weathering. Heavy rains remove the topsoil. The water flow has little time to recharge the water table and soil-moisture store, and just carries the topsoil in sheet wash down into the valleys.

Machine damage Where there are vines and olive trees, there is visual evidence of their having been planted vertically up the slope rather than to the contours of the land. Ploughing up and down the slopes loosens the topsoil and encourages future wind and water erosion. Furrows increase the rate of run-off. Farming is very machine intensive. Bulldozers are used to work the soil on steeper gradients. The weight compacts the soil surface producing 'platypeds', inhibiting aeration of the soil and reducing its water infiltration capacity.

Monoculture Many of the wine farms are organic. There is little sign of chemical erosion through overuse of chemical pesticides. Wild flowers can be seen in abundance during spring. However, monoculture is indicated. Repeatedly cultivating the same crop each year on the same piece of land uses up the same nutrients. It is not an area of animal farming and therefore dung is not applied to the fields as a source of soil nourishment.

Soil damaged by machine-intensive farming.

Erosion of buildings

Plant erosion Wedging by plant or tree roots that grow between joint blocks and along fractures exerts an expansive force and tends to widen the openings. Plant erosion is common in San Gimignano, which has a climate conducive to seed germination and plenty of birds to transport the seeds. Occasionally, the towers are cleaned of vegetation, and netting is placed in the old scaffolding apertures to discourage birds.

The presence of lichen on terracotta roof tiles dramatically reduces the extent of physical weathering. It also indicates a 'clean air' environment which may be less susceptible to chemical erosion.

Temperature changes and sun erosion Alternating temperatures plus the effect of sun and moisture can cause stucco to flake, as substances repeatedly expanding and contracting will crack away from the main building. Stucco buildings are also subject to discolouration through bleaching from the intensity of the sun's rays. Both types of sun erosion are common throughout the area.

Materials Even though materials for building are taken from the locality, there is a variance in the rate of erosion of sandstone, limestone and brick. When they all come together because of the composite nature of building construction, stresses and rates of erosion cause cracks and derangement.

Plant erosion on the north side of the town walls.

Below: Wedging by plants on Becci arch.

Above: Lichen on a four-year-old terracotta roof.

A composite form of weathering on the north wall of the town. Tree roots are exposed as a result of the part collapse of the wall. Whether they were responsible for pushing the blocks apart or for holding the matrix at the centre of the wall together for so long, is questionable. The matrix of the wall – shale and lime mortar – disintegrates through the action of water. Limestone is particularly susceptible to erosion through the action of the carbonic acid in rainwater.

Spalling on the walls of a house, San Gimignano.

Below: Sun bleaching on the walls of a house, San Gimignano.

Building materials in varying stages of erosion, Piazza Cisterna.

Building materials in varying stages of erosion, San Giovanni.

The erosion of clay bricks leaves limestone mortar, east walls of the town.

Erosion as a result of changes of use, Piazza Cisterna.

Facades A characteristic of this area is the erosion of the surface appearance of buildings due to changes of style, changes of use, repair and the utilisation of old materials and the desire for a more authentic medieval appearance. Local opinion about the disappearance of San Gimignano's numerous towers is that owners who could no longer pay their taxes had a layer of their towers taken away as a substitute. The materials were then used in the repair and construction of other buildings.

Traffic erosion The road on the west side of San Gimignano passes close to the town walls. It carries moderately heavy traffic as this is the main route from south to north or north to south. Traffic no longer passes through the town, which has limited access only. However, every Thursday morning a town market is held in Piazza Duomo and Piazza Cisterna. This may be causing considerable damage to the surface of the latter. Tunnels dating from the 13th and 14th centuries and probably used as internal town links, run under the town. These have collapsed in places thus increasing the risk of subsidence to both buildings and surfaces.

Erosion as a result of changes of use, Piazza Cisterna.

The use of waste building materials, Piazza Cisterna.

The use of waste building materials near Arch Becci.

Historical erosion, Palazzo Podestà. Plaques were removed from the building in the 18th century and taken to the Louvre in Paris.

Historical erosion, Piazza Cisterna. Grooves remain where the roof alignment had been.

Traffic erosion, tower on the western town walls.

Traffic erosion, eastern town walls.

The traffic-damaged surface of Piazza Cisterna.

Physical Conditions: Summary

Initiative

Many of these forms of erosion are not of a critical nature. Some, such as soil erosion, need to be corrected by improved methods of farming. From past photographs of around 1900, evidence suggests that the landscape not only looks healthier today, but has improved in productivity. To make good the effects of the many forms of erosion on buildings is very costly. If erosion does not present a danger to human safety, it may be regarded as an enhancing the character of a place. Lichen-covered roof tiles, for example, are not only an enhancement but are also sensitive indicators of air pollution. Lichen will not grow where there are too many gases or smoke. It is also thought to have a chemical action that removes substances such as iron from the air and materials.

Further Investigation

An investigation of the stability of landform, especially the hill San Gimignano is built on and the implications for architecture.

i.   Cracks are appearing in some buildings. Recently one appeared at the top of the Cugnanesi tower. This may be because of the addition of a metal-framed window which, not having the same flexibility in contracting and expanding as the surrounding natural materials, has caused stresses resulting in a crack. However, it may mean there has been subsidence at foundation level and that a change in alignment has caused the crack.

ii. Most disturbing is the extent of erosion in the walls, areas beneath the walls and around the base of the walls. The implication is of a movement in the sedimentary formation on which San Gimignano is built. Many of the houses and roadways, particularly on the southeast and northeast sides, are built directly on to the walls. Although the land on the east side has acted as a buttress for these the gradient is steep, and the formation sedimentary and subject to gravitational force. The implication is that there may be mass wasting, which could cause the collapse of part of the town.

Functional Needs: Indicator Matrix

Indicator	Positive	Negative	Comments
Resource efficiency and effectiveness	/		Traditional and established use of local geological resources for building requirements, although import of modern materials for recent development needs to be monitored. Traditional design and materials used, together with climate idiosyncrasies, suggest a passive low-energy approach to development and efficient and effective use of resources.
Passive systems	/		Passive systems of cooling and humidity control in both building and master planning.
The town and its plan	/		Master plan excellent within the medieval town of San Gimignano – provides thermal comfort. Effective and efficient layout encourages human interaction in public spaces.
Boundary	/		Boundary – convenient to geographical areas – determined by topography. Rural with urban nucleus.
Efficiency technologies	/	/	Efficient traditional technologies but little attempt to adopt modern technologies, ie solar shading, brise-soleil.
Relief, climate and buildings	/		Used to maximum effect to bring thermal comfort to inhabitants of the town of San Gimignano and in traditional settlements within boundary area. Lowland modern development disconnected from traditional methods.
Mixed-use development	/		The town of San Gimignano is exemplary as a compact mixed-use development.
Polycentred development	/	/	Town monocentred; unique and dynamic centre for maximum population of 13,000, surrounded by rural hinterland.
Reduced need for public transport	/		Walled town limited access only. Quick and easy access to all parts of town for pedestrians. Safe, pleasurable, functional and free of traffic pollution. Car parks around perimeter of town.
Spaces: prospect/enclave;	/		Extensive use of prospect vistas and enclave – enclosed, sheltered, refuge – spaces.
private/public; transitional	/		Enclosed building plans plus building design mean clear distinction between private and public space.
	/		Spaces within town walls act as transitional space between habitation and landscape outside walls.
Landscaping and amenities		/	Functional – to bring climate relief rather than being a conscious effort towards ecological restoration or aesthetic pleasure.
Place gives pleasure	/		San Gimignano created especially in response to people – human scale, thermal cooling – built and adapted in response to human needs and cultural identity.
Recycling: materials; resources; waste	/		Natural building materials extensively recycled.
		/	No regulated effort to replant woodland, recycle water or towards ecological or soil restoration.
		/	Responsibility on individual to take waste to collection points – although not sophisticated, system tends to work. Limited toxic industrial emissions and use of plastics.
Reuse of buildings	/		Regulations forbid change to the outside of traditional buildings. Buildings within San Gimignano have proved adaptable to change in use throughout time.
Information technologies		/	The scope information technologies could give to the area in terms of efficiency and generation of small businesses has not been developed.
Totals	15	6	

Functional Needs: Statement of Assessment

The Town and Its Plan

There is no evidence to suggest San Gimignano had a preconceived master plan – rather that it had an organic type of growth based on function, population and relief of the land, and the need for protection from enemies and the elements. The indication from the amount of building packed between the town walls is that at some stage it reached optimum growth. Being in the town is like being in a large house or interior. Streets are narrow and seem less to separate housing lines than act as spacious corridors for movement over the natural hilly site. A converging network of passages and squares functions to provide inside communication. At the centre are three vertical towers. From the top of the highest tower, the Torre Comunale, the horizontal prevails. The roof line establishes the design of buildings precisely for providing shelter. Public space is practically every space that is clear and open. The whole of the landscape outside the town walls can be viewed from the gates or the tops of roofs and towers, but can only be experienced by going out of the gates.

The town of San Gimignano is bound within its walls. Although some traffic is allowed inside, most people have to leave cars in one of the many car parks on the south, west and north sides. Entry into the town has to be through one of the gates and most people visiting it for the first time will enter through San Giovanni or San Matteo, the original entrance and exit route of the Via Francigena. The town is so precisely bound, enclosed within itself, protected, that to enter through one of the gates is like going through the doorway of a house.

A footpath goes all around the outside of the town walls; it is 2177 metres long and it takes just about an hour to walk it. En route are a number of small arched entrances. The path is tree-lined, mostly pines and cypresses. The wall and path undulate according to the contours of the land. Outside the walls, on the lower slope of the south side are hotels, residential buildings and a supermarket. The lower slope of the north side accommodates more residential building plus schools and a sports centre. On the east side the vista is much the same as it must have been for the last 1000 years as the steep, rocky, tree-lined slope is impracticable for development. The prospect this affords is aesthetically pleasing – rural and agricultural, with small cultivated fields of vines and olives, farms and villas, half-encircled by cypresses.

The main axis of the walled town runs in an arc: from San Giovanni it rises up through the Piazza Cisterna and the Duomo piazza and down through San Matteo. It reveals a clear form in its unity, arrangement and boundaries of a medieval town. Here the architecture and spaces are of communal significance – the Duomo, Palazzo Comunale, Palazzo del Podesta, the Cisterna (a cistern dating from 1237 with a capacity of 911.68 hectolitres, which was in use until 50 years ago), the towers of great families and large banking houses. The tourist information office is also here. The spaces are meeting places for the townspeople and accommodate public communal activities, festivals, spectacles and religious occasions, and, every Thursday from 8.30 am to 1.00 pm, a town market. San Giovanni and San Matteo are lined with shops which cater almost exclusively for the needs of the many tourists who visit each year. Behind this arc are the parallel, or cross streets, for smaller commercial activities, and houses. This transversal slash through the middle of the town is the dynamic sign of the entering and exiting spaces, delineated by walls. Whether people are actively engaged in business, crafts or just visiting, the gates both open up, and close, this space to them. Defined boundary is an indicator of both the town and its specific functions.

Boundary

A little exploration of the parameter outside the wall will explain the location of the town and its relationship to the topography of the site. San Gimignano covers the tops of two hills, the contours of which define its shape and boundaries. If the site had been flat the town plan would probably have been circular.

Horizontal line of building, San Giovanni.

Cross section and plan of the town.

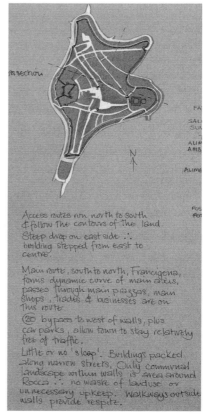

Access routes run north to south & follow the contours of the land.

Steep drop on east side .'. building stepped from east to centre.

Main route, south to north, Francigena, forms dynamic curve of main areas, passes through main piazzas, main shops, trades & businesses are on this route.

(20) bypass to west of walls, plus car parks, allow town to stay relatively free of traffic.

Little or no 'sloap'. Buildings packed along narrow streets. Only communal landscape within walls is area around Rocca .'. no waste of landuse or unnecessary upkeep. Walkways outside walls provide respite.

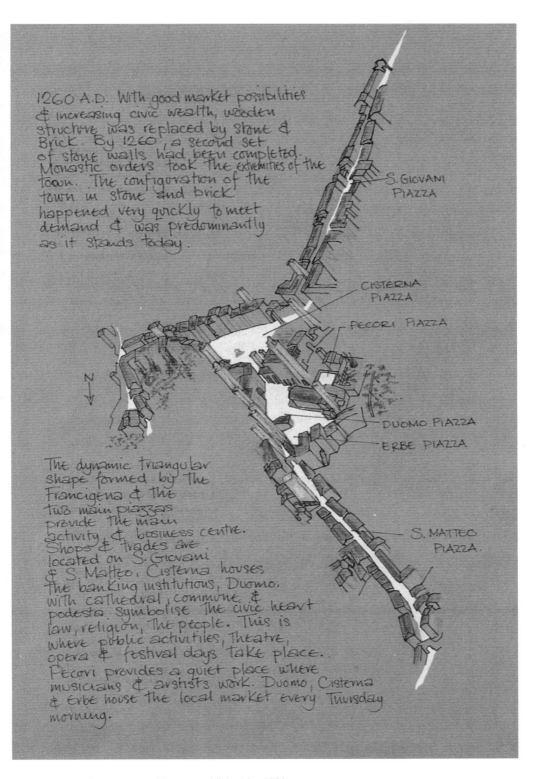

1260 A.D. With good market possibilities & increasing civic wealth, wooden structure was replaced by stone & Brick. By 1260, a second set of stone walls had been completed. Monastic orders took the extremities of the town. The configuration of the town in stone and brick happened very quickly to meet demand & was predominantly as it stands today.

S. GIOVANI PIAZZA

CISTERNA PIAZZA

PECORI PIAZZA

N

DUOMO PIAZZA

ERBE PIAZZA

The dynamic triangular shape formed by the Francigena & the two main piazzas provide the main activity & business centre. Shops & trades are located on S. Giovani & S Matteo. Cisterna houses the banking institutions, Duomo, with cathedral, commune & podesta symbolise the civic heart law, religion, the people. This is where public activities, Theatre, opera & festival days take place. Pecori provides a quiet place where musicians & artists work. Duomo, Cisterna & Erbe house the local market every Thursday morning.

S. MATTEO PIAZZA.

The main axis of the town had been established by 1260.

Stage 1: AD 800–1000 The first town, probably made of wood, was composed of a castle, now the site of San Domenico, Via del Castello, and the two piazzas now called Cisterna and Duomo. The first walls were built in 998 around these two central piazzas which embraced a forum used for legal, political and public business and a *mercantum* used for the buying and selling of produce, merchandise and commercial exchange. Included within the walls were Towerhill, the castle to the east and the hills of Montestaffoli (today the Rocca) to the west. It was 1108 metres in circumference, with four gates: the Cancelleria to the north, Becci to the south and Santo Stefano and the Arch of Goro to the east and west.

Stage 2: 1000–1200 During the next 200 years two large suburbs grew around the main north-south axis, the route of the Via Francigena or Via Roma. The Via del Castello, a main street running from east to west, intersected with this axis and connected the two hills, Towerhill and the hill of Montestafolli. As San Gimignano grew in importance strategically, so economic growth increased. Opportunities existed for trade, business, commerce, related services and markets, including the sale of locally produced luxury goods such as gold, silk, wine and honey. The provision for the needs of a growing number of travellers and the improved spending power of the townspeople caused a tremendous growth both in the quality and quantity of the population during the middle of the 12th century, with banking institutions and professionals such as lawyers coming from other large centres including Rome, Siena and Florence. San Gimignano was also able to profit from the unsettled situation within the locality. To give an example, in 1198 Florence began attacking Semifonte, now Petrognano, whose inhabitants had for some time disturbed their business activities, and in 1200 it destroyed Semifonte and took the instigators of the disturbances to Florence for a lifetime of surveillance. The remaining inhabitants were allowed to go free. They went to San Gimignano and at first would have squatted on either side of the main gates, Becci and Cancelleria, along the Francigena – the route beside which they were most likely to make a living. The triangular form of the town plan was dictated by these two suburbs along the Via Francigena, which would have been at first squatter camps for refugees. With good market possibilities and increasing wealth, wooden houses were replaced by stone or brick. The design and size of the houses varied according to the means of the owners.

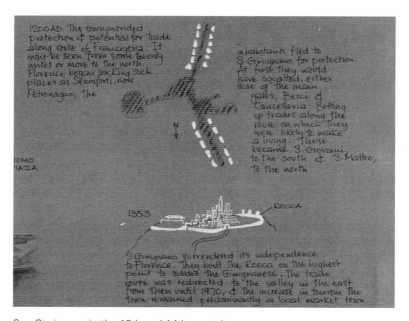

San Gimignano in the 13th and 14th centuries.

One of San Gimignano's many towers.

13th-century building regulations defined the way San Gimignano still looks today.

Stage 3: 1200–1350   The configuration of the town in stone and brick happened very quickly to meet demand. In 1207 a second town wall measuring 2177 metres in circumference was built. Episcopal power managed by Volterra through vice-directors and important families had gradually passed over to the townspeople, who governed themselves through a committee of four consuls. In 1199 they named their first *podesta* or chief magistrate. In 1253 Santa Fina hospital was built. A commune was reponsible for the look of the growing town, controlling the height of its towers and the width and depth of its buildings. By 1255 communal statutes stipulated proportions that were not to be exceeded and thereby defined an image which still exists today. One building regulation states that no house can exceed 12 *braccia* (a measurement based on a man's arm span) across the facade or 24 in depth (Pietro Toeska, private communication 1996). This explains the external discontinuity and asymmetry of the palazzi on the two large streets. The harmonious look of the buildings is greatly indebted to common abeyance of boundary. The highest tower was the Torre Grossa, at 53.28 metres. It was planned in 1298 and built from 1300 to 1311. This was the tower of the commune. No private one was allowed to go higher as this would have been considered an attempt by a private individual to usurp the power of the town. The height of the central towers defines the triangular shape of the town vertically. So the place is characteristically triangular vertically and horizontally.

Medieval culture was fundamentally based on Roman Catholicism and consequently churches are found on most of San Gimignano's principal streets. The gates bear the names of saints and the Convent of Saint Agostino stands as a landmark at the walls' edge.

The town is representative of medieval Tuscan architecture. Examples of Sienese, Pisan and Florentine influences are symbolic of both the wealth of its inhabitants and wider communication. The mullioned windows of the Palazzo Comunale are Florentine; the Romanesque facade of San Francesco, originally San Giovanni of the Order of the Knights of Malta and now a trattoria, is of Pisan origin, dated 1247. San Gimignano is not without renovation, reconstruction and alterations as a result of changing needs and preferential styles.

Here we see growth as interdependent with topographical location, the town's strategic geographical position on the main communication route affording opportunities for economic advancement and the ability to attract a quantity and quality of population. Equally, we see rapid decline when these qualities are lost. Common abeyance of boundary both in plan and building provides an indicator for clarity of function, identity and visual harmony. Diversity of architectural style indicates the extent of external communication.

The town plan and its present function

With pride, the inhabitants of San Gimignano claim that the quality of life is so good in the town because it has not succumbed to industrial or worldly pressures, as have many of the similar walled hilltop towns within the area. However, the implications are that it would make an unsuitable location for industrial or commercial activities because the possibilities for communication are inadequate. San Gimignano has probably capitalised on its best options: good agricultural conditions for wine and olives, and historical significance for tourism.

The town plan shows that a definite area is defined by the boundary of the walls. This is classified as a traffic-free or limited access zone. San Gimignano's configuration can be seen

Duomo piazza before 1900 and after renovation in 1988. It is obvious that throughout the 20th century alterations – not all of them improvements – were made to the building conurbation to emphasise an authentic medieval image.

clearly as a landmark from all directions. The main axis identifies the public area and the area for trade and business. The town has the benefits of a clear identity and imposing image.

The arc formed by the Via Francigena constitues the main axis. Everything of importance to merchant trade or commercial business was, and still is, accomplished on this route. Laws were, and are, passed to protect this axis from obstruction. Alignment of buildings is smooth and continuous. House projections under second-storey level are forbidden. This is the widest throughway and predominance is given to pedestrians. Whether for buying, selling or any other business, everything required is still in this main axis arc of which piazzas are the centre. Cisterna houses the banking institutions while Duomo is more of a public meeting space where public activities, theatre, opera and festivals take place. Pecori provides a quiet place where musicians and artists work. Duomo, Cisterna and Erbe house the market every Thursday morning.

This layout allows other areas to serve visitors in search of peace and the town's inhabitants, with a library, hospital, convents and private housing. The area bound by the walls functions almost exclusively for people. Its size is such that one can reasonably negotiate the whole of the interior, on foot, in a morning. Entering by any one of the gates will give quick and direct access to the centre and limited traffic access allows pedestrians to negotiate the area comfortably and in safety. The whole town functions as a place for people who are uninterrupted by traffic and not frustrated by the divisive systems set up by traffic routes. It also means that San Gimignano is free of the pollution caused by traffic fumes.

This arrangement demands adequate traffic routes and car-parking facilities around the town walls. Car parks in areas of outstanding beauty always present a problem. From the point of view of appearance, San Gimignano would be better off without them. However, none of the car parks are multistorey or ugly encroachments on the natural beauty of the landscape. There are plans to make a further underground car park. The indication is that on occasions, when all the car parks are full, the town has a maximum density of people. This is because visitors populate certain areas only – the main axis arc, Rocca which houses the Vernaccia association and possibly San Augustino piazza which sometimes houses a Sunday market. Sunday is the day when the people of the locality visit San Gimignano.

Buildings and gardens Adequate existing architecture within the walls has been adapted to accommodate public or community needs, including a library and hospital on the Via Folgore. Unfortunately, the schools are outside the walled town in newer development to the northwest. This would imply that the town is not used by an important part of the community – the young – thus forces exist that

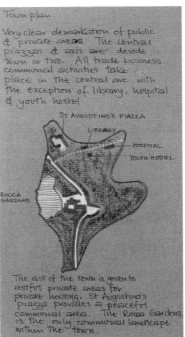

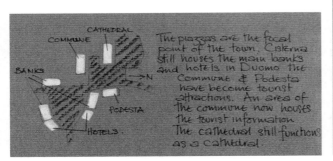

The layout of the town today.

Public and private spaces.

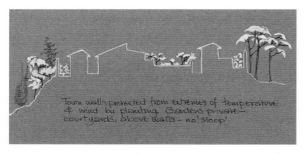

San Gimignano's town walls.

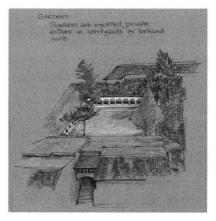

Private gardens in the town.

separate the town from the whole of the community. The important stimulus for change and opportunity that could have been presented by the active participation of the youth of the population is lost. With the advantages gained from its hill location, the town itself acts as a very large house, built on many levels. This is experienced as though one were moving through a series of corridors, streets and alleyways, doorways, arches, large rooms, small rooms, quiet places, activity places – the various roles and sizes of the piazzas and open spaces – and coming across what represent large windows: vistas, views through arches into piazzas, small intimate openings giving small framed vistas of landscape or gardens, an open space beyond confinement.

All buildings are of an enclosed design with the exception of San Domenico, the former prison, which has an open plan of a much later date. Although most houses have a garden, these too are enclosed by walls or are within gates or within groups of buildings. The town is densely built and enclosed within its walls. Within the town, visual surprise and interest are created by voids, alleys, arches, narrow and wide space projections, stairways, doors, small gardens at differing levels; nothing is symmetrical. As the streets are narrow, it is the sudden widening of space, the openings of piazzas, that affirms the relationship between horizontal and vertical. It is a place of human proportions; there is nowhere too confining or overexposing. The private world of gardens can only be seen from the tops of towers. However, walking through the town, this private world is occasionally glimpsed above a wall or through an open doorway. Within the town, the Rocca gardens are the only public gardens. Views of the surrounding landscape are to be experienced through gates on the east side and by walking along the pathway that follows the walls. The impression is of a refuge that presents unlimited vistas. A stimulating environment visually, without repetition.

Relief, Climate and Buildings

Certain advantages regarding thermal comfort for the inhabitants of San Gimignano are gained from the relationship of the relief of the land, climate and building conurbation. The town configuration also suggests that specific strategies may assist the control of excessive heat and humidity. The most obvious, which has been practised for centuries, is that when the heat and humidity of the lowland areas become uncomfortable during the summer months, people retire to the higher altitude of hilltop towns where the airflow makes for a more comfortable environment. In San Gimignano, the temperatures are likely to be lower than in the surrounding lower areas such as Ulignano, Certaldo and Poggibonsi, as there is more air movement and less mosquitoes. However, a comparison of temperature and relative humidity in San Gimignano and Siena shows that both places can be thermally uncomfortable in the summer months.

Transitional and intermediary spaces.

CORRIDORS

Trees help form windows
between walls &
surrounding landscape

Creatin
peacefu

Av
to
P

Outside of buildings the
whole town acts as a
large house or transitional
space between the
protection of urban
conurbation & the
landscape or world
outside the walls.

Arch leading
to Duomo
Piazza

Some narrow alleys
lead to views of open
landscape about city walls

Narrow entrance into large
communal space of Cisterna
Piazza.

(Table 2) That the daily swings of both temperature and humidity are greater in San Gimignano is probably a reflection of the town's hilltop site, its adiabatic climate and an abundance of landscape vegetation which aids night-time cooling

On the southeast side of the town, the side most subject to radiation, building conurbation and streets are terraced up the slope and follow the contours of the land. Therefore streets and many of the buildings are in shadow for most of the day. The experience of being in the walled town on a hot humid day is considerably more comfortable as regards temperature, humidity and airflow than being in the area outside the walls. At various points around the town, and at its entrances, a warm breeze may be experienced even on the most hot, humid and still days in the middle of summer. Standing on the balconies of buildings on the south-east a rising hot and humid airflow from the landscape below can be experienced. A hypothesis about the passive cooling of the town is that hot humid air rising from the lower tree-lined valley area outside San Gimignano is resisted by the walls and only drawn in through the openings – the gateways. Once in, it passes up the hilly site, through narrow shaded streets which, with the overhang of the roofs, act as cooling tunnels. As all the streets rise upwards, opening into the central piazzas, it is reasonable to assume that the hot air passes through the narrow cooling tunnels and comes out in the central open areas, cooler, drier and faster. The height

Table 2: A comparison of temperatures and relative humidity in San Gimignano and Siena which lies 32 kilometres to the south. The figures for San Gimignano were taken on a farm just outside the walls of the town, the ones for Siena were taken in the *campo*. They apply to May, June, July and August 1995 (Convento Capuccini, Siena). Note that for San Gimignano there is a considerable daily swing of approximately 20°C in temperature.

	Temperature °C			Relative humidity %		
	Med	**Min**	**Max**	**Med**	**Min**	**Max**
6.5.95						
San Gimignano	17.3	7.1	28.0	57	21	94
Siena	16.65	11.5	21.8	45.90	22.30	69.50
29.5.95						
San Gimignano	20.9	14.3	29.6	69	37	96
Siena	18.5	14.6	22.4	70.55	41.90	100
7.6.95						
San Gimignano	18.2	9.3	27.3	71	34	98
Siena	17.18	10.25	24.10	64.60	38.30	90.90
20.6.95						
San Gimignano	24.3	14.7	33.7	56	16	93
Siena	23.84	17.14	30.54	49.90	21.80	78
1.7.95						
San Gimignano	23.5	15.5	31.3	63	32	94
Siena	22.94	16.97	28.73	83.70	40.30	83.70
27.7.95						
San Gimignano	28.0	17.9	38.4	51	16	83
Siena	27.70	21.30	34.10	60.50	43.00	78.00
6.8.95						
San Gimignano	25.7	17.9	34.5	60	21	92
Siena	24.90	18.17	31.63	53	22.80	83.20
26.8.95						
San Gimignano	22.3	15.9	31.1	77	37	96
Siena	21.75	16.00	27.50	64.80	44.60	85.00

of the towers in the centre of the town means they could conceivably cause downdraughts or in some areas, upcast, like chimney-stack ventilation.

Passageways, which may or may not be connected to town wells, go under San Gimignano and may cause a certain cooling airflow to circulate under the town itself. Whether these were built as places of refuge during times of siege or as a means of internal communication, the likelihood is that they were built after the town. Certain places have a pleasant resonance of sound. One noticeable one is the entrance into the Duomo piazza from San Matteo – a passageway runs from the southeast side of Via di Capassi up into the piazza. Some entrances to the passageways, outside the walls, are at a lower level than the town. As a strategy towards cooling this is not uncommon in Italy – the hill on which San Marino is built has many passageways and butcher's shops have been built against them because of their cooling effect (Giovanni Flores, private communication 1996).

Buildings and climate control   The walled town and the majority of farms and villas in San Gimignano and district were built for the functioning and comfort of a society that is now history. The town is medieval, the rural properties of 17th- and 18th-century origin.

The plan of rural villas and farmhouses is enclosed and deeply square, sometimes with a small asymmetrically positioned tower which may provide ventilation or bring light into the interior. Roofs are of a shallow pitch and have an overhang, giving shade to the top-storey windows. Sometimes villas and farms have small central towers, which allow light into the centre of large square buildings. Windows are deep set and the more prestigious buildings have louvred shutters.

Winters in San Gimignano and the surrounding district are cool enough to require some extra interior heating, but the most difficult period for human thermal comfort is the summer months from June to September when the sun's radiation and high humidity are threatening. As with the town's layout, buildings belong to a time when man had little option other than to interact with the climate and geological or geographical resources and materials for the provision of human thermal comfort. In the satisfaction of this many passive and low energy design strategies are implemented into planning and architecture for the control of temperature, humidity or airflow.

San Gimignano from the southeast.

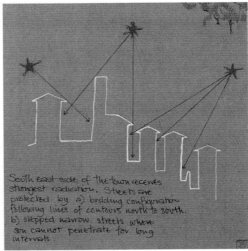

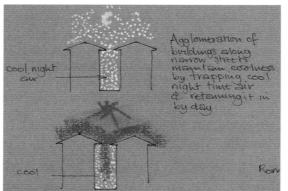

Agglomeration of buildings along narrow streets maintain coolness by trapping cool night time air & retaining it in by day

cool night air

cool

Ron

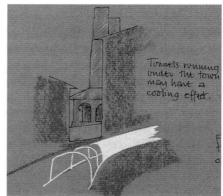

Tunnels running under the town may have a cooling effect.

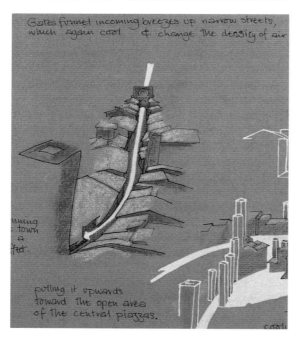

Gates funnel incoming breezes up narrow streets, which again cool & change the density of air

pulling it upwards toward the open area of the central piazzas.

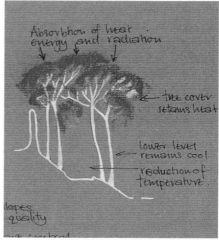

Absorbtion of heat energy and radiation

tree cover retains heat

lower level remains cool.

reduction of temperature.

Towers give a further cooling effect by creating down draughts, or in some areas, upcast like chimney stack ventilation.

Passive cooling within the walls of the town.

Consequently, the available materials, building design and lifestyle had to come to some agreeable compromise with climatic conditions. It has been the human response to live with these conditions rather than combat them.

Although the summer temperatures and humidity in San Gimignano can be uncomfortably high this is not constant. Rather there is a cycle each day of high and low, and therefore we may assume that suitable building materials would absorb and retain during the high periods, and release during low periods. Daily fluctuations would suggest that there is a need for some sort of daily human control.

Building materials   Traditional building construction is dependent on the mass of the materials – stone, brick, cement and terracotta – that are available within the locality. Do these materials interact with climatic conditions in such a way as to be of benefit to human comfort? An important prerequisite for this is preventing a house overheating in summer. Winters are cool and there is the need to prevent heat from escaping; and the daily swing of both relative humidity and temperature is considerable in winter as well as summer. It is desirable that a building has good thermal inertia and in some way aids the balancing out of temperature and humidity. In this area this is achieved through the use of natural materials which have the ability to absorb, retain and then release both heat and moisture. In the summer months, the exterior walls and roof slowly absorb heat and moisture throughout the day then slowly release them at night. The mass of the materials allows the interior to stay cool. In winter the same materials, from the interior, benefit from low constant heat which they are able to absorb, retain and release as needed to balance internal temperature. However, within this system many unseen modern innovations such as insulation, improved windows and sealers are incorporated. It is unusual for temperatures to drop below freezing, so a large amount of energy is not needed for heating. This is fortunate, because most places within the area have a low electricity supply of 3 kilowatts. A Bavarian stove, which consumes very small amounts of wood as fuel, is a good solution to the need for low constant heat. In this region its use may be facilitated by the natural fall of dead wood or the thinning of overcrowded areas of trees so as to strengthen woodland.

In San Gimignano itself the fact that materials for building came from the locality gives a harmonious effect to the whole. The warm grey of travertine, and buff and brown sandstone, blend with the pale terracotta of bricks. Plants are seeded and grow between joints, lichens cover terracotta roof tiles. In the more important streets and piazzas the paving is brick or stone slabs. Today building regulations (*piano reggelatori*) provide a strict code of conservation prohibiting any changes in external appearance. Most buildings are made of stone or brick and some have stone – travertine, sandstone and serpentine – on the lower levels for strength and brick, which is lighter, on the higher levels. Rural properties take advantage of waste materials – walls are constructed of bricks, pebbles and old tiles and then given a coat of stucco. It was common in the time of the *mezzadre* (feudal agricultural system) for each large estate to make its own bricks for its farms.

Design for climate control   Certain design features, characteristic of the area, give a degree of climate control. Windows are small in relation to wall area, and shuttered. Doors are substantial, and usually made of hardwood. The roof is terracotta tiled, at a shallow angle to account for moderate rainfall, and has an overhang of about 50 centimetres which protects upper walls and windows.

The main door of a house often opens into a windowless, inner lobby which, by means of a stairway, leads to an inner door to the living accommodation; or an outside stairway may lead to a covered balcony and entrance. In both instances there is some kind of cooling of the air before it enters the living area. The ground floor of a building is usually surrounded by

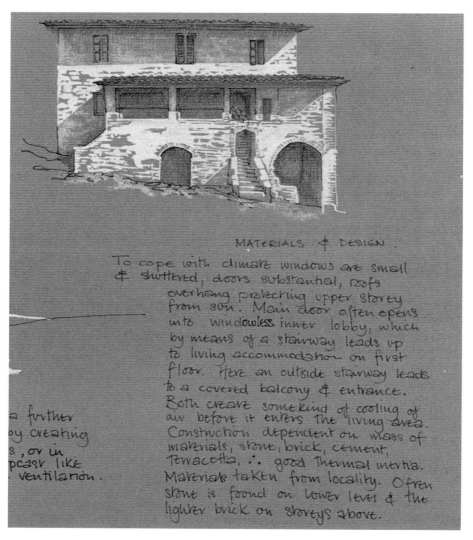

MATERIALS & DESIGN.

To cope with climate windows are small & shuttered, doors substantial, roofs overhang protecting upper storey from sun. Main door often opens into windowless inner lobby, which by means of a stairway leads up to living accommodation on first floor. Here an outside stairway leads to a covered balcony & entrance. Both create some kind of cooling of air before it enters the living area. Construction dependent on mass of materials, stone, brick, cement, Terracotta, .: good Thermal inertia. Materials taken from locality. Often stone is found on lower level & the lighter brick on storeys above.

a further by creating s, or in peask like ventilation.

The design of buildings and the materials used in their construction help their occupants to cope with the climate.

planting or stands within the shadow in narrow streets, methods of keeping cool at the expense of natural daylight. This floor is used for storage or as a workshop. Accommodation is on the upper floors. This elevation has advantages as regards site and living conditions, better airflow and quality of light, privacy and fewer biting insects.

Windows that have replaced more traditional ones are of good quality, usually with heavy hardwood frames. A common size for the window and frame is 1.2 metres high by 90 centimetres wide, with glass at least 5 millimetres thick. On average there is one window to 16 square metres of floor area. The intensity of light is such that this gives adequate daylight for most domestic tasks. However, taking into consideration shade from the building's location and the part of the day when windows are obscured by shutters, allowing sufficient daylight into the interior can be a problem. To keep air cool and dry inside demands a certain daily procedure during the summer months, which the majority of people adhere to as part of their lifestyle. Windows

Private houses in the town.

HOUSING
Housing is enclosed.
Often the ground floor
is a windowless lobby
accommodation being
above ground level
Housing is two to four
storeys. There is very
little 'sloap' within the
town walls .

are shuttered, but not always with the traditional wooden louvres – there are some raffia or aluminium shutters. The indication is, however, that louvred shuttering is the more desirable both in appearance and in the way it gives protection without preventing airflow.

In summer, cool air may only enter the building during the evening, night and early morning. In the middle of the day, any air that comes in is hot and humid. The sun's radiation through a glass window would only intensify the internal temperature and windows and shutters are opened only between late afternoon and early morning, letting in cool air and allowing warm internal air to cool. Throughout the day they go through varying degrees of closure. Complete closure restricts ventilation. In the morning, at 10 am, shutters are closed with the bottom area angled to allow a draught to rise from below, which is then trapped and cooled between shutters and slightly opened windows. Later, towards midday, windows and shutters are closed, preventing the hot, humid air and the sun's rays from entering. The layer of air between the shutter and window acts as a further insulator throughout the hottest part of the day. Later in the afternoon windows may be opened, allowing some airflow, and finally shutters are opened when the sun is not so intense and the humidity is lower. This system works to the benefit of human comfort. However, the compromise is the reduction of daylight into a building, and a demand on lifestyle.

Roof materials and structure   As the sun is the most threatening element to thermal comfort, the roof becomes the part of the building that is most vulnerable to exposure. But again, as with the rest of the structure the threat is not consistent throughout the year, but only in the summer months of June to September. The roof has to fulfil other functions such as keeping

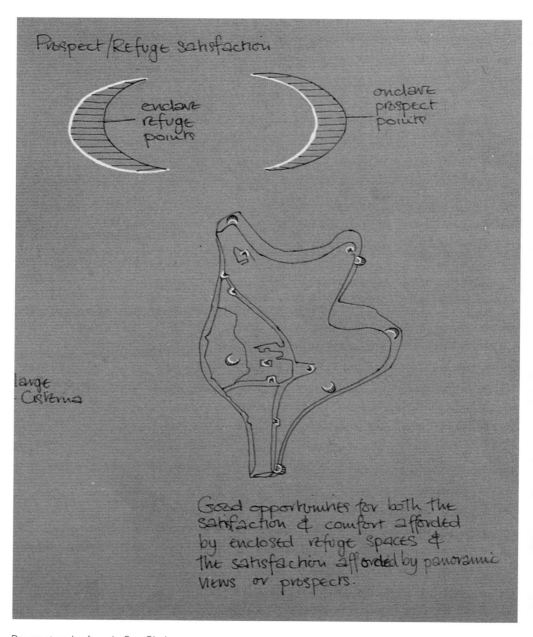

Prospect and refuge in San Gimignano.

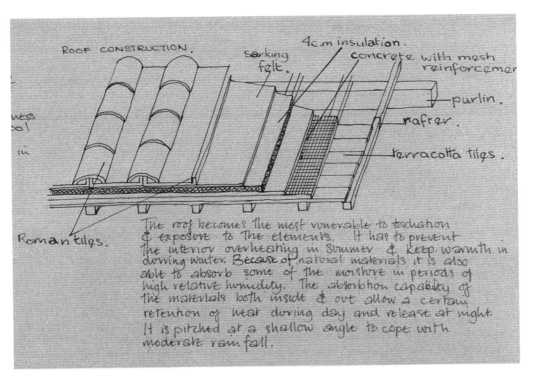

ROOF CONSTRUCTION.

4c.m insulation.

sarking felt.

concrete with mesh reinforcement

purlin.

rafter.

terracotta tiles.

Roman tiles.

ness ol

in

The roof becomes the most vunerable to radiation & exposure to the elements. It has to prevent the interior overheating in summer & keep warmth in during winter. Because of natural materials it is also able to absorb some of the moisture in periods of high relative humidity. The absorbtion capabilty of the materials both inside & out allow a certain retention of heat during day and release at night. It is pitched at a shallow angle to cope with moderate rain fall.

Typical roof construction used for the renovation of properties.

The interior of the roof of a property that has been renovated.

rain and wind out, and warmth in during winter. The indication is that it would be advantageous if the roof showed good thermal inertia plus an ability to absorb moisture during periods of high relative humidity.

Typically, in the roof of a property that has been renovated concrete insulation and tarred fabric form a barrier between the functioning of exterior and interior – traditionally, the roof did not have the fabric and, sometimes, not the concrete. The layer of insulation varies, but is usually not more than 8 centimetres which is considered to have the maximum effect. Terracotta tiles have some porosity both inside and out, allowing an absorbtion of heat and moisture which may be retained and then released during a cooler or dryer period. Rooms on an upper storey are open to the rafters and the tiles. It is also common to find flat terracotta ceiling tiles forming the ceilings of lower floors. During the winter months heat absorbed from an internal stove in the daytime may be released at night thereby helping to keep an even temperature. However, the tone and nonreflectant quality of the tiles does not improve the daylight factor.

Spaces

The whole town and the footpath that circles the walls form a composition of interconnected intermediary spaces. The tree-lined path that connects the landscape and town acts as a cool corridor, the trees forming the frames of large windows that look on to landscape vistas. Spaces give psychological comfort, prospect and enclave, prospect and refuge. They dictate activities: large public piazzas for occasions when members of the community are gathered for markets and festivals; small enclosed squares for more intimate, but still public, groups. Streets become intermediary space. People often wonder why it costs them more to sit outside to drink a coffee than inside. One reason is that the proprietor of the bar pays a high rent to the town commune for his outside street space. In concept, spaces are meeting places for people who possess a town in common. They are accessible and enjoyable, yet defined, limited and enclosed and protected by the buildings. They are both aesthetically pleasing and functional. Inside the town walls the only communal landscape is the Rocca gardens, again indicating that San Gimignano is of a size and proportions to act as a large house within the walls. The entire landscape beyond becomes a communal garden to be viewed from many prospect points.

Functional Needs Summary

Initiatives

This section has given the human response to building in this specific environment. It has asked how well landscape and architecture are functioning to improve human biological and psychological comfort while being sensitive to the abuse of artificial energy sources. San Gimignano may have originated in the need for a safe resting place at a strategic geographical point on a much-used and important communication route in the early Middle Ages or, even earlier, in Etruscan times as a hilltop refuge for Romans. However, its form is a clear and truthful reflection of what its purpose and functions were. Although these may have changed, all who live here or who visit, respect the sincerity and clarity of identity that exist, and are prepared to adapt. The creative significance of this will be discussed in the section on cultural identity. There are many advantages in San Gimignano's size, layout and concept of boundary that could be assimilated into the overcrowded, outgrown and confused layout of some industrial cities and their suburbs, in particular relation to 'compact' urban planning.

Purposeful growth dictated the town plan in relation to topographical location and strategic geographical communications, incentive structures that attracted a desired quality and quantity of population.

Further Investigation

In many ways, what has been said here of building design, materials and climate control is only a reflection of something that people have known by trial and error, and have made use of for centuries in preindustrial built environments. Applying traditional passive methods of climate control is of importance in the reduction of harmful energy consumption globally. A logical corollary is the application of monitoring, scientific method and measurement, which will enable decisions to be made about calculated repetitions. To quote Michael Hough (1995): 'Creating favourable habitats by natural means combines traditional wisdom, modern science and intelligent planning.'

1. Analyse and compare performance of traditional and modern:
    i.   Roof design and construction; house design and construction;
    ii. Cost and availability of materials and skilled workmanship;
    iii. Cost to the environment, that is, depletion of natural resources, transport, embodied and operational energy.
2. Test hypotheses on methods of cooling connected with climate, relief and building conurbation through model and simulation.
3. What lessons may be drawn about traffic control that may be pertinent to the city:
    i.   Clear boundary;
    ii. Arrangement of built conurbation for people;
    iii. Town covers an area reasonably negotiable on foot.
4. Design solutions. Efficient daylighting is forfeited during the summer months in order to maintain the coolness of interiors. Without the use of excess artificial energy, how may the amount of daylighting entering into these buildings be increased?
5. Advocacy. Climatic comfort has to some extent dictated a type of lifestyle – most businesses close between 1.00 pm and 3.00 pm. Is this a disadvantage in terms of expectations of efficiency in the 21st-century lifestyle?
6. How important is the sense of boundary as a prerequisite of place? San Gimignano presents many examples for analysis:
    i.   Triangular plan and building conurbation;
    ii. Common abeyance of street alignment and units of measurement;
    iii. Treatment of whole area within town walls as a large house;
    iv. Boundaries separating activities, spaces and qualities, for example, axis, piazzas, public and private, prospect and enclave, enclosed and open.
7. The interaction of landscape, town configuration and climate poses many questions of how human biological comfort may be improved in an urban environment. This is not unique to San Gimignano. Local common opinion tells:
    i.   When the walls surrounding Florence were removed in the 19th century temperatures increased during summer and decreased during winter.
    ii. The hill on which the old town of San Marino is built is full of passages. In places, butcher's storerooms are built up against these passages because of the cooling effect.
8. Further beneficial research, progressing from this section, would be to make an accurate reconstruction model of the town and the hill on which it is built. Applying simulated climatic conditions would enlighten researchers as to what is actually happening.

Institutional Requirements: Indicator Matrix

Indicator	Positive	Negative	Comments
Economic base	/		Very good in the region generally: wine, olives, tourism.
Integration or reductionism		/	Tourism detrimentally monopolises business and threatens the healthy existence of the town.
Systems that reward efficiency and saving resources		/	No common legislation or guidance regulations towards energy efficiency, alternative energy or conservation of natural resources. However, very common-sense approach by indigenous people – building waste from natural materials is recycled in other buildings.
Incentive structures	/	/	Few institutional incentives for sustainable development. Landscape and architecture plus slow pace of life make San Gimignano an extremely desirable place to live.
Professional government: local; national; international		/	No local authority autonomy – money from taxes passes to national government which people perceive as being indifferent to their needs.
Communication and infrastructure: local; national; international		/	Wine industry has good business communication – international. Some international interest through Eupolis in future fabric of town.
Legislation: taxes; building regulations; conservation		/	Local taxes go to national government and are then proportioned back to locality, therefore local people are disconnected from the concept that money earned benefits the public activities of the area.
	/		Very rigid regulations about exterior appearance of vernacular building – good for conservation and protection of heritage.
Pattern of conservation	/		Clear – change as little as possible to exterior envelope – use similar local materials of a similar age to original.
Welfare services: health; education; social services		/	Adequate – trend to move essential services to large cities, ie:
		/	Fino hospital no longer state-funded; people must go to new hospital 10km away in Poggibonsi.
		/	Schools outside city walls.
Land tenure		/	Dissolution of medieval systems of land tenure has been mismanaged, exposing rural and urban areas to exploitation by private speculative external forces.
Opportunities		/	Quality of life very good for those who have already bought into the area; property prices and escalating rents prohibitive for those wishing to progress within the area.
Public transport		/	Inadequate and infrequent.
Property speculation	/		Extensive from 1950s to1990s: farms, property, holiday retreats, tourist-connected buisinesses. Now an expensive area to move into.
Population changes	/	/	Extensive – indigenous population of San Gimignano dropped from 7000 to 1700 in less than decade. Agricultural economy benefited from improved technologies and methods of management brought in by northern European immigrants
Civic responsiveness: societies; organisations		/	Elitist groups – disunited. Piazzas are focus for communal interaction and exchanges of ideas when not monopolised by tourists.
Totals	6	14	

Institutional Requirements Statement of Assessment

Economic Base

Prosperity is reflected in the landscape and architecture of the area and the source of that prosperity is tourism, agritourism, and the production of wine and olives. There are no large industries within the area. Edmund Gardner, who in 1902 described the inhabitants of San Gimignano as being 'miserably poor' in contrast to the inhabitants of Poggibonsi and Certaldo, went on to say that 'living is exceedingly cheap; but there is no trade, and what little work there is, is but scantily paid'. Traditional crafts such as weaving had almost died out and practice in arts and crafts was negligible. The inhabitants of the surrounding area were mostly peasant farmers who made a meagre living selling their products in the town. However, by 1965 a tourist information service had been established (a private body supported by local administration); and in 1993, 86,172 foreign and 147,673 Italian tourists visited and stayed in San Gimignano. In 1995, 180,608 foreign and 200,508 Italian tourists visited and stayed in hotels and other forms of holiday accommodation (Commune records 1996).

Integration or Reductionism   The number of tourists visiting San Gimignano would indicate that the place is conducive to the growth of tourism. How sustainable is tourism as an economic system for the whole of the area? What effect has tourism had on local identity, landscape and architecture? And is there evidence to suggest that tourism points the way towards growth in the future?

Conditions conducive to the growth of tourism   The growth of an affluent 20th-century urban culture has been very much dependent on the increase in industrialisation in the towns of northern Europe and America. San Gimignano and district is an area of outstanding natural beauty at a time when industrialisation has put this type of environment under threat. It has a pleasant climate (although it can be uncomfortably hot and humid, and mosquito-ridden in July and August). It represents an exemplary and nostalgic glimpse into a kind of preindustrial style of urban living, one that has almost vanished from modern industrial society. Improvements in communication and transport have made it more accessible – San Gimignano is easily reached from the main Tuscany tourist route. However, Tuscany is full of such hilltop towns and these have not experienced a similar growth in tourism. Significant indicators towards San Gimignano's encouragement of tourism are: a number of population changes; availability of very desirable low-cost housing in the 1960s and 1970s; proximity to a major tourist route; and its refusal to embrace the industrial revolution which has swept northern Italy since the Second World War.

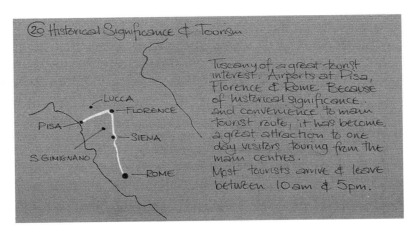

San Gimignano's position on Tuscany's tourist route.

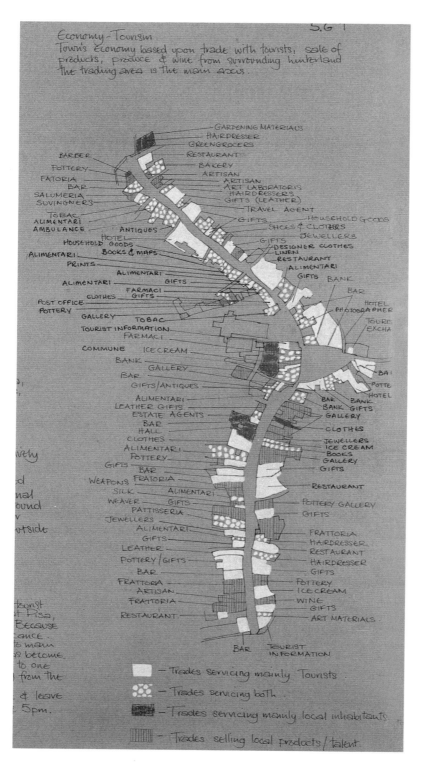

The use of buildings in the arc from San Giovanni to San Matteo. Most of the shops and restaurants are predominantly dependent on tourism.

Indicators of tourism   From the end of March to the end of October the town has a high density of people between 10.00 am and 5.00 pm, when large numbers of day tourists arrive in cars and coaches to visit. During these hours tourism becomes uncomfortable. In the evenings and mornings it is a pleasantly and comfortably populated place. The whole commercial axis of San Gimignano, from San Giovanni to San Matteo, is given over to exploiting the tourists' spending capacity, exemplified in the number of retail establishments dependent on the tourist trade. Local trade is insignificant. In the whole of the walled town only a proportion of public buildings – churches, library, hospital (since early 1996 the hospital of San Fino is no longer supported by the state) – and piazzas is shared with the local inhabitants. Looking on the positive side, most shops and restaurants promote and sell local crafts or produce, thereby providing some employment within the locality. The quality of art and food products is very high.

There are only four hotels within the town: Bel Soggiorno on Via San Giovanni with 45 beds; La Cisterna in Piazza Cisterna, accommodating 92 visitors; Leon Bianco, also in Piazza Cisterna, with accommodation for 34; L'Antico Pozzo in Via San Matteo with 32 beds. All four hotels offer three-star facilities. There is a youth hostel on Via delle Fonti, which is able to take 75 travellers. Small bed and breakfast places and self-catering accommodation provide for the remaining tourists who wish to stay in the walled town. The indication is that the town can comfortably accommodate the number of people who are there between 5.00 pm and 10.00 am.

Within the landscape there are no obtrusive indications of tourists, such as camping sites or picnic areas. The only other factor that might infringe on the natural beauty of the countryside is the growing number of hotels. However, these are not incongruous with the general appearance of the area. Many tourists stay in agritourism centres which have recently gained the approval of the planning authorities. These are farms, farm buildings or large villas in the surrounding countryside that have been especially converted for the tourist trade. The most noticeable effect of tourism is the increasing number of car and coach parks on the southwest and north sides of San Gimignano. Fortunately, these are at a lower level than the town, so even walks around the outside of the walls give views of landscape beyond foreground car parks.

With the exception of a very good three-laned road from Poggibonsi, which has been widened and straightened over the last 10 years, roads are narrow and full of bends. Heavy traffic such as coaches and lorries usually arrives on the Poggibonsi road which feeds off the Florence-Siena autostrada. Its presence may have contributed to the large proportion of day visitors to San Gimignano. There is concern about the large number of cars and heavier traffic that travel the road close to the walls of the town on the west side. This arouses fear about traffic erosion to the walls and foundations of the town. An attempt has been made to prevent heavy traffic passing near the walls, with a large coach park and turn-around point to the south of the town. The commune is considering a plan for a ring road that will bypass the town walls. The problem here is not only finance, but genuine concern that any large bypass would in some way defile the natural beauty of the surrounding landscape. One suggestion is to build a large tunnel through the landscape, so that the traffic would be out of sight. The underground parking development which is under consideration would also meet the demands of the growing number of tourists. Parking around the walls of San Gimignano is expensive, which acts as a deterrent to local inhabitants, although a certain number of permits, to park both outside and inside the walls, are granted to local residents and businesses.

Property prices are high, both in the town and surrounding country. In 1996, a modest terraced town house might have sold for £250,000. People wishing to buy second homes or holiday accommodation to rent out have greatly inflated the property market. The indication is that this is having an adverse effect on the permanent local community. And as rents are high, little use is made of the town by local private, professional or commercial businesses. Taken with the declining population – figures for the walled town are 4121 inhabitants in 1971, 3500 inhabitants in 1985 and 1760 in 1996 – it looks as though there will be an increasing amount of residential building owned by people who do not live in the town full-time, or who rent to tourists. There is obvious concern for the survival of local identity as projected by an indigenous permanent population. It is not that tourism is in itself a malign force. However, if it is not held in balance with the needs of local community it may turn this place into a museum town instead of one that is developing its still-living culture. Tourism and the lack of provision for local employment are forcing an artificially high cost of living on the area. The implication of these changes is a rapid decline in the population of local inhabitants, who are usually placed in new housing near to Certaldo or Poggibonsi, and loss of local identity and community.

San Gimignano has become symbolic of good quality, prosperity and culture. It attracts tourists visiting for the day; people wishing to buy or rent a property for longer periods; those whose jobs allow them to live and work here for many months of the year; and people buying retirement homes. They are not the people concerned with earning a living within the area. Local inhabitants come under increased pressure to sell their properties as greatly inflated prices are offered by the newcomers. At present, people who have rented properties at prices commensurate with their earning ability as artisans within the area are threatened by demands for ever-increasing rents by landlords. Landlords are aware of the more lucrative opportunities provided by renting these properties to tourists.

Pattern of Conservation

Of the architecture within the walled city, nothing has been specifically built for tourists. Visual appearance provides an indicator of a town in a commendable state of preservation. The disturbing incidences of vandalism and negligence attributed to tourist activities in larger cities such as Florence are not apparent here. Of the many forms of erosion, it would be difficult to determine the percentage caused by tourism. Most forms seem to add a pleasant patina to the surface of buildings. Because there is limited access to the town it is almost free of traffic pollution.

The building regulations are very rigid. Within the town, it is impossible to make even minor alterations without the permission of the commune. Planning permission for new building, extensions or even change of use is seldom granted within its walls. Materials used in repairs or renovations must be of similar age and appearance to those used in the original building. In the 1960s, when many small rural properties were renovated, the advice given to their owners was to renovate as little as possible, but to make realistic allowances for needs and habits. It is difficult to gain planning permission to change the external appearance of a building, even down to louvred shutters (traditionally these were not allowed on peasant farmhouses). Thus a homogeneous balance of landscape and architecture has been maintained. Whereas this may have enhanced the appearance of the area, as old buildings were protected from the whims of style often associated with do-it-yourself owners and poor insensitive renovations, it has also prohibited any creative infusion of architectural design representative of 20th-century culture.

Legislation and building use   The indication is that building regulations have safeguarded the appearance of the town. However, they have not safeguarded the use made of these buildings in any way that encourages the survival of a local community. The way buildings are used is monopolised by tourism, which explains why San Gimignano seems empty and deserted from November through to March. The majority of shops open as infrequently as possible during these months.

Although the commune has authority as regards the look and shape of the place, the taxed proportion of income generated in the area does not come to it, but passes to Rome. Rome then gives back the public funds for administration. Wealth earned here is not commensurate with money invested in public concerns. This has repercussions on the motivations of indi-

The main tourist entrance into Piazza Cisterna.

viduals towards community responsibility. If people see few physical benefits from the payment of taxes they become self-interested and evasive, with a predilection towards declaring only what is absolutely necessary of their income and business activities. For example, the commune controls the giving of licences to anyone wishing to run a small business or shop within the town. The licences are free, but the commune controls what kind of business should operate or what the shop should sell. You cannot buy an *alimentari* and reopen it as a *farmacia* or, in the case of reapplying for a licence, be sure of running it as an *alimentari*.

However, because of tourism shops and businesses are very lucrative concerns. Licences obtained free are of considerable value when a business property changes hands. A practice exists called '*buon'uscita*' (a good way out), whereby the incoming tenant or buyer gives large sums of money, undeclared, to the previous occupant in exchange for the licence. There are few public structures that encourage civic responsiveness. However, certain groups of people – artists, craftsmen, artisans, traders and academics – form community groups out of common concerns, and the town's conurbation is conducive to social intercourse with its communal central piazzas and proliferation of enclave and prospect spaces. The indication is that community spirit exists between certain elite groups. This is not the same state of reciprocity that existed during the building of the town, where money earned through the town was relevant to what was built, and worked for the common good of all citizens. Money earned through tourism profits private individuals or passes as taxes to national government.

In 13th-century society the idea of citizenship implied that money made had a direct impact on the appearance of the town, for the common good of all its inhabitants. People who had come to San Gimignano either to take refuge from Florentine attacks or merely to make a fortune in a place of business were expected, when given opportunities to make money through the town, to invest in public concerns – architecture, paintings, hospital, public meeting spaces like the piazzas – as part of a sense of public duty. The implication was that these people would not have made money without the town. This was the basis of citizenship and the patronage of artists and craftsmen that established an attractive and functional town and an urban lifestyle. A good indicator would be to see the opportunity presented through the town balanced with civic response.

Population Changes

With the running down of the *mezzadria* system after 1945, significant population changes began to take place. The *mezzadria* was a series of agreements between peasant farmers and landowners. The peasant farmer used materials provided by the landowner and the produce was divided between them. Many small peasant farms were in attractive locations, and the quality of the local materials with which they were built made them very desirable. Changes and increases in the taxation system after 1945, compounded by the effects of poor crops, put increasing pressure on both landowner and farmer. Thus, a disintegration of the system took place. There was new industry and housing in newly developed valley areas around Poggibonsi and Certaldo and many peasant farmers abandoned their farms in search of work in these industries. Therefore, cheap desirable property came on the market. A small farm bought for £4000 in 1950 would now be worth £1,000,000. In the 1950s and 1960s the farms were attractive business propositions to people from the more northern part of Europe where land and property prices were much higher. Germans, Swiss, English and northern Italians, discontented with the quality of life in the larger industrial areas, sought a new beginning here. With the influx of money made in the industrial towns, improved farming methods and mechanisation, the small farms around San Gimignano became very profitable concerns. Now they are orderly and well run, and have great visual appeal. A high proportion are organic and show awareness of environmental concerns.

The success of wine farming is evident from the appearance of the landscape. Vernaccia, exclusive to this area, became Italy's first *Denominazione di Origine Controllata* (DOC) wine in 1966. In 1993, Vernaccia of San Gimignano entered the category of fine Italian prestigious wines with the title *Denominazione di Origine Controllata & Garantita* (DOCG). The Vernaccia consortium began in 1972 and is housed in the Villa della Rocca. Seventy per cent of Vernaccia is exported, mostly to Europe and America. Figures are not available prior to 1990. The number of producers in that year was 179, and in 1995 there were 170. The output in 1990 was 43,111.60 litres and in 1995, 41,602.37 litres. It is remarkable that there is only a slight decrease in both these figures, taking into consideration the more stringent standards required for the DOCG label after 1993. Wine that does not reach this standard, together with many wines from differing grapes, is sold as ordinary table wine. The majority of wine farms are private family concerns – only one cooperative exists within the area.

The implications are that the area has sought to promote an image of quality. This has involved improved mechanisation, technology and efficient management; a side effect is the decline in the need for manual labour. Most of the wine farms are family owned and managed. In 1951, 79 per cent of the population were employed in agriculture. By 1961 the figure was 57 per cent and in 1991 only 32 per cent were employed. From 1961 to 1971 the number of owner-worked farms increased from 20 per cent to 51 per cent and the surface of useable farm land increased by 9 per cent. The people who were pushed out of the area were the indigenous peasant farmers and labourers. They have moved to the industrial valley areas, Certaldo and Poggibonsi in search of employment. Their homes and properties have been taken over by people such as artists, artisans and craftsmen, who are able to make an income in this area, especially from tourism.

Population changes over the last 40 years have undoubtedly contributed to the recent prosperity of the region. By the 1980s it had become an area of creative artisans and small family-run businesses. These individuals have both respect for, and an understanding of, the character and importance of this place – they are artists, craftsmen, academics and wine producers who value the place and the heritage which contributes to their quality of life. From a local association of these kinds of people comes a proposal for an institutional form of sustainable development suitable for San Gimignano – a plan that could rejuvenate a more significantly local and serious attitude to the area and, paradoxically, a more long-term and worldly sustainability.

Civic Responsiveness

In 1993, in opposition to a plan to make the redundant prison of San Domenico into a hotel, the Citizen's Association put forward a rough outline for a cultural centre and territorial university, with the possibility that it would be connected to Eupolis, a network of historical cities of cultural artistic and environmental value in central Italy. It was a form of development that would have had definite advantages for the town, coexisting with, and even complementary to, tourism, and providing serious and permanent forms of employment. However, the plan never reached fruition and the former prison is now a hotel.

Unfortunately, in the 1990s the local administration and national government seemed to have a reductionist and short-term perspective on development. Ironically, the instant wealth from increasing tourism and inflationary property prices, created by people who wish to live in San Gimignano for part of the year only, are considered to be benign cultural forces because they bring instant wealth and business, instead of being viewed as destructive forces. In this economic climate the bid to turn San Domenico into a hotel seemed desirable. A crucial factor in sustainability is this stifling of all possibilities for future growth through parochial forms of local government which, because it has no real influence over the long-term direction of a town's finances, encourages short-term incentives (funding for a programme like the territorial university has to be approved by the minister of works in Rome and by the European Community).

The decrease in population, inflationary property prices, high cost of living, closed practices, trade monopolised by tourism and the inability to plough wealth earned in San Gimignano back into local community projects are unsustainable trends. The rigid regard for conservation, together with the commune's protection of areas of cultural and historical heritage, provides the only balance between private and public concerns.

Institutional Requirements: Summary

Initiative

Many towns of historical significance face a similar problem, namely: how to sustain their development without the loss of their cultural and environmental heritage. If they are not to become museum towns they must come up with particular solutions to this problem. The people of San Gimignano have tried to do this through proposals for a territorial university, sadly rejected.

Further Investigation

1. Investigation into possible types of long-term and sustainable development for tourist centres that would encourage considered growth, permanence of population and community spirit.
2. The movement of people from affluent industrial areas to areas of outstanding environmental beauty has caused malign effects through property speculation.
   i. What legislation would protect indigenous local populations against the effects of property speculation?
   ii. How to encourage a state of reciprocity so that money earned through the town is relevant to what is built or works for the common good of all citizens?
3. What incentives could be given to encourage parochial authorities of historically significant areas to invest in creative architectural expressions of cultural relevance to today's populations?
4. How are such towns as San Gimignano affected when institutional infrastructures, such as schools, hospitals, libraries, etc are relocated many miles away because of government efficiency methods?

Cultural Identity: Indicator Matrix

Indicator	Positive	Negative	Comments
Equilibrium	/		Looking behind the disruptive influence of large numbers of day tourists, on which the area depends economically, there is a healthy coexistence of diverse occupational activities and stability of communities.
Human scale	/		Architecture and planning respond to human scale and need, providing space and comfort for human physical and psychological functioning.
Humane housing	/		Traditional housing successfully provides sufficient shelter from adverse climatic conditions. Not so with more modern housing – mainly because of materials used. Water supply to the majority of individual homes within the town of San Gimignano has been an advantage since the 13th century – mainly due to siting of town on good natural springs. Generally, area has intermittent breakdowns of power and water supplies.
Individuality	/		Often the strength behind community groups is the respect for, and freedom allowed to, individual expression.
Enlightened behaviour and attitudes	/	/	Great diversity of behaviours and attitudes. Some may be described as cosmopolitan and enlightened in a 21st-century global sense – some may be described as traditional and parochial.
Heritage: environmental; historical	/	/	Laissez-faire attitude towards natural environment. Acutely aware of human, cultural and political history.
Cultural stimulation	/		Age-value, states of erosion, cultural heritage, diverse interests and occupations of bohemian population make this a stimulating environment.
Permanence of population		/	Area disrupted by population movements over last 40 years – immigrant and indigenous.
Regional character	/		Passionate regional identity – local dependency on regional wines and food products. Products that are imported tend to be costly.
Sense of community	/		Strong sense of caring and belonging among indigenous peoples and bohemian immigrants. However, this is being constantly degraded through tourism and large numbers of wealthy second-home inhabitants.
Religious and ethnic toleration	/	/	Not really tested – some adverse reaction to numbers of wealthy Europeans and Americans buying into the area. The region does not have to adjust to large numbers of immigrant economic refugees.
Creativity: 'Creativity, if it has any meaningful boundary, lies within the moment when potential begins to emerge into reality.'	/	/	Transitional – 50 years ago a very poor area dependent upon agriculture, San Gimignano has gone through tremendous changes and the upheaval of population movements and increased tourism. It is questionable whether or not these changes will bring a stable economic prosperity or an all-year consistent population. Could degenerate into affluent holiday home area, with San Gimignano as a museum town.
Human misery	/		No immediate evidence of abject material, psychological or spiritual poverty.
Local particularity	/		Most place have their own particular wine, cheese or delicacy. Local festivals part of culture and heritage. Much good-humoured rivalry between localities.
Totals	13	5	

Cultural Identity: Statement of assessment

The style, unity and compactness of form of San Gimignano's architecture and town plan are unique and arise out of a medieval background. It is a place constructed for a medieval lifestyle. How resilient is this place in terms of 21st-century sustainable development? Because San Gimignano exhibits this unique medieval configuration, uncluttered by later periods, its aims, purpose and function have clarity. This has enabled an evaluation of a whole and different approach to urban planning, location, site, design, building methods and materials in a partic- ular climate, in a place constructed in a preindustrial age. Nor is this by any means a return to medieval living or architecture. It is more a study that allows a hypothesis of what constitutes San Gimignano as a town to emerge from what has, for hundreds of years, resisted historical change. Do the actual needs for seeing, making, communicating, exchanging things and ideas, find operational space in this place?

The type of people who made up the population of the growing town were serfs, fleeing their masters; feudal laymen, seeking refuge from the authority of the bishops of Volterra, who had been compelled to give up their properties; merchant families and professionals who came from other towns as the potential for making a more prosperous living grew; and people whose towns or villages had been sacked by the Florentines. In 1214, special dispensations were offered to those who built a residence within the walls. Families, such as the survivors of the town of Semifonte, who had had their castles in the surrounding area destroyed by the Florentines in 1202, were the first to seek protection. Towards the end of the 13th and in the 14th centuries, the great mendicant orders entered San Gimignano's walls: Franciscans to the south, Augustinians to the north and the Dominicans to the west. This gave a triangular definition to the town plan. Thus this place has a triangular shape, horizontally and vertically.

Indications are that today's population has a widely differing identity. The immigrants who came in the 1960s and 1970s injected an affluence that symbolised San Gimignano as a good place to be. In the late 1960s and during the 1970s the area received stimulation to thought and culture through the influx of people who came to be artisans. Many came out of discon- tent with the lifestyle forced on them by modern, industrial city living and were seeking an alternative. Opting out of the 'rat race', they were looking for peaceful, rural locations where the concept of community mattered and they could make a living using their hands. They were not wealthy people. Many had difficulty meeting the rising prices of the property market and renovating their dwellings. Many had to find new occupations – artist, craftsman, writer, cottage- industry producer. These people physically renovated their own homes. What they produced added to the attraction of San Gimignano as 'a good place to be'. The artisans had a rapidly growing market for their work as tourism increased. The indication is that they have formed a new kind of community identity. Possibly this is creating a new image of what constitutes San Gimignano's local identity. However, this community does not have the civic institutional infrastructure of the 13th century, when an incentive structure based on the idea of citizen- ship implied that money made here had a direct impact on the appearance of the town, for the common good of all its inhabitants.

Cultural Stimulation

The value of erosion The cultural value of erosion may be looked at through an aesthetic of 'age value'. The indication is that in this place the presence of erosion in landscape and architecture actually acts as a stimulating force culturally. It provokes creativity. 'Age value can be identified with the notion of ageing as enhancement and the idea that the various markings and layers of a surface record and allow one to recollect earlier stages in the history of a building and the human life associated with it' (Mostafavi & Leatherbarrow, 1993).

The constituent parts of this aesthetic are the homogeneous relationship of buildings and landscape; the look of buildings and materials, especially the effect of the natural environment on the exterior surfaces of buildings; how erosion may have infinite possibilities for creating anew a sense of presence; the implication of these for the creative quality of life experienced in and around San Gimignano.

The homogeneous relationship of landscape and architecture   In most areas of the world where there is a strong tradition of vernacular architecture, with materials and inspiration for the architecture coming from the locality, time has looked kindly on the whole and allowed a fusion, a melding together. Subtle land movement, plant growth, the effects of the elements over a prolonged length of time bring an integration and harmony so that the two parts seem to grow as one. This becomes a reaffirmation of man's dependence on, and harmony with, the land. It is questionable whether a new building can at first seem an integral part of its environment. It needs a period of assimilation by nature, not least in the mind of man himself. Large developments of completely new buildings encourage a feeling of separateness and disconnection with nature.

Detail from triptych by Taddeo di Bartolo: *San Gimignano and Stories of His Life* (*c* 1393).

In San Gimignano and district the harmony of landscape and architecture that comes from the passage of time is apparent everywhere. The beauty of much of the art in the area lies in its loyal reflections of home ground. In San Gimignano these reflections, such as a detail from Taddeo di Bartolo's triptych, *San Gimignano and Stories of His Life*, are patriotic and intensely urban. To be in San Gimignano today is to experience the pleasures of urban living, the stimulations and comfort of moving through an architectural configuration and communal spaces created for the interaction of people. Given this love of urbanism, one might expect to encounter disregard for the rural areas, but this is not so. The region's history features few significant disturbances of the traditional agricultural landscape. It has successfully overcome the potential shocks of mass tourism and retained its character against all odds. The progressive farming methods of the new immigrants have enhanced the area without changing or dominating local distinctiveness. The cultivated landscape looks greener, and the villas, farms and towns have just enough maintenance to allow them to function, otherwise the graceful eroding effects of the natural environment recreate a new picture at every step in what is the dissolution of buildings.

A gradual ageing process without the violence of demolition, clearance and annihilation can be comforting to the human psyche. Here one can accept the inevitable passing of life as something that is familiar, reassured by the knowledge that it is nothing strange or threatening – these buildings are evidence that it has happened many times before. Ageing can be aesthetically pleasing and acceptable. This concept may seem too romantic for life in an age of high technology. However, a large proportion of the immigrant population that has come to live here over the last 20 years comes from countries of high technology, Germany and Switzerland in particular.

Creativity and materials

Erosion forms the strongest visual stimulant to creativity within this area. Through the process of weathering, rain, wind, sun and humidity have sculpted, modelled, bleached and stained the highly receptive sedimentary materials of buildings and landscape. The effect is often very beautiful. In architecture, it is of subtle gradations of warm, earthy colours and soft textured surfaces. The landscape provides enough change to either complement or contrast with this. In periods of intense sunlight and dryness the pale, silver-green of olive trees and pale yellows of the landscape give an impression that the whole scene has been dipped in bleach. After rain, and during spring, the vibrancy of the greenery and flowers provides a dazzling contrast. The dissolving layers of buildings, the cracked and crazed textured surfaces of landscape, combined with the dramatic changes of light, provide inspiration for the arts of weaving, ceramics and painting, in the colour, forms, lines, textures and shapes of the place.

Unlike in the Middle Ages, when artistic achievement was an affirmation of citizenship politically, economically or socially, and was coupled with a cultural dependency on Christianity, present-day work is more an affirmation of the state of place. It does not make a moral comment about place. If it makes a comment on the environment this is without judgement or moralising and is made by people who are happy just to 'be' here. San Gimignano belongs to craftspeople: potters, who have used the eroding surfaces and shapes within the environment as inspiration for the textures and forms of their ceramics; weavers who have used the colours and irregularities within the lines of architecture or landscape strata as a basis for their designs; etchers and printmakers who are able to extract a design out of the rich visual stimuli of this place's legacy.

These people could not exist if there was not a need within the market. The market force which sustains artists and craftsmen here is tourism. It is both fortunate and interesting that there are enough wealthy and enlightened visitors to patronise this work. Interesting because it hints at what the visitor is looking for, and has found here. An object that is essential, uncomplicated, made by human hands. This is a living interaction between inhabitants and visitors and not just based on economics. Unfortunately, to supply the demands of the tourist industry there is also a great deal of tedious play on historical connection, exhausted traditional crafts and pretty postcard images of the town and surrounding areas.

Doorway, Petrognano.

Landscape, Bagnano.

Regional Character

The indication is that architectural and environmental heritage exert a powerful influence on regional character. History bears witness to the strong purpose behind the construction of the town – construction that gradually defined a plan guided by the needs of living. The architecture and plan are the result of a sincere attempt at urban living during the 12th and 13th centuries. Human needs were elaborated on, creating a very precise image and a very clear identity. This has suffered through neglect and been threatened by tourism, but the essential message has never been compromised.

The buildings are of good design, good craftsmanship, good local materials, and the landscape is natural, with the exception of the recent formal garden outside Porta San Giovanni. Nothing here could compare with the more decorative and opulent architecture to be found in larger Italian towns. The cathedrals of Florence and Siena have intricately decorated facades in a variety of coloured stones and marbles. Places convey a message. The Florentine and Sienese cathedrals are saying, 'Look at me, I am splendid and beautiful, made by the very best artists and craftsmen, of the most expensive materials. Oh!, and by the way, I have something to say about this place.' San Gimignano is saying, 'Look at me. I have something to say about urban lifestyle. It is so important that I have said it with care, using the best craftsmen, artists and materials at

Piazza Cisterna.

Duomo piazza.

my disposal and, in its form, there is truth and beauty.' The civic actions and pride that fashioned San Gimignano are no longer practised here, but the message is in the town's physical configuration; a state of presence for all who are within its walls. Its people may be said to practise a kind of cultural and civic parasitism on the past. However, people collect here to see people, to be seen by people, in a place built specifically with people in mind. Henry James aptly described this state of presence as follows: 'Presenting itself, more or less in the guise of some rare silver shell, washed up by the sea of time, cracked and battered and dishonoured, with its mutilated marks of adjustment to the extinct type of creature it once harboured, figuring against the sky as maimed, gesticulating arms, flourished in protest against fate.'

After centuries of anonymity and poverty, having stubbornly refused to court the possibilities of industrialisation, or to make too many physical changes to accommodate tourism, San Gimignano remains as an alternative form of urban environment. For the people who come to visit, it is an image of a utopian town, a visionary place outside time and space. But, it is very real. It has not as yet been turned into a showpiece or museum for the many tourists, despite decreasing population figures. The piazzas, with or without tourists, testify to the effectiveness of good urban planning and vitality. However, this place could not survive except through the intrinsically unsustainable tourist activity.

Cultural Identity: Summary

Initiative
1. A case has been presented in favour of the creative effects of 'age value' in this environment and the potential stimulus this affords the present-day community. The homogeneous characteristics of landscape and architecture take time to develop. In effect, nature carries on its creative process through weathering and erosion, long after man has finished his. With reassurance, man receives affirmation of his purpose and existence in the identity of place. The richness of sources and the visual appeal of the materials of building and landscape have a liberating effect on restrictive, traditional or historical preoccupations and complicated ideologies. It is enough just to be, to see, and to appreciate and recreate through craftsmen's skills in another material. Paradoxically, man starts to create anew from the environment.
2. The truth and purpose of the town's conception have been preserved in its physical configuration through time. This gives an alternative understanding of urbanism to that of the 21st century and is beneficial to our knowledge of the type of arrangement of spaces and forms that encourages the development of urban community. 'Places, spaces and objects, combine meaning and beauty with utility. Settlements are "human" in scale and form. Diversity and local distinctiveness are valued and protected' (Agenda 21 1996).

Further Investigation
1. Is San Gimignano sufficiently protected against the onslaught of mass tourism and property speculation?
2. The movement of people over the last 30 years has led to a change in cultural identity. How important is it to see some expression of this in the architecture of place?

STAGE 3: CAPABILITY ASSESSMENT

The capability matrix quantifies positive and negative indicators, as well as giving the most significant incentive and problem for further investigation in each of the constituent parts. This enables an evaluation of sustainable development capability in terms of low, moderate and high.

Capability Matrix

PHYSICAL CONDITIONS	FUNCTIONAL NEEDS
NO. OF INDICATORS PRESENT POSITIVE. 7. NEGATIVE. 12.	NO. OF INDICATORS PRESENT POSITIVE. 14. NEGATIVE. 5.
INITIATIVE. If erosion does not present a danger to human safety, it may be regarded as an enhancing characteristic of place. Some, such as lichen-covered roof tiles are not only enhancing but also a sensitive indicator of air pollution.	INITIATIVE. Origins of town:- Purposeful growth dictated the town plan in relation to, topography, geology and strategic geographic communication route – Francigena. Incentive structures given to attract a desired quality and quantity of population.
FURTHER INVESTIGATION. Investigation of the stability of landform – especially the hill on which San Gimignano is built – what are the implications for architecture?	FURTHER INVESTIGATION. Analyse and compare performance of traditional and modern: i. roof design and construction; house design and construction; ii. cost and availability of materials and skilled workmanship; iii. cost to the environment i.e. depletion of natural resource, transport, Monitoring of embodied and operational energy use.
CAPABILITY OF Low.	CAPABILITY OF Moderate – High.
INSTITUTIONAL REQUIREMENTS	**CULTURAL IDENTITY**
NO. OF INDICATORS PRESENT. POSITIVE. 6. NEGATIVE. 14.	NO. OF INDICATORS PRESENT. POSITIVE. 13. NEGATIVE. 5.
INITIATIVE. Town developed on foundation of civic responsibility – people could not have prospered without the presence of the town – therefore citizens expected to give back to the town.	INITIATIVE. The creative effects of "age value" in this environment are potentially a source of stimulation.
FURTHER INVESTIGATION. Possible types of long-term and sustainable development for such tourist centres that would encourage considered growth, permanence of population and community spirit.	FURTHER INVESTIGATION. The impact of the movement of people from industrial countries on cultural identity.
CAPABILITY OF Low.	CAPABILITY OF Moderate – High.

Summary Statement

It is ironic that in San Gimignano the greatest risk to sustainable development – namely, the geologically recent sedimentary land formation, the climate, and the degree of erosion of both the landscape and the architecture – are also the source of its attractive character and appearance. Where as certain forms of erosion are not particularly threatening and may even be classed as contributing to an aesthetic of 'age value' which contributes to a definitive cultural identity, subsidence of both the landscape – the two hills on which the town is built – and the built form of the town warrants concern. This seriously threatens the stability of the town walls and dwellings on the east side.

The institutional prerequisites, such as good communication with national government and locally meaningful legislation, are weak and give a low capability reading although the function of the master plan of the town was originally intended to encourage civic responsiveness with its many meeting places. The population of the town has decreased from 7,000 to 1,700 in less than a decade, which suggests severe degeneration of societal and community capability. This is in part linked to demographic changes and in part to reductionistic local and national policy. Throughout the 1980s and 1990s this area has become economically dependent upon day tourists and settlers from the more prosperous northern European industrial centres. These changes upon an indigenous population have not all been equitable. Many local inhabitants have sold their homes to people who are prepared to pay high prices to use the town as a holiday retreat. And rents have been raised to levels only tourists can afford. However the economy of the rural area is based upon wine and olives and many of the immigrants have brought enlightened methods of farming to this area based upon new technologies and progressive and sustainable agricultural processes.

Taxes are paid directly to the national government in Rome, which local people perceive as indifferent to their needs. The local government, with little economic power, is unable to counter the speculation and commercialism arising from tourism. Policies that require a long-term investment and would cause a qualitative development, such as the establishment of a Territorial University, cannot be made locally. Citizen-led organizations are ineffectual because communication links with national government are weak. Similarly, no common legislative guidance or incentives exist toward major environmental concerns such as establishing a local source of renewable energy. The potential for solar energy on south facing slopes is extensive and would be more than adequate for the low energy requirement of this region. There exists a very common sense approach toward energy efficiency generally and building conservation regulations dictate that building waste of natural materials is recycled in other buildings.

The capability of the urban configuration to accommodate the functional needs of a town population is high. The master plan evolved, making maximum use of the topography of the land, outward from the two central piazzas, as commerce and population grew. Thus the dynamic curve of the main axis was formed by the main trade route as it passed through the pivotal spaces of the central piazzas. This is an extremely effective design strategy to focus business activity efficiently and effectively while leaving the rest of the town space and peace to function in a less public fashion. The compact nature of urban development within the town walls, the exclusion of traffic, the stimulating arrangement of public and private space and the considerations of design to provide a pleasant urban micro-climate make this environment both thermally and psychologically comfortable for its inhabitants.

Together the town master plan, architecture and the use of local materials cope with a difficult 20°C swing in daily temperature and humidity in what may be described as a traditional, passive low energy approach to development with effective and efficient use of resources. Natural materials are able to absorb some of the moisture and cope with the expansion and contraction caused by alternating wet and dry periods. The master plan makes use of the contours of the terrain and the hilltop site to allow for good airflow and shading.

Many very practical considerations have gone into the planning of the town: efficient land-use, almost all the land inside the town walls has been utilized; the predominance of enclosed building plans helps to ensure a clear distinction between public and private space; the town boundary defines an area that people may reasonably negotiate without the need for mechanical transportation; the impact or ecological 'footprint' of the town is counteracted by the landscape immediately outside the town walls.

Despite the eroding influence of a large number of day tourists, population movements and the lack of policy infrastructure to encourage stable consistent long term socio-economic development, a strong sense of cultural identity is experienced in San Gimignano and surrounding area. The history and longevity of settlement plus the attractive character of states of erosion in landscape and architecture, have established a potentially creative and stimulating environment. A diverse mix of nationalities and occupations and passionate regional autonomy, realized through the dependence and promotion of local wines and produce, suggest the rather laissez-faire approach toward development is of significance here.

STAGE 4: DETERMINING

In terms of global environmental problems and risk assessment ground subsidence presents the single most serious risk to sustainable development.

The strongest incentive directive is the creation of a benign urban microclimate and a comfortable, functional and livable urban environment conditioned by the interaction of topography, built form, spaces, building type and materials. The replication of such urban microclimates is of interest to the advancement of sustainable design in city regeneration and new city form. Investigation through monitoring, simulation and utilization of appropriate technologies such as remote sensing, will enable accurate prediction and evaluation.

Chapter Six
Case Study 2: Ludlow, UK

INTRODUCTION

The area of this case study falls between latitudes 52°20' and 52°24' north and longitude 2°36' and 2°52' west. Within the midlatitude, temperate zone it is part of the internal landmass of England that borders Wales to the west. Ludlow is situated in the Welsh Marches, halfway between Chester to the north and Chepstow to the south. Local government identifies this area as the South Shropshire hills. Upland terrain and the Welsh mountains to the west and, to the east, Clee Hill, have influenced the positioning of the main road, the A49, which runs north and south of Ludlow.

This is a rural environment dependent on agriculture, some tourism and forestry. Ludlow, the one main town, functions as a local market town and tourist centre of historical and architectural interest. The rural areas are designated of outstanding beauty. Habitation is in small villages, hamlets, isolated farmsteads and cottages. The land undulates between 100 metres and 500 metres, although most slopes are gentle enough to be cultivated. The highest points occur on Titterstone Clee (533 metres) in the northeast, and High Vinnals (377 metres) in the southwest. Drainage is by the rivers Clun, Teme, Corve and Onny. In the southwest forested scarplands, small copses and timbered hedgerows give most of the area a well-wooded aspect. To the northeast, Clee Hill is sparsely wooded grazing land. This difference arises out of specific geological conditions.

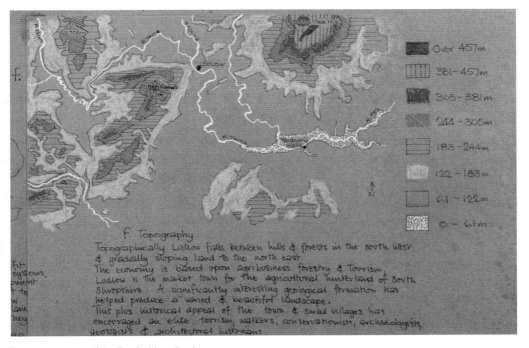

The topography of Ludlow's hinterland.

The Growth of the Town

By the time of the Norman Conquest in 1066 the area had passed through various stages of development and had a thriving agricultural or rural community, but no town. When the Domesday Book survey was made in 1085 the site of Ludlow was part of the Saxon manor of Stanton, immediately to the north. The place name 'Lodelowe' was in use by 1138, suggesting a town had been created (Lloyd 1997). Ludlow was termed a 'new town' and was part of a deliberate policy of town plantation by the Normans. Such towns helped to pacify the surrounding countryside. They were usually managed by the king or seigneurial lords and were dependent on market tolls, court fines and rents paid by burgesses. So what was the potential for the sustainable development of a town at this location?

The area was part of a vulnerable boundary between England and Wales, running from Chepstow in the south to Chester in the north. Offa's Dyke, and later the Roman Watling Street and the fort at Leintwardine, testify to centuries of trying to defend the English border against Welsh attack. If the Normans were to hold on to their conquest, permanent stability and strong defence were needed. All along the Welsh Marches, castles were built. Strategically, Ludlow falls halfway along an ancient Chepstow to Chester route, conveniently at the point of a crossroads of another ancient west–east route running from Clun to Clee. Ludlow Castle was built as a major fortress on the defensive frontier with Wales and was used as a base for assembling military campaigns in the 12th and 13th centuries (Faraday 1991). Such an enterprise would not have been possible had there not been the potential for adequate supplies and services, not only for military garrisons but also for building, energy and a degree of pleasure and comfort. Natural resources were plentiful and an established rural population would, as needs be, have serviced the growth of a market town. In reciprocation for this Ludlow has never forsaken its original function. Its main role today is that of a viable market town serving a rural community.

The first Norman lords, Walter de Lacey and his son Roger, were given the management of the Saxon hamlet of Stanton and decided on a site to its south for the castle and town. This has stood the test of time, through the need future generations felt to enhance its physical conurbation and settle there. Initially, it was a site with a view, easily defended and defined, with natural boundaries on three sides created by the Teme and Corve rivers and the ancient north–south road on the fourth or eastern side. The castle is focused on the western tip of a spur of land aligned approximately east–west and rising to 105 metres. The positioning of the castle and marketplace is on the crest of the hill, with residential streets sloping southwards

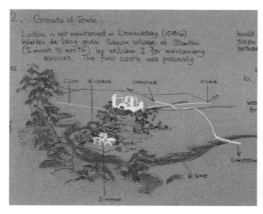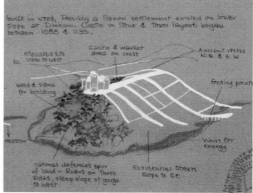

Ludlow in the 11th and early 12th centuries.

to the Teme and, to a lesser extent, northwards to the Corve. The castle overlooks a gorge and a clear view to the northwest.

Until the mid-19th century the town was confined within these boundaries. Since then, there has been considerable growth to the north and east. However, there is a consciousness of the importance of a clearly marked boundary, or setting a limit to growth. In the middle of the 19th century the coming of the railway provided a boundary for development. In 1979 the modern A49 bypass provided one which has all but been built up to. Local district policy is to limit growth of the town beyond this boundary for the foreseeable future. It is considered that the town's population of 9000 is at an optimum for its historical centre. Beyond this boundary development runs the risk of becoming decentralised, sprawling suburbs.

SUSTAINABLE DEVELOPMENT ASSESSMENT

STAGE 1: OBSERVATION STUDIES
The Observation Studies are illustrated in the six colour plates 11–16. The series as a whole aims at establishing a comprehensive record of sustainable development as it is embodied in the landscape, architecture and planning of this place. This record includes the plan and cross section of the town, the location, geophysical infrastructure and topography of the boundary area; an account of growth and change within the town; the characteristics of surrounding landscape; the functionality of plan and architecture, including building with space syntax, climate and natural resources and proposals for future development.

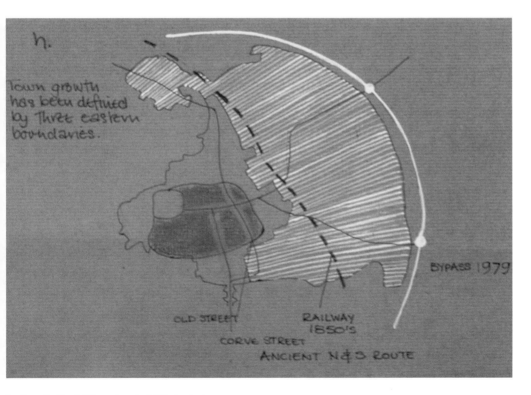

Ludlow in the 11th and early 12th centuries.

STAGE 2: INDICATORS ASSESSMENT

Physical Conditions: Indicator Matrix

Indicator	Positive	Negative	Comments
The countryside	/		Area of outstanding natural beauty. In southwest forested scarplands and timbered hedgerows give a well-wooded aspect; to the northeast grazing land.
The climate	/		No climate data available for southwest glacial valleys – summer highs of 20°C and winter lows of 1°C – moderate rainfall 700 mm.
Geological formation	/		National and international significance – many different outcrops in region. Richness of visual amenity and natural resources – glacial valleys to the west.
Topography	/		Land undulates between 100 metres and 500 metres – most slopes gentle enough to be cultivated.
Geographical convenience		/	Upland terrain to the east, Clee Hill, and west Welsh hills have conditioned the positioning of the main road, A49, and railway – communication routes east and west inconvenient.
Agriculture and fishing (ecologically acceptable sufficiency): locally; for export	/ / / /		Mixed farming. Good regard, care and protection of natural environment; organic farming methods practised. Area could be self-sufficient in food. Many people practise self-sufficiency at cottage garden, small-holding level (vegetables, fruit, dairying, meat). Figures not available to say how much goes to supply local markets or export – considerable amounts of good quality local produce (jams, cheese, cakes) and organically produced meat sold locally.
Vegetation and forestry: indigenous; cultivated	/	/	On the southwest scarplands much of indigenous broad-leaved forest land taken over by the planting of coniferous variety. In farming and forestry (main form of economy) foreign types are cultivated for profitability. Quality and condition of vegetation are excellent.
Resources (materials, minerals, water, soil, air): regeneration; depletion; unexploited	/ / /		Extensive forest regeneration over many centuries. Many disused sites of limestone-quarrying in west and coal mining on Clee Hill – scarred landscape healed. Rich resources of good soil, pollution-free water and air – many rural properties have private water supply from spring or well.
Renewable energy	/		The county council energy audit favoured energy crops, ie, modified conventional forestry (MCF).(hydro, wind, wave, solar, biomass)
Biodiversity	/		Excellent.
Degeneration of the environment: erosion; pollution;acid rain; heat island; exploitation	/ / / / /		Negligible erosion – most caused by tourism. Extensive woodland keeps environment pollution free. No observance of acid-rain effects. No observance of heat-island effect. Generally little exploitation – although there are beginning to be signs of damage and harm to wildlife and erosion particularly to forest paths through increasing tourism.
External dependencies		/	Although passive energy method used the area is dependent on external supplies of oil, gas and electricity.(oil, gas, electricity, other)
TOTALS	19	3	

Physical Conditions: Statement of Assessment

The Countryside

The great Ice Age of two million years ago strongly influenced the shape of the landscape south-west of Ludlow. Great torrents of meltwater cut overflow channels through previous watersheds, causing rivers to be diverted from their earlier courses. Before the last advance of the ice, the predecessor of the Teme flowed south to Aymestrey, but when that route was blocked by ice in what is now the Clun forest, a proglacial lake was formed at what is now Leintwardine, which eventually overflowed into what is now Downton Gorge, a course which the Teme subsequently continued to follow. The steep-sided valley of the Teme, between Whitcliffe and the town of Ludlow, is another overflow channel created by the river's flow southwards. The dramatic slopes of Whitcliffe and the opposite slope towards the castle were a major factor in the choice of the castle site (D Lloyd, private communication 1998). Equally important for the town's medieval development were the natural rapids along this stretch of the river, especially between what is now Mill Street and the bottom of Holdgate Fee, where the river has a gradient of 1:16. These rapids caused the 'loudwater' which gave the place name Ludlow its prefix 'lud' (D Lloyd, private communication 1998). The noise is less apparent now than formerly because of the weirs built in the 12th and 13th centuries to provide the head of water needed to drive the town's numerous mills.

Taken together with climate data, a further consequence of this glacial southwest area is its unique microclimate. This provides an indicator of relief affecting climate. The glacial action has formed basin-like areas where air drainage is impeded. Many of the valleys are sheltered from the predominantly southwest wind and retain heavy moist air, making mists and fogs common. The area also suffers from radiation frosts and frost pockets which are especially harmful in late spring. Therefore careful siting of habitat and arable crops is important. Height and slope must be taken into consideration – concave slopes and hollows suffer more than convex steeper slopes from air drainage. The low sun in winter means that many places are in shadow for part of the winter months.

The proglacial lake at Leintwardine.

Two million years ago glaciers formed the landscape southwest of Ludlow.

'S.W. of Ludlow glacial action has formed basins where air drainage is impeded & heavily moist air is retained — and the area subjected to mists. Radiation frosts & frost pockets are especially harmful in late spring'.

The impact of extracting limestone at Whitcliffe for use in Ludlow in former centuries.

The Climate

Climatic records for this area are few. Meteorological Office information held for Birmingham 30 miles to the east is given in Table 3 as an indication of comparative temperatures for a similar latitude but varying topography. The climate data in Tables 4, 5 and 6 were recorded for the period 1926 to 1960. Tables 7 and 8 were taken from readings by Mr D Small, a local farmer, who consistently took daily temperature and rainfall measurements over a period of 10 years. Information is given for 1986, 1991 and 1996. Climate data cover a period of almost 70 years. Tables 4, 5 and 6 are for Kimbolton, approximately 10 miles south of Ludlow, Tables 7 and 8 for Greete, 4 miles southeast of the town. Neither of the latter reflects fully the conditions of the glacial valleys to the southwest of Ludlow. This raises the question of how local information about climate should be used if it is to be effective in the design strategy of building: should it cover an area of 100 square miles, 50 square miles or less? The indication is that microclimate bears relationship to the relief of the land.

Climate data reveal monthly temperatures averaging highs during June, July, August and September of around 18°C to 20°C and lows during December, January and February of around 1°C. From May to late September is frost-free. This gives a good growing season of approximately 250 days from mid-March to late November (Hodgson 1972). The mean temperature falls 1°C for every 165 metres altitude, altering the start of the season by almost 14 days over the area (Hodgson 1972). The wind force averages 4.5 metres per second and is directionally from the southwest. Gale force winds occur less than twice a year. When they do, they are directionally from the northeast and can cause damage to upland forest areas (D Bole, private communication, 1997).

Most of the area lies within the rain shadow of upland Wales. It has a moderate rainfall, ranging from 700 millimetres in the west to 1000 millimetres in the east. Rainfall is well distributed

Table 3: Monthly averages of maximum and minimum temperatures (°C), Birmingham 1941–70.

	Jan	Feb	Mar	Apr	May	Jun	Jul	Aug	Sep	Oct	Nov	Dec
Max	11.1	11.4	15.8	19.2	23.0	25.5	26.6	25.6	23.0	19.2	13.8	12.0
Min	−5.0	−4.1	−2.7	0.1	2.3	6.2	8.2	8.2	5.6	2.1	−1.1	-3.7

Table 4: Monthly averages of maximum, minimum and mean temperatures (°C), Kimbolton 1931–60.

	Jan	Feb	Mar	Apr	May	Jun	Jul	Aug	Sep	Oct	Nov	Dec	Year
Max	6.0	6.7	9.5	12.6	15.9	19.2	20.4	20.2	17.5	13.2	9.3	7.1	13.1
Min	0.7	0.8	2.0	4.0	6.4	9.4	11.3	10.9	9.0	6.1	3.7	1.7	5.5

Table 5: Average potential transpiration and rainfall (millimetres), Kimbolton 1926–60.

	Jan	Feb	Mar	Apr	May	Jun	Jul	Aug	Sep	Oct	Nov	Dec	Year
Rainfall	71	46	44	47	57	52	58	69	60	71	85	67	729
Potential transpiration	1	10	30	55	77	93	93	71	44	19	5	−1	498
Cumulative potential moisture deficit				7	28	68	103	105	89	37			
Excess water	70	36	14								43	69	231

Table 6: Average hours of sunshine, Kimbolton 1931–60.

Jan	Feb	Mar	Apr	May	Jun	Jul	Aug	Sep	Oct	Nov	Dec	Year
1.6	2.5	3.6	5.2	5.9	6.6	5.9	5.5	4.3	3.0	1.8	1.5	3.9

Table 7: Monthly averages of maximum and minimum temperatures (°C), Greete 1986, 1991, 1996.

1986

	Jan	Feb	Mar	Apr	May	Jun	Jul	Aug	Sep	Oct	Nov	Dec
Max	5.3	0.4	7.5	11.6	15.3	18.5	20.2	17.0	16.1	13.5	9	6.8
Min	0	−4.5	1.6	1.8	6.7	10.2	10.8	9.2	6	6.6	4	2.3

1991

	Jan	Feb	Mar	Apr	May	Jun	Jul	Aug	Sep	Oct	Nov	Dec
Max	4.4	4.6	11.5	11.1	16	15.9	21.0	22.2	19.7	12.9	9.1	6.5
Min	0	0	4.4	3.6	6.1	7.6	10.8	11.5	8.6	6.7	3.1	2.0

1996

	Jan	Feb	Mar	Apr	May	Jun	Jul	Aug	Sep	Oct	Nov	Dec
Max	9.7	5.4	6.9	13.1	12.5	19.7	20.4	20.1	18.1	13.6	8.2	4.5
Min	1.6	−1.6	1.7	3.9	4.3	8.7	11.0	11.7	9.2	7.5	2.4	0.3

Table 8: Monthly and yearly rainfall (millimetres), Greete 1986, 1991, 1996.

	Jan	Feb	Mar	Apr	May	Jun	Jul	Aug	Sep	Oct	Nov	Dec	Year Total
1986	105	6	50	56	59	48	46	128	12	50	104	91	755
1991	94	38	82	67	6	77	87	20	60	57	73	27	688
1996	60	57	52	62	53	42	59	52	15	82	76	38	648

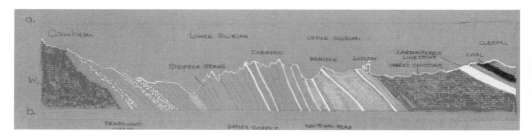

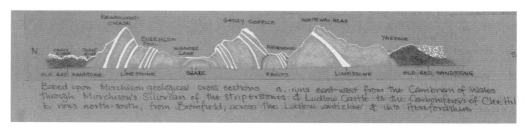

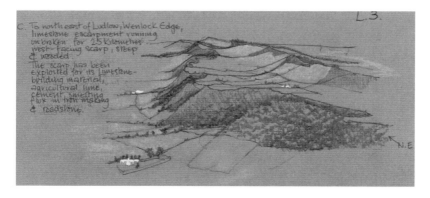

The geological formation of the area surrounding Ludlow.

throughout the year with a November and January maximum and an August submaximum. However, rivers with sources in the Welsh uplands often bring heavy flows of water to the area in winter causing flooding in glacial valleys. The potential transpiration indicates that soil moisture deficit is unlikely to occur (Table 5). It also indicates excess of moisture in the air from November to March. The climate is generally moist and sustains mixed farming and forestry.

Geological Formation

Geologically, this is an area of national and international significance with many different outcrops within a comparatively small area. The benefits of an ancient landscape are indicated not only in the richness of visual amenity but also in the extent of natural resources. Older Silurian rock formation lies to the southwest and younger, old red sandstone to the east. The Silurian rocks were laid down in tropical seas more than 400 million years ago. Conditions changed throughout the period, at times causing fine mud, which has now hardened into shale and mudstone, to be deposited while at other times, when the sea was deeper, corals and other lime-producing creatures thrived, forming limestone. These rocks were later folded into an anticline, the softer shale being eroded to form valleys while the more resistant limestone was left upstanding as escarpments. The most famous escarpment is Wenlock Edge to the north of Ludlow.

Resources

The geological formation has provided the area with a wealth of natural resources, materials and minerals for building and industry. Most local areas have building stone of varying qualities. Limestone from Whitcliffe, although prone to weathering, has been used for most stonework within the town; red clays from old red sandstone were fired for bricks from the 17th century on and until recently a brickworks existed in Fishmore Road, Ludlow. The coal mined on Clee Hill provided Ludlow with an important source of fuel, while ironstone gave the basis of a considerable rural iron industry. Exploitation of these resources has now mostly ceased, although they are not completely depleted. Stone gravel is taken from Aymestrey, and dolerite for road building from Clee Hill.

Agriculture

Agriculture is the largest industry within South Shropshire and there is little variance over the whole of this area. The emphasis is on mixed farming, sheep being more important over Clee Hill. Traditionally, cattle are sold in the local market town, Ludlow, as 'stores' (young cattle sold on for further rearing, not slaughter). The average farm is 40 hectares (100 acres). Over Clee Hill, small farms are worked part-time, and men have secondary occupations in quarries or industry (Ministry of Agriculture, 1966).

Agriculture has been practised in the area since prehistoric times and has brought about great changes in the landscape and the soils. It probably goes back to the Neolithic culture of 3000 BC (Chitty 1963). There are over 50 pre-Roman hillforts within Shropshire, most of them in the southwest region near to Ludlow (Watson & Musson 1993). Excavations on hilltop Iron Age settlements(1500–700 BC) such as Croft Ambrey and Caynham Camp reveal abundant evidence of pastoralism and cultivation (Stanford 1967; Gelling 1996). At Croft Ambrey numerous granaries and bones of domesticated animals (sheep and pigs) were found. It has been estimated that the population of this area averaged 29 people per square mile at that time and may have been roughly equivalent to this much later, in medieval times (Hodgson 1972). The rural population is roughly equivalent today, excluding the population of the town of Ludlow.

Aerial photography has revealed extensive relict field systems of probable prehistoric origin (Watson & Musson 1993). If this is the case, it would mean that large areas of the Shropshire uplands were given over to arable farming, and that this was a major part of the overall economy of the region by 1500 BC. These uplands are now used mainly for sheep grazing or forestry. Arable farming was possible during prehistoric times because a warmer and drier climate permitted the raising of crops (Wilson 1982). This type of analysis reveals the changing patterns and sites of farming as it has adapted over the centuries to meet human needs. The indicator is that maintaining a set level of agricultural prosperity has come through adapting to changing social, economic and physical conditions, and that skills, experienced management built up over time, are important factors in sustaining the level of amenity present in the area.

The present agricultural landscape was laid down during Saxon times and incorporated into the Norman manorial system in the 11th century. Hence the pattern of nucleated villages and solitary farmsteads or farmsteads with a cottage attached. The following indicators suggest that resilience and adaptability have played a vital role in maintaining human rural settlement. In the 13th and 14th centuries, epidemics of the Black Death and the consequent decline in population

Burrow Hill camp at Hopesay, one of more than 50 Roman hillforts in Shropshire.

facilitated enclosure and enabled surviving tenants to buy their farms from manorial landlords (Hodgson 1972). The unreliability of labourers made the management of large manorial estates difficult, so the risk element was allowed to be passed to individual tenants. The emergence of the town with mills, and the medieval wool trade, provided incentives for enclosure into sheep farms with a consequent decrease in arable land. In the 17th century estates broke up in the aftermath of the Civil War, and large royalist estates passed into the ownership of Parliamentarians as the spoils of war. In the late 17th century low prices for corn gave little incentive to farmers to grow arable crops and consequently more land was given to grass (Jones 1961). An agricultural depression which started in the late 19th century, accompanied by a series of years with poor weather, resulted in yet more reversion to grassland (Buchanan 1944), which the Second World War partly reversed. Land was used to its maximum to feed the nation's people. Britain as an island was cut off from many external food suppliers. This raises the issue: how vulnerable do we render ourselves both locally and nationally by reliance on external dependencies, whether these be food, natural resources or energy sources (gas, oil, electricity)?

Since the Second World War, a system of mixed farming has until recently been both prosperous and stable, with increased technology and fertilisation making more arable and livestock possible for the acreage. The latest threat to the agricultural economy, and therefore the ability of farmers to maintain the look of the landscape, has been the outbreak of BSE and the 'foot and mouth' crisis, together with the stringent national measures taken for their eradication. Locally, farmers' incomes have obviously been affected as most farms rear some beef cattle. However, the tradition of mixed farming practice and accountability to local consumer outlets indicates that farmers were able to respond quickly and efficiently without devastating consequences. In response to the local and national market an emphasis is being placed on qualitative production. Butchers are being asked to guarantee local products; farmers are accepting responsibility for safety and quality with many moving towards organic methods of farming. The outlet for agricultural produce has traditionally been through local markets, especially Ludlow. This raises the issue of the need for accountability. How important is the link between supplier and consumer, especially where food products are concerned? A system of mixed farming allows for the natural goodness of the soil to be maintained as long as production is not exhausting; crops receive trace elements and minerals from the soil which are passed on to humans through the food chain. Intensive farming methods rely on chemicals of dubious nutritional value to animals or humans.

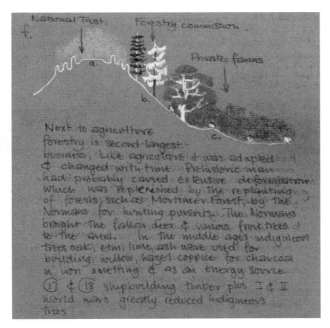

A typical farm location.

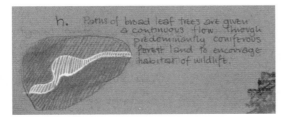

Forestry

Forestry is the second largest industry within the area. The scarplands to the southwest of Ludlow are dominated by Mortimer forest, which is run by Forest Enterprises and covers approximately 2130 hectares. It averages about £1.5 million turnover a year of which probably £1 million goes to provide local employment, services, planting, cutting, surgery, conservation, rangers and administration.

A view of Mortimer forest from Burrington, looking east towards Ludlow.

On the Silurian scarplands, which rise to a little over 300 metres over much of their length, exposure and acid soil conditions have encouraged the planting of conifers. Elsewhere the more sheltered valley woodlands, rarely rising above 250 metres, often have base rich soils and support a better growth of broad-leaved trees. In contrast to most of Britain, forestry is practised on land that could be used for agriculture. Mortimer forest has the highest growth rate in England, soil and climate being conducive to forestry. Only 15 per cent of forest is native broadleaf, of which there are 35 species. Only 2 per cent of that is oak which, discounting the economic disadvantage of its long-term investment – 25 to 70 years – does not grow well here. Forest Enterprises runs the forest as a business and does not receive subsidies to help with the long-term maintenance of broad-leaved trees. Many farmers do receive grants to maintain them. Hence the landscape has the pleasant appearance of conifer-covered hilltops merging into the broad-leaved woodland of farmland on the lower slopes. This landscape is an indicator of visual amenity, biodiversity and the environmental benefit of trees in control of climate and pollution.

Tradition of sustainable forestry development   Forestry management has contributed to the life quality and economy of this area since at least 1500 BC and has sustained human need through many changes. This must have been achieved through an awareness of when it was advantageous to exploit, and when to sustain before serious depletion of natural stock occurred. At the postglacial optimum woodland covered all but the wettest valleys. The indigenous trees were sessile oak, ash, wych elm, birch, alder, holly and hazel. Six hundred years or more before the Roman invasion, much of the area was deforested by the Bronze Age and the Iron Age inhabitants to facilitate clearance for agriculture, building materials and fuel. It is reasonable to assume that much of the forest in the valleys as well as around the hilltop sites was cleared by the time of the Saxon invasion (Voysey 1972). Anglo-Saxon place names with 'leah' or other such endings that suggest woodland clearance are very few (Hodgson & Bayliss 1958). Bayliss has based his evidence on Domesday records and accounts of the extents of the lordship of Wigmore held in the Public Record Office, Hereford. He further notes systematic reforestation within the vale of Wigmore in the 14th century. This suggests that woodlands may have been less extensive at the time of Domesday than at present.

Prior to the Norman Conquest there were three Saxon hunting forests on the scarplands. After 1066 William the Conqueror gave these to the Mortimers for services rendered at the time of the invasion. Hence this land is covered mostly by what is known as Mortimer forest. The forest was extended and maintained for hunting and fallow deer were introduced from France. Wood was felled and used for building and firewood, Ludlow Castle being perhaps the largest single consumer of domestic firewood. The beams for local timber-frame houses were usually pit-sawn in the forest which also supplied the lathes or wattle for walls (Voysey 1972).

In the 16th century, increased demand for timber to make charcoal for the iron-smelting industry resulted in extensive coppicing. Bringewood Forge on the River Teme used local wood and ironstone from the Titterstone, Clee Hill. Eventually, owing to local shortage of timber, the forge had to draw its charcoal from Clun, 20 miles away to the northwest (Voysey 1972). Charcoal was also used in the pottery and clay-pipe cottage industry, together with outcrops of fine white Silurian clay found within the Elton beds. Wood was also the main source of fuel for the numerous lime kilns on the Aymestrey and Wenlock limestone. Economic stability and developing craftsmanship were dependent on wood as a natural resource: builders used oak in timber-framed houses; wheelwrights used ash, wych elm and oak; coopers required oak staves and ash hoops; tanners favoured oak; and itinerant clay-makers worked from one alder coppice to another (Voysey 1972).

In the 18th century there was a demand for oak for shipbuilding. This had to be found on the better land and private estates sold much of their timber. Harries, in 1791, thought that between 1760 and 1790 some £200,000 of oak had been sold in Shropshire for the navy and that no single estate could then supply enough timber for a 70-gun ship (Wakeham, 1892).

From the 16th to the 18th centuries forestry was based on coppice, mainly oak, although ash, alder, hazel and willow were also coppiced. Oak coppice was cut over every 18 to 25 years; the other species had a shorter rotation. The larger trees were in demand for building and coppice gradually gave way to high forest systems as demand grew for navy oak and for hop poles for the hop yards in Worcestershire and Herefordshire. In the 18th century woodland under management yielded between £12 and £20 per acre after 12 to 14 years' growth, a return which was better than that for arable crops (Clark 1794).The indication is that sustainable forestry practice is nothing new, and that we have much to learn from previous generations as regards reforestation, harmful depletion of natural resources and the value of good management of the economic, functional and recreational amenity of trees as a renewable resource.

Forestry today Since the end of the 19th century, there has been a decline in the availability of oak and consequently in the traditional uses of oak throughout Britain. Demand for fast-growth coniferous timber has increased. Good quality hardwood still fetches high prices, and therefore the limited acreage of broad-leaved trees on better soils can be justified economically, as well as for amenity and ecological reasons. Top quality oak, ash and beech can be grown in this area, in sheltered sites with base rich soils, using selected strains of trees and a high standard of silviculture. If grown in a mixture with conifers, the income from these crops can be greatly enhanced. Under the present economic conditions, the proportions of conifers grown is likely to increase. Of the 2130 hectares of woodland managed by Forest Enterprises, only 142 hectares are now broad-leaved trees. If the balance is tilted further in favour of conifers, this could be detrimental to wildlife and biodiversity of species, as well as human amenity.

The choice of tree species grown is determined in part by soil, in part by the market value of timber and in part by the rate of growth but, most of all by climate (rainfall, exposure to wind, frost and average summer temperatures). The economic criteria are for short-term investment. A thriving industry has been built on coniferous trees: Douglas fir, Japanese and European larch, and some Scots pine. The lower quality end product is used for paper, chipboard, pallet wood and fencing; the best for construction. Forest Enterprises keeps a wildlife conservation map which marks the location of wildlife and plants, monitoring such wildlife as *Scoparia ancipitella*, a moth that feeds off lichen which only grows in especially pollution-free environments. This rare species has recently been sighted in Mortimer forest. (Conifers, because of their dense foliage cover, are able to scrub more pollution from the air than most broad-leaved trees.) This sighting is an indication that the air is becoming purer. Unfortunately, the wildlife conservation map has to remain confidential because of intrusive damage to habitat and harm caused to animals by visitors to the forest. The poaching of fallow deer is a particular problem. Mountain bikes have caused erosion of plant life. These indicators would suggest that, as the forest is increasingly opening up to tourist activities, careful monitoring of the impact of tourism should be carried out.

Renewable Energy

In theory the county council structure plan, and the district council local plan, support a movement towards the development and use of renewable energy. It would seem that in this area, with such an abundance of natural resource, rivers, windy hilltops and extensive woodland, there should be little difficulty in choosing one or maybe a combination of a few renewable energy resources.

A policy guidance statement issued by the county council says it 'recognises the environmental benefits which can be achieved by displacing fossil fuels with more benign forms of energy generation. However, the wider environmental benefits must be balanced against the visual and physical effects which the necessary development would have on the locality.'

In the Shropshire structure plan for 1989 to 2006 the criteria most relevant to renewable energy proposals are:

- The scale and design of the development in relation to its location and setting;
- Appropriate landscaping of the site;
- The protection of wildlife habitats and geological features;
- Nuisance, danger or damage to neighbouring areas;
- The ability of the surrounding road network to accommodate traffic generated by the development (including during the construction phase);
- Pollution and hazards;
- The stability of the land;
- Flood protection;
- Protection of water resources and patterns of drainage;
- Retention of the best and most versatile agricultural land;
- Conservation of trees and other natural features;
- Conservation of the landscape character of the area;
- Conservation of the historic environment;
- Protection of public rights of way; and
- Protection of land to which the public has access.

Two things are clear. This is a place much valued and not amenable to random experimentation; and development towards renewable energy supply will have to meet the stringent competition of enhancing what is already an area of outstanding natural environmental character. Visual amenity becomes part of an aesthetic for sustainable development. The indicator suggests there is a conflict between visual amenity and power generation.

In response to a government directive, *Climate Change, A Discussion Document* (Department of the Environment 1992), 1500 millivoltes of electricity-generating capacity should come from renewable energy sources by the year 2006. This has not happened. As with many other local authorities nationwide Ludlow looks to national government initiatives on energy. However, lack of funds and an increased emphasis on environmental protection may delay the development of renewable energies on a large scale in this area. In the structure plan, Shropshire County Council's energy audit states: 'It is unlikely that any very large scale schemes will be viable in Shropshire in the short-term. Therefore, progress is likely to be made through a variety of small scale applications rather than major capital schemes.'

Passive forms of energy saving are stressed and encouraged: 'Developers are to be encouraged to design and orientate new buildings to maximise passive solar gains and improve insulation. Schools and offices should utilise natural daylight.' In the county council's supplementary planning guidance, *Renewable Energy* (1994), it is recognised that 'there is considerable scope in the rural area for small scale schemes, for example, individual wind turbines or small biomass generators to serve farms, other small businesses or homes'. However, this goes on to state that this is conditional on what seems visual amenity: 'Although these developments which could assist in improving economic viability as well as achieving broader environmental benefits would normally be welcomed, their effect on the locality will still be of primary importance.'

The local authority's approach to renewable energy seems overcautious and biased towards the visual amenity of the area. So what is the potential for renewable energy? Consider the sources under three categories:

Primary: physical   Determined by: geography; geomorphology; climate

Secondary: biological   Determined by: energy crops; biomass wastes

Tertiary: municipal waste   Determined by: landfill gas; scrap, tyres, etc

Primary
Given that the technology is available for solar energy, wind energy and hydro-energy, of what benefit could these prove to this area?

Solar energy: The average sunshine hours per day and the sun-path chart for latitude 52° **(Figure 14)** do not fully reflect conditions in the glacial valleys where mist can linger all or most of the day, and north-facing slopes are in shadow for part of the winter. The indication is that climate is not conducive to the large-scale development of solar technology and that this would not be economically viable.

Wind energy: This is viable at wind speeds in excess of 7 metres per second at a height of 25 metres above ground level. Average wind speeds in this area are 4.5 metres per second. The only place where wind energy may be possible is on Clee Hill. The Countryside Commission has recommended that this should not be permitted as it would be detrimental to visual amenity in an area of outstanding natural beauty.

Hydro-energy: Ludlow town weirs have produced energy in the past for the running of mills. Schemes exist to gain charitable status for the weirs so that lottery funding may be applied for

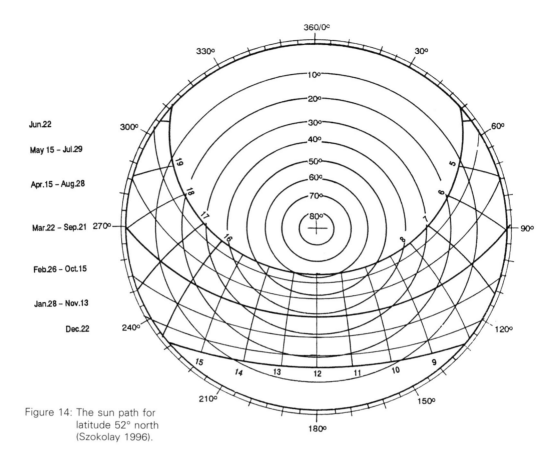

Figure 14: The sun path for
latitude 52° north
(Szokolay 1996).

to renovate them (Lloyd 1997). In its energy audit the county council suggests this would have a detrimental effect on drainage and the environment and would not be economically justified by the small amounts of electricity generated.

Secondary

Biomass: Whereas anaerobic digesters could be possible on a small scale such as farms, it is suggested in the audit report that this would be only marginally economically viable for the town of Ludlow (9000 population).

Energy crops: These came out of the audit report as the most favoured long-term solution given development constraints and restricted local government funding. The report looked towards what is called modified conventional forestry (MCF). This would involve short-rotation coppicing, two to three years, of poplar or willow, and possibly eucalyptus; power is the product of either charcoal or alcohol. Potential wood waste from forestry such as 'lop and top', sawmills, etc could also be used in the process. The county council regards this as increasing support for the Shropshire countryside strategy, productive forestry, as it would:

* provide more area for wildlife and diversity;
* provide opportunities for leisure and recreation;
* enhance the landscape.

The embracing of MCF was by no means mutual (Bole 1997) and views were expressed that: this type of coppicing on an extensive scale could limit ecological diversity; more research is needed into the technology; nowhere in the country is there a commercially operating scheme that uses MCF; and that the town of Ludlow should provide its own energy through utilising its waste through biomass generation.

Tertiary
This would be disadvantageous, both economically and environmentally, if it involved considerable transportation side effects in this rural area. At the moment municipal waste is disposed of at a site 4 miles north of Ludlow, in the village of Brimfield.

Physical Conditions: Summary

Initiatives
A large number of positive indicators are present suggesting the excellent potential of physical conditions; energy and food demands for the town can potentially be met locally, and the pollution created by a town the size of Ludlow is absorbed by its rural hinterland. This is one of the few areas in England where such favourable conditions still exist. This is not 'wilderness'. The high standard of visual amenity and the productive possibilities of the landscape are the consequence of significant and varied geological wealth, favourable climate and efficient, consistent and unexploitative land management over a long period of time. The history of agriculture and forestry stresses the importance of enlightened management in adapting to changing needs in use and renewing depleted natural resources. At present the management of the land is shared. The National Trust manages hillfort sites, English Nature protects small areas of special scientific interest, the Severn Water Authority monitors the rivers, Forest Enterprises maintains forest areas and farmers manage agricultural land. This balance seems to work well, maintaining a richness of diversity and some protection from exploitative forces.

Further Investigation
1. Analysis of local accountability in agricultural methods and consumerism.
2. Monitoring the impact of increasing tourism on the landscape.
3. Solution of the conflict posed by:
    i. insufficient technological advancement in certain areas of renewable energy sources;
    ii. visual amenity and renewable energy supply.
4. Geologically this area provides excellent opportunities for investigating how climate differs over locality as a consequence of the relief of the land and physical conditions.

A typical farm location.

Functional needs: indicator matrix

Indicator	Positive	Negative	Comments
Resource efficiency	/		History of efficient resource use in agriculture and forestry – local resources used for industry, energy and building. Decline in use over last century but area would still justify positive resource efficiency.
Passive systems	/		Encouraged in SSDC's local plan and energy audit.
The town and its plan	/		Norman planned 'new town' – coherent master plan of streets, plots and units of measurement satisfying efficient land use and demarcation of public/private space.
Boundary	/		Clear concept of boundary – formed by geological landform on three sides and main north–south access route to the east.
Efficiency technologies		/	Negligible use other than standard insulation in building.
Relief, climate and buildings	/		Implicit regard of relief, materials, town conurbation and climate to maximise human comfort.
Mixed-use development		/	Divided into specific zones – however, Ludlow does not cover a large land area therefore ease of access to retail, industrial, residential and business areas.
Polycentred development		/	Medieval market area provides central focus.
Reduced need for public transport		/	Taking town and country, car use essential.
Spaces: prospect/ enclave; private/public; transitional	/		Good balance between spaces emphasising enclosure and spaces offering prospects of landscape beyond walls.
	/		Clear definition between public and private space.
	/		Good examples of use of transitional space in cool climate.
Landscaping and amenities		/	Public landscape within the walled town is negligible – few trees – however compensated for by extensive common land outside town walls.
Place gives pleasure	/		Town – combination of views of landscape, richness and diversity of architectural conurbation and human scale to spaces.
			Country – area of outstanding natural beauty – many country, forest and riverside walks.
Recycling: materials;	/		Oak beams, stone – considerable renovation of older properties.
resources; waste	/		Extensive woodland pollution from the air.
	/		Recycling for paper, bottles, tins and plastics in Lower Galdford car park – municipal waste not recycled but taken to a site 5 miles north of town, Onibury.
Reuse of buildings	/		Basic timber-framed structure – adaptable to many changes of facade and use.
Information technologies		/	This will be a way of overcoming employment and transport difficulties in the future.
Footprint	/		Light.
TOTALS	14	6	

Functional needs: statement of assessment

The Town and Its Plan

Ludlow offers a number of insights in terms of man's interaction with place to facilitate functional needs. The following are particularly indicative of initiatives which encourage sustainable development:

- A coherent master plan of streets, plots and units of measurement which has satisfied both efficient land use and the need for demarcation of private and public space;
- A predisposition, throughout time, towards adaptability in urban development;
- An implicit regard for relief, materials and climate in maximising human comfort; and
- A recognition of the amenity of landscape and architecture for human psychological comfort.

Very little evidence, either architectural or documentary, exists for the initial period of the town's growth and discussion of the 'master plan' is based on the few known facts and speculations. Of particular importance are the postulations of MRG Conzen (1966, 1988) and research carried out by D Lloyd on burgage and architecture (private communication 1997–8).

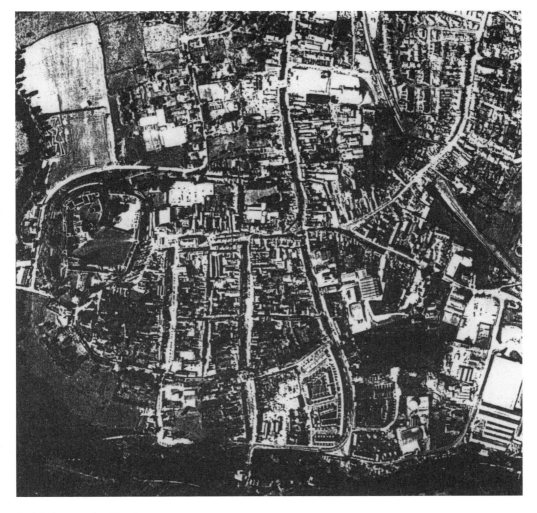

Aerial photograph of Ludlow.

Beresford describes Ludlow as one of the Norman new towns, founded between 1086 and 1094 and laid out on a grid plan oriented on the castle (Beresford 1988). Butler describes it as one of only five towns in England laid out on a grid before 1140 (Butler 1976). Hindle suggests it developed as a linear settlement focused on the ancient north–south route, crowning the River Teme below Old Street and the River Corve at the bottom of Corve Street (Hindle 1984, 1990). Opinion differs. Aerial photography suggests the implementation of a 'master plan' because of the town's strong internal logic.

Conzen's definition of 'town plan' consists of three distinct complexes of plan elements:

- the streets and their mutual association in a street system;
- the individual land parcels or plots and their aggregation in street blocks with distinct plot patterns; and
- the buildings or, more precisely, their block plans and the arrangement of these in the town plan as a whole.

The sense of interconnectedness is stressed. Each element conditions the other's origins, physical relations and functional significance, not just in historical time but also in the present.

Conzen posits that the single-period 'grid plan' interpretation for Ludlow, in the sense of a single act of rectilinear planning as may be exemplified by other medieval towns – Flint and Conway – is untenable (Conzen 1966). He postulates that Ludlow has a 'composite plan', and identifies a sequence of 'plan units' that correspond to periods of development. This would suggest that, if there was an initial master plan, it allowed for a qualitative use of time, with building taking place as and when the need occurred and according to the readiness for development. Conzen identifies five plan units which are distinguished by the shape and size of burgage plots as well as by street arrangement. **(Figure 15)**

Plan units   With the exception of a possible pre-existing Saxon settlement at Dinham, Conzen and Lloyd (private conversation 1997) agree on four 'plan units'. The pre-urban nucleus is the castle, probably begun between 1086 and 1095; the wide high street unit occupying the ridge running east from the castle to the Bull Ring, which was probably well established by the middle of the 12th century; an eastern plan unit merging into the previous one and probably a spontaneous follow-on development, consisting of the Bull Ring, top of Corve Street and the top of Old Street; and a central and southern plan unit containing Broad Street and Mill Street with internal back and cross lanes completed during the 13th century. There is a difference of opinion over what Conzen terms a fifth plan unit immediately south of the castle. For him this is the fifth unit of development whereas Lloyd posits that it may well be an interruption of the original town plan and is another unit such as Broad Street, only not fully developed before the extension of the outer bailey of the castle and the building of the town walls truncated the shape. Figure 16 suggests how the grid might have extended, had the outer bailey and town walls not been erected (Faraday 1991).

Burgaging   Burgaging represented a positive indicator towards guided investment and was designed to release the energies and tap the resources of all the people of an area and to be a means of encouraging the external skills and influences needed for the growth of a town. This was at a time when people and capital were scarce and land plentiful.

A burgage plot was a piece of land held of the king or lord in burgage tenure – for payment of a standard yearly rent. Ludlow was one of 33 towns whose charters were influenced by that of Breteuil in Normandy. Most of these towns, including Ludlow, had a fixed burgage rent of 12d a year (Bateson 1900). Burgage plots are the basic cells of a medieval town plan. They are

Plan Units

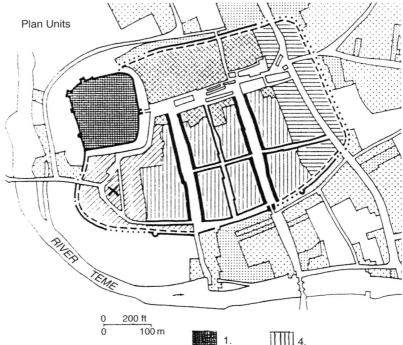

Figure 15: Conzen's five 'plan units'. The creation of the odd shape marked X, together with the fact that it represents 'sloap' not found anywhere else, would suggest some inconsistency of town plan logic.

1.

2.

3.

4.

5.

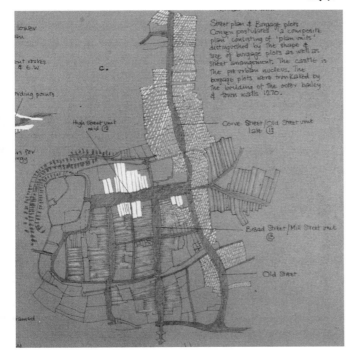

Plan units in Ludlow.

characteristically long and narrow and are arranged in series along streets. Once laid out, the boundaries of burgages were often divided again, both lengthways and widthways, for greater functional flexibility. However, such plot divisions did not normally remove or alter earlier boundaries. Burgages for rent, natural resources in good supply for building and energy, and the possibility of trade constitued a town's package of attractions. It had to offer incentives to attract the skills and labour on which its development depended, and burgage plots, as well as the possibility of trade and protection, were important in this process. This indicates a strong relationship between the master plan, units of land and the socioeconomic status of the desired population.

Ludlow is one of a large group of new towns initiated by a lay lord. David Lloyd (1997) explains: 'New towns were an investment where profits could be made from burgage rents, market tolls and judicial fines. For the Normans, they also served wider strategic and economic needs, especially that of creating trading links between the new towns and a still largely hostile peasantry.' Having carried out extensive research into Ludlow burgages, Lloyd has found evidence that they were originally laid out over a greater area than is suggested by the town plan, such as in the Linney in the north of the town. They were never developed there, possibly because the land was subject to flooding.

The burgage plots must have been set out before the building of the town walls towards the end of the 13th century. It is evident by looking at the town plan that the walls, which were built to the contours of the land, have in many areas truncated the burgage plots. However, the layout of burgages is extensive and this and the unusually large market area (High Street) indicate that a large town was anticipated from Ludlow's early beginnings. Map 2 shows the efficiency of land use in comparison with the 19th- and 20th-century development carried out to the north and east of the town.

There are certain distinguishing features of the Ludlow burgage that have left a unique imprint on the town form. The standard medieval unit of measurement at Ludlow was the

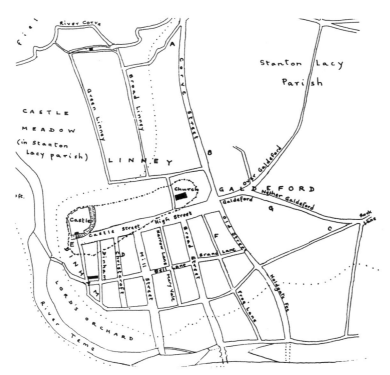

Figure 16: The grid plan
         suggested by
         Faraday
         (1991).

134 Sustainable Place

'perch', approximately 16 feet 6 inches. The basic Ludlow burgage is 33 feet (2 perch) widthways and multiples of that lengthways. Many are exceptionally long. The width of the burgage
reflects the conditioned proportions of early timber-framed buildings. The average two-bay structure was approximately 33 feet (Lloyd 1997).

Plan units and burgages To go back to Conzen's postulations of a 'composite plan' of at least
five plan units that were distinguished by the shape and size of burgage plots as well as by
street arrangement, he argues that these plan units reflect phases of growth. Conzen actually
identifies seven plan units. However, six and seven are most certainly later adaptations to a
basic layout. The following looks at stages of development through plan units two, three and
four.

Plan unit two: High Street (mid-12th century) This is the first town unit as such. The whole
complex measures 300 metres long and averages about three burgage plots in width. Before
the extension of the outer bailey of the castle it was probably 400 metres in length. Originally,
the complex formed the marketplace, its considerable size reflecting the probability of an
important livestock market. Taking the reputed burgage front of 33 feet, the elongation – the
ratio of burgage depth to burgage width – is about 10:1 in the western part and 7:1 in the
eastern (Conzen 1988). These burgages are therefore reminiscent of agricultural selions and
are the longest in medieval Ludlow. Some have a depth of 105 metres. Their general character
suggests they were derived from manorial agricultural practice, adapted to a standard width of
2 perches to give adequate street frontage for a timber-framed town house of two structural

19th- and 20th-century development in Ludlow.

bays (Conzen 1988). As well as suggesting the need for a high degree of self-sufficiency, they set a precedent for further town form. The first inhabitants were probably craftsmen for the castle who would have been dependent on their own plot of land for space for crafts such as weaving and for food and shelter, not just for themselves but for their animals.

Plan unit three: Corve Street/Old Street (late 12th century) This signifies the early success and expansion of Ludlow along the route of the ancient north–south roadway. It consisted of a bilateral ribbon development of traditional long burgages, but these were not as large as those of the High Street unit. Here the original inhabitants came not as craftsmen for the castle but probably as traders. Before the building of the new Ludford Bridge in the middle of the 13th century the best place for passing trade would have been along this route. Traders would have benefited not only from people visiting the castle and market, but there would also have been travellers en route from Chepstow to Chester. The plots facilitate a trade frontage, with workshop and habitation space behind, and land at the rear enabling a degree of self-sufficiency. The deep burgage in plan units two and three is the period index of early development.

Plan unit four: Broad Street/Mill Street (13th century) This unit brought a major innovation of medieval town planning to Ludlow (Conzen 1988). Its technical features are:

- A rectangular street system for rational accommodation of a maximum number of burgages (91 units);
- A distinction between streets of different function:
  (a)   wide multipurpose main streets providing front access to burgages;
  (b)   narrow occupation lanes for cross-connection between main streets or for provision of rear access to burgages;
- The introduction of a standardised type of medium burgage of a ratio 6:1; and
- The fitting of the plan unit to the site so as to:
  (a)   make it contiguous with the original town;
  (b)   incorporate the recently constructed new main access which came over the new Ludford Bridge up Broad Street to the market or High Street; and
  (c)   maintain reasonable access to the town mills from all parts of the town.

This was a sophisticated step forward in urban development and implies a progressive quality of urban lifestyle. It prompts questions about the origin of such design and of the local sociopolitical situation that instigated its installation. Conzen provides information that helps answer these questions.

Most of the features belong to planning devices of the time with the exception of Raven Lane, first recorded as Narrow Lane in 1270, which is a rare example of a bilateral occupation lane (original width 1 perch/16 ft 6 in). This was intended exclusively for the provision of rear access to burgages and 43 out of the 91 standard burgages had this advantage. The device is not used in any of the other medieval towns listed by Beresford for England and Wales (Beresford 1988). However, it can be linked to practice in Gascony under the kings of England and dukes of Aquitaine. The land of the *bastides*, as it is known, features this development. Conzen gives the example of Monpazier, founded in 1285 by Edward I and a local French baron, as a 'mature text book plan of a "bastide"', with literally no part of the intramural area left unserved by bilateral back lanes. The Gascon basic burgage differs from that of Ludlow. It is a short burgage of 7.9 metres by 23.77 metres (24 × 72 *pied*) working to a ratio of 1:3.

The Ludlow and Gascon planned units were put into practice contemporaneously, which suggests vital links and communications. We know Edward I used Ludlow Castle as a base for attacks on the Welsh so there may have been a royal link. The changing socioeconomic

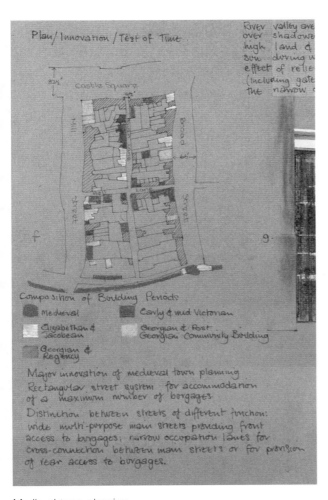

Plan / Innovation / Test of Time.

Castle Square

Composition of Building Periods:

- Medieval
- Elizabethan & Jacobean
- Georgian & Regency
- Early & mid Victorian
- Georgian & Post Georgian Community Building

Major innovation of medieval town planning.
Rectangular street system for accommodation
of a maximum number of burgages.

Distinction between streets of different function:
wide multi-purpose main streets providing front
access to burgages; narrow occupation lanes for
cross-connection between main streets or for provision
of rear access to burgages.

Medieval town planning.

conditions suggest another. Close commercial ties existed between Bordeaux and Bristol and Gascon wine reached Bristol and all the towns within the drainage basin of the Severn and its tributaries, such as Ludlow. Similarly, wool, cloth and hides from Ludlow and the Welsh Borders could reach Gascony. The idea of the bilateral back lane could have reached Ludlow via this route (Conzen, 1988)

Conzen makes an astute evaluation of the constitutional town development: 'Only a constitutionally competent corporate body of townsmen could have tackled the major town planning tasks within one century: the division of the main north–south highway to go through the middle of the existing town soon after the beginning of the thirteenth century; the construction of Broad Street–Mill Street unit in stages and its completion by late mid-century and the town walls and gates by the end of the century.'

This master plan imposed a discipline, clarity and unity on the developing town up to and including the present day. In layout, the planned units and burgage plots give little room for manoeuvre. Some flexibility may be seen in the encroachments of later centuries such as the High Street infills. However, future generations of townspeople have been forced to leave their imprint in the vertical conurbation. Here we see initiatives towards the enduring qualities of consistency and stability through the clear urban logic of the master plan, enabling stability of socioeconomic conditions favourable for external communications, design initiatives and rational development.

A predisposition to adaptability

Within the discipline of the town plan with its system of streets and the measured units of the burgage plots, Ludlow shows great adaptability in architectural development. It is by no means a museum town and every century and stage of development is represented in its configuration, including the 20th century. It is symbolic of its periods of prosperity and town pride that Ludlow has 469 listed buildings – one to every 16 inhabitants (Lloyd & Klein 1984)

There is one important exception to the suggestion that the town defies radical reshaping in its horizontal layout – the very wide, former medieval market area along the ridge. Free burgage tenure had always been liable to upset the corporately established order among burgage plots to some degree, through subdivision and amalgamation, but was kept in check by the custom of longitudinal division which resulted merely in complicated sequences of frontage amounts (Conzen 1988). Conzen explains: 'Arguably the most important interference with corporately established order came from private encroachments on public spaces.' These were of two kinds:

- lateral encroachments on the sides of street spaces, resulting from the actions of individuals and characterised by randomness and irregularity, for example, the south side of King Street;
- island encroachments – market colonisation which virtually produced a second plan unit within the High Street unit.

These encroachments occur throughout the period 1270–1500. They probably originated in open retail stalls in the market street, which in time became shops and eventually shops with residential accommodation above. 'Though contrary to corporate intent, they were condoned for their general convenience and for the extra tax income they brought' (Conzen 1988). Mercantile interests had progressed to a stage where holding land for reasons of self-sufficiency was not necessarily an advantage. It was possible to make a living by buying and selling and the exchange of money. However, space as amenity has been recognised over the last 20 years. Ludlow has had two town halls in its history and, after the second was demolished in 1986, a proposal to enhance Market Square (also known as Castle Square) was accepted. The thriving market still functions there on four days of the week.

The private space provided by the burgages is enclosed and the streets with their continuous line of buildings define the public area. Versatility is experienced vertically in the changing facades. If one thinks of the town plan as a large stage with certain points for fixing the flats, the facades of houses and streets become the flats which have been continually adapted to suit various needs or developments. And like all good props, the structure behind the facade is amenable to change. Many medieval timber-framed buildings were covered with stucco to give an impression of Georgian elegance and then stripped again in the 20th century to give an air of authenticity.

Island encroachment.

Town Council initiative for Market Square Enhancement

Bringing trees, bandstand & seating into the town centre giving more public amenity & providing pleasant community meeting area.

Enhancement proposals for Market/Castle Square.

Broad Street, the most affluent residential area of Ludlow, has an enviable predisposition to change. This is not radical disconcerting demolition and rebuild but gradual adaptability to trends or changing needs. Extensive research into Broad Street has been carried out by the Ludlow Historical Research Group and in particular by David Lloyd. The findings are published in a research paper (Lloyd 1979). The following information is taken from that paper and from unpublished material by David Lloyd.

Broad Street spans eight centuries and for most of that time has been fully occupied. What we see there today is a building achievement reflecting many architectural styles, materials and stages of development over history. Few properties were planned and built as a whole, the earlier buildings having been completely dismantled. In the research paper number 32 Broad Street is discussed: 'The great majority of Broad Street houses . . . are the compositions of two or more architectural styles. Thus No. 32 at first appearance another mid-eighteenth century house, is in fact the result of at least five periods of building, from before 1431, when the house was described as "newly built", to 1969, when an extension was added at the back using plate

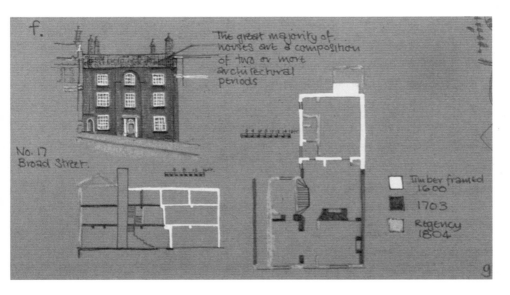

Adaptability of architectural building structure.

glass and other materials produced by twentieth-century technology.' Most of the buildings in Broad Street have timber-framed structures behind their facades. It is interesting to note how the builders have related the buildings to each other and to the natural slope. As far as possible eaves, lintels and sill levels are carried through to the nearest corresponding features of the next building. So the eaves of No. 37 follow through with the sills of No. 38, and the eaves of No. 38 follow through with the shoulders of the Venetian windows at No. 39.

Although virtually all its buildings are listed, Broad Street has adapted to 20th-century functions and use, and is constantly changing. There are: ten shops, numerous offices, two antique businesses, one bank, one hotel, one café, two restaurants, one public house, one chapel and houses for approximately 200 people. The basic timber-framed structure serves as an indicator of adaptable building structure.

Relief, Climate and Buildings

Very little documentary evidence exists to suggest that the medieval builder applied theories of passive energy control in determining the layout and configuration of a town. However, as he had to build at a time when artificial energy was not available, it is reasonable to suppose he was adept at maximising the benefits natural physical conditions could bring to human comfort. An implicit regard for relief, climate and indigenous building materials in conjunction with design helped to maximise the potential for human comfort. The following posits a reasonable hypothesis that would need to be simulated before quantifiable data could be verified.

Natural boundaries such as rivers or steep high land were not only used as protection and defence but also as wind breaks and energy-generating sources. Finding the best orientation towards the sun denoted the logic of the town's physical layout and configuration. Ludlow is afforded protection from southwesterly winds by the higher escarpments of Whitcliffe, Bringewood and High Vinnalls. Some protection from northeasterly weather fronts is afforded to the land that slopes up towards Clee Hill and Wenlock Edge. The slope on which most of the town is built faces south and slightly east, giving maximum advantage from solar gains. **(Figure 17)** Further, the gradient of the slope, averaging one in three but much steeper in the middle, is almost parallel with the low angle of the sun in winter. Therefore, the maximum benefit that can be achieved from solar gains in winter, is capitalised on.

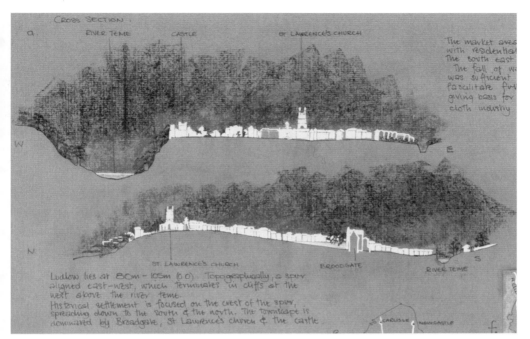

CROSS SECTION:

a.

RIVER TEME   CASTLE   ST LAWRENCE'S CHURCH

W   E

The market area
with residential
The south east
The fall of wa
was sufficient
fascilitate fu
giving basis for
cloth industry

N   S

ST LAWRENCE'S CHURCH   BROADGATE   RIVER TEME

Ludlow lies at 80m – 105m (o.o). Topographically, a spur
aligned east-west, which terminates in cliffs at the
west above the river Teme.
Historical settlement is focused on the crest of the spur,
spreading down to the south & the north. The townscape is
dominated by Broadgate, St Lawrence's church & the castle.

Cross section and
plan of Ludlow.

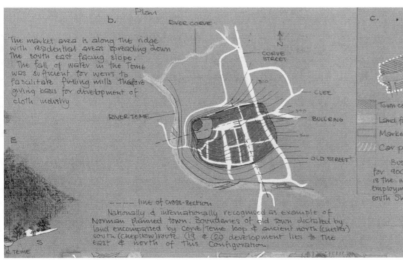

Plan

b.   RIVER CORVE

CORVE
STREET

The market area is along the ridge
with residential areas spreading down
the south east facing slope.
The fall of water in the Teme
was sufficient for weirs to
fascilitate fulling mills therefore
giving basis for development of
cloth industry

CLEE

RIVER TEME

BULLRING

OLD STREET

Town ce
Land f
Market
Car p

Bus
for 900
is the n
employm
South Sw

c.

------ line of cross-section
Nationally & internationally recognised as example of
Norman planned town. Boundaries of old town dictated by
land encompassed by Corve/Teme loop & ancient north (Chester)
south (Chepstow) route (13 & 20) development lies to the
east & north of this configuration.

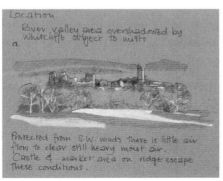

Location
River valley area overshadowed by
Whitcliffe subject to mists
a.

Protected from S.W. winds there is little air
flow to clear still heavy moist air.
Castle & market area on ridge escape
these conditions.

The relationship between Ludlow's location and its
climate.

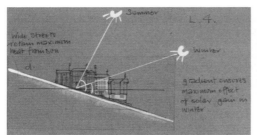

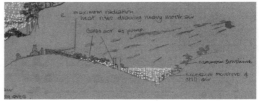

The relationship between Ludlow's location and its climate.

Relief
Generalised form lines at 10ft (3·048 metres) vertical interval interpolated from OS spot heights and adjusted to published OS contours

N

0   100 metres

Figure 17: Ludlow town plan in relation to the contours of the land.

The relationship between Ludlow's building conurbation, relef and climate.

Three very wide streets run up the slope to the ridge. Building conurbation is enclosed giving a continuous effect along the street line. Given that the streets are tarmac and the building facades are mostly brick or timber framed, which absorbs rather than reflects radiation, we may make the supposition that the streets act as trenches for the maximum collection of solar gains on sunshine days and slow release of heat during the cooler night period. Burgage plots run east to west and are terraced up the slope enclosed by buildings; thus gardens have ideal sheltered and sunny positions, providing an indicator for maximising the potential for comfortable outdoor relaxation in a cool climate. As the sun moves from east to west all the housing, at some point during the day, will benefit from sunshine front and back, with the exception of housing on narrow service lanes and housing on the lower slope which is shadowed by Whitcliffe.

Disadvantages of site location
The river valley area to the southeast and southwest is overshadowed by Whitcliffe and receives very little sunshine in winter. Given the temperatures and excessive moisture levels generally in the air between October and March for this area, plus the mist off the river and further transpiration from the densely wooded slopes of Whitcliffe, the lower areas of the town are subject to mists, radiation frosts and poor light quality. This condition is further exacerbated because these areas are protected from the southwesterly winds that might flush out the heavy moist air. Of course, this may be one of the reasons for building the main part of the town along the ridge and higher slopes where, through altitude and greater air movement, these conditions are not as prevalent.

We are aware of the importance of town walls and gates as regards protection but not much is known about their effect on climate. The detail from Ludlow observational study 4 (architecture and function) shows a simplified diagram of the town with the walls in place and makes a reasoned hypothesis of likely climatic benefits. **(colour plate 10)**

Building materials
With few exceptions Ludlow is built with materials from its own environment: oak from Bringewood Chase and Whitton Woods, unpolished Silurian limestone from the Whitcliffe quarries, bricks fired from old red sandstone clays outcropping in Galdeford and behind what is now Portcullis Lane. Superficially brick, much of which is not of good high-fired quality and has a tendency towards porosity, predominates. Stone has been used for some of the architectural focal points such as the castle, town walls, St Lawrence's Church and the 18th-century Buttercross. It is rarely used as the major material on residential buildings, but provides effective contrast to wood and brick. Extensive research by David Lloyd and the Ludlow Historical Research Group suggests most buildings of the old town and suburbs are timber framed. To the north and east, 19th- and 20th-century developments are of brick. The timber-framed buildings are often obscured by the Ludlow trait of adding new facades to existing buildings. The materials, especially the timber frame, have good expansion and contraction qualities and are suitable for the climate. Therefore favourable indicators exist to suggest resource efficiency in materials and energy use, and the reuse of buildings.

A number of research papers give details of famous framed buildings such as number 112, Corve Street (Speight 1989) and The Feathers (Lloyd et al 1986). During the period from 1550 to 1642, which David Lloyd terms the first of the 'great rebuilds', a number of important conditions, including wealth and status – Ludlow was now the seat of the Council of the Marches – existed for the successful development of timber-frame buildings. Materials were readily available locally and skilled craftsmanship was present within the town.

David Lloyd (1979) explains that 'oak for the box frame, wattle and daub for infilling and tiles or thatch for roofs remained the chief building materials, all of them obtainable within a

Examples of materials used in buildings in Ludlow.

few miles of Ludlow. Stone was used for the chimney stacks which had replaced open hearths . . . There was a "brick close" in Galdeford by 1561 and bricks may have been used for particular purposes e.g. the wall enclosing the "Fayre House" garden has stretches of "English bond" that may date from its construction about 1570.'

The signs are that an amalgamation of the skills and crafts necessary for the building trade existed in Ludlow: 'Occupations given in the parish registers between 1550 and 1620 show that there were numerous carpenters, masons, plasterers and tilers in the town at this time. The styles and mannerisms of surviving buildings confirm that Ludlow has its own native school of carpentry, distinct in many details from those which flourished at Shrewsbury or Worcester. Among the craftsmen, the carpenters enjoyed the highest social status and some of them were leaseholders or tenants of substantial Broad Street properties, e.g. "Wright the Joyner" who leased No.14 between 1559 and 1572' (Lloyd 1979).

Plentiful and varied local building materials, developed local skills in the use of those materials, and the advantageous circumstances presented by the Council of the Marches, were conducive to the development of architecture. With this potential the creativity expressed in the facade of The Feathers was possible, and provides an indicator of architecture to bring pleasure.

The domestic timber-framed building
Timber-framed buildings are not the exclusive tradition of this area, but occur in other areas where oak forests grew and vernacular architecture was able to make the best possible use of local building materials. Areas of Kent, Essex, Sussex and the Forest of Dean have regional variations of the building style. Timber-framed building generally became unsustainable in the late 17th and 18th centuries when demand for naval timber caused a relative shortage of good

The construction of a Border Oak property.

Left: The Feathers hotel, Ludlow.

quality oak, and the introduction of alternative building methods, especially the use of brick, led to a decline in the craft. In the last two decades a company called Border Oak at Kingsland, part of the hinterland of Ludlow, has revived this traditional method of building. Their buildings are mainly in country or village locations. They stress their regard for sustainable development of the environment: the importance of gnarled old oaks to the English landscape is recognised. The company uses only straight coppiced trees from large college estates which operate approved replanting and regeneration programmes. Their promotional literature states that they use English oak as a renewable resource and do not rely on vast quantities of finite resources such as oil, coal or gas for converting it into a building component. Further, they allege that they play a contributing role in the regeneration of British hardwoods (Border Oak 1991). They do not say where the oak comes from, but it does not come from Mortimer forest (Bole 1998).

It is possible to compare materials, processes and costs for number 16L Broad Street for when it was built in 1924/25 and a similar 946-square-foot cottage (two bays) by Border Oak built in 1991, using information from an extract from the accounts of the steward of the Palmers' Guild, as transcribed by MA Faraday and Dr M Speight (SRO) and cited in the Broad Street research paper, and a cost analysis of the cottage. Both houses use the same basic construction of a box-frame or post-and-truss building. Of necessity this divides the house into bays, which can put limitations on plan and structure. However, units of measurement thus created do tend to give unity and harmony and the method is flexible enough to allow almost any room size and configuration needed within a domestic building. The width of the Ludlow burgage is based on two bays of 16 feet 6 inches each. Bays, however, can vary in size from 5 feet to 20 feet. They take structural loads to points where main columns are placed. The system is flexible, using variations of open and closed cross-frames on different storeys, and it is possible to create almost any configuration.

Both houses are basically 'design and build' packages, although the term would not have been used in 1424. The timber frame is fabricated in a workshop, tested and assembled in a 'framing ground', and carpenter's marks are incised into the frame which is then disassembled and delivered to site where subcontractors reassemble it and take over the completion of the building.

The extract from the Palmers' Guild accounts gives details of time, materials, labour and costs for the building of number 16L immediately outside the Broadgate. The house is no longer there, but we are told it was of medium size, two-storeyed with a solar – a small upper room that receives sunlight – which suggests it would be comparable to Border Oak's small two-bay cottage. The total cost of building was £5 3s 6½d, the annual rent 4s. Consequently, the Palmers' Guild, which leased the property out, recovered the cost of building over a 26-year period (SRO 356, Box 322: 1431, 1439 and 1461).

The cost analysis of the two-storeyed Border Oak cottage assumes the use of direct labour with the client organising subcontractors. Border Oak could assist with finding a suitable site within the area of Worcestershire, Herefordshire and Shropshire. The cost of this, plus the cost of planning consent and the total cost of the cottage package, is borne by the client. The total cost of the cottage package is £62 per square foot (1997 price) – not dissimilar to that of estate houses to the east of Ludlow town centre. The property is not likely to come up for rent.

With 16L Broad Street, wood or wood products such as boards and wattle consumed over half the materials budget – £1 9s 11d out of £2 2s 4d. This proportion is similar to the Border Oak cottage where about £30,000 out of £59,516 goes on skeletal frame and roof structure. In 1424 the 1300 roof tiles at 1s 8d is considerably less in proportion to the total costs than the Border Oak tiling at £5984 to £59,516. From the number of days craftsmen worked on 16L, we may assume that the house was put up in a relatively short period of three to four weeks. Border Oak estimates three to four weeks to build the frame and a further few weeks on site before the building is weathertight. With the 1424 house, hinges and hooks at 1s 6d are relatively expensive, probably reflecting their scarcity and the expensive and skilled production involved. In the cost analysis of the later cottage, these are considered too insignificant to mention.

When we come to probable use of materials other than for the frame, the benefits of 20th-century technology are apparent. This provides an indicator of the effective use of efficiency technologies and also the recycling of traditional skills in craftsmanship.

With the 1424 house, the spaces between the timbers of the frame were wattle and daub. Oak staves were fitted between horizontal beams about 12 inches to 18 inches apart and hazel rods were woven between them to form the 'wattle' panel. This was then 'doubled' on both sides with a mixture of clay, dung and straw or hay. When dry, the complete panel was limewashed. The final result was seldom weathertight. Through the utilisation of 20th-century technology, the Border Oak property has tremendous advantages in terms of 'weathertightness' and energy efficiency. A sophisticated system of PVC waterbars, neoprene panel seals and joint seals, together with lead trays, is introduced in conjunction with the fitting of 90 millimetre Styrofoam infill panels. The panels are so thermally efficient they have a 'U' value of 0.25 (Border Oak 1991). Many individual design capabilities are possible using this form of basic kit. Some of the other advantages are:

- After an initial painting of the wood with linseed oil the buildings need very little maintenance.
- Because very little water is used there is no disruptive drying out process, condensation or cracks.

- There is no cavity wall: 'We consider this to be a totally illogical way of building, particularly as the cavity is susceptible to a process known as the latent heat of vaporisation, i.e. the evaporation of the moisture from the outside skin sucks heat from the inside skin. This is the same principle that is used in clay wine coolers. It is disturbing that this phenomenon is never taken into account when assessing the 'U' value or efficiency of a conventional built cavity wall' (Border Oak 1991).
- It is interesting to note that, proportionally, materials and labour costs are not dissimilar to those for 16L Broad Street. The serious difference is in land tenure, the cost of the site, the form of tenure and the availability of sites. In the 21st century many people are denied the liberty and opportunity of designing and building their own homes through restrictive forms of land tenure and inflexible conditional forms of borrowing finance.

Spaces

The old town of Ludlow makes a clear definition between public and private space. It is only possible to find one area of sloap – land that is neither public nor private – within the walled town. There is also clear distinction between public landscape and urban conurbation.

Public space within the walled town Spaciousness while emphasising enclosure is the overwhelming feeling in Broad Street, Mill Street and Castle Square. Henry James in the 1870s noted of Broad Street that, except for the 'dramatic constriction of the Broad Gate with its narrow passage "arousing curiosity", it was one of those wide handsome streets' (James 1877). From all parts of the street, the end vistas are, architecturally, effectively closed with the Butter Cross to the north and the Broad Gate to the south.

Enclosure is not felt to be restricting because of the spaciousness of the street – 66 feet wide and approximately a quarter of a mile in length. Mill Street is of similar proportions and, as in Broad Street, house frontages are almost continuous, emphasising its urbanity. However, the slope of the street affords a prospect of the surrounding wooded hills of Whitcliffe.

Looking up Mill Street into Castle Square there is something of a lack of focal point. This is soon to be rectified by proposals to enhance the whole of the market area. Castle Square is a large rectangular area with the castle gates to the west and the end of the rows of market colonisation to the east. The proposal of enhancement will make this area more conducive to public leisure and pleasure for both visitors and the community, with seats, a bandstand and trees which are otherwise absent from the large public areas.

Ludlow's town plan speaks of generations of controlled infill – the modern concept is 'compact' urban development. It is surprising that after all its centuries of development it can still find a corner of space for a building of importance to time and place. Such a corner has been found for a £4 million public library, presently under construction (September 2002). The plot is inconspicuous, an irregularly shaped piece of land formed by the various trunkations to burgages off Corve Street, hidden from main streets. Approach to the site, through a narrow passage between dwellings on Corve Street or from the back of the Somerfield building on Upper Galdeford, intrinsically holds elements of aesthetic stimulation and surprise. From the potential shown by the building framework in place at the moment citizens and visitors should be well satisfied with the design and construction of the library. Architects Aldington, Craig and Collinge have given Ludlow something new and exciting – of the 21st century yet respectful of place. After the confines of the approach, the building opens up with paleness of colour and grace of form; it sits lightly and projects light in its place. It is also exciting because it looks as if it will be the first building in Ludlow to incorporate all the benefits of new technologies and materials, bringing grace of form amid the mass of traditional wood and brick.

There is only one area of 'sloap' within the walled town, site of St. Thomas's Chapel in Dinham (now a house).

Broad Street closes to the Buttercross in the north (left) and the Broadgate in the south (below).

Transitional spaces Space that is neither obviously public nor exclusively private has been governed by the town plan and its system of burgages. Over time, encroachment and subdivision have produced an interesting arrangement of enclave spaces. They are not spaces for sitting in but rather for walking through en route from one part of the town to another: narrow streets and entrances to burgage plots that, over time, have become public pathways to burgages that have become small squares.

An interesting transitional space occurs at the east top side of Broad Street, as a consequence of the standardisation of Butchers' Row, as it was known in the 18th century. Corporation members designated improvement commissioners and charged them with the provision of public services such as paving, lighting and street cleaning. In 1795 predecessors of today's town planners ordered that various projections and encroachments be removed (Lloyd 1979): 'Then the Commissioners agreed to pave under the Butchers' Row in Broad Street and to Regulate Shop Windows and put up Cast Iron posts in the same manner as the Angel posts (hotel) are done on the several proprietors adjoining Agreeing to pay for Iron Posts.' The cast-iron posts are still standing and the result is similar to a covered arcade which provides shelter from the weather and a comfortable enclave experience in contrast to the exposure of the spacious Broad Street.

A hypothesis may be made that these type of spaces, which are not sitting out spaces, bring psychological comfort to everyone moving through the town.

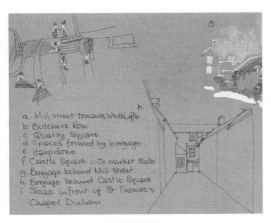

a. Mill street towards Whitcliffe
b. Butcher's Row
c. Quality Square
d. Spaces formed by burgage
e. Harpdone
f. Castle Square with market stalls
g. Burgage behind Mill street
h. Burgage behind Castle Square
i. Stoap infront of St Thomas's Chapel Dinham

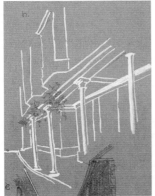

Transitional spaces.

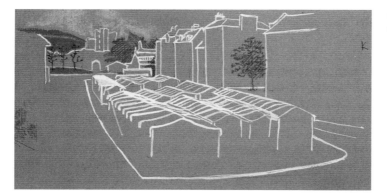

Public space: market square.

Private space: garden taking up rear of a burgage.

Private spaces   The town's building configuration encloses the private space of gardens on the former burgage plots, with the exception of those burgages on the west side of Corve Street which open on to the flat land of the Linney. Many of the properties on the south side of the town have beautifully terraced gardens which command prospects of Clee Hill, Whitcliffe and Bringewood while being maintained within the privacy and seclusion of the urban configuration.

Landscaping and Amenities

The areas known as the Castle Walks and Whitcliffe Common provide public amenities for the town and its visitors. The Castle Walks circle the castle wall and cover the slope to the river on the west and north side. Some seating is provided, mostly on the east side facing the town. Recent proposals for tree-work show evidence that the slopes have become steadily more overgrown since they were laid out as walks in 1722. The majority of the larger trees on the site (excluding individual limes, old sycamores, a beech and a yew) are regrowth from former stumps selected in a previous management scheme about 20 years ago. The extensive growth of young elm, sycamore, etc is indicative of a lack of any management over recent years (Norman 1995). A present proposal attempts to balance the objectives of security, amenity and wildlife conservation, introducing various elements to create visual interest, such as the exposure of rocky outcrops and opening areas which give a view outward towards the surrounding landscape or inward and upward towards the castle.

Whitcliffe, which covers the higher land to the south of the river, provides walks along the side of the river and over well-wooded slopes with outcrops of stone. Here, too, there is an enhancement programme involving clearance and tree thinning. Horse power is proving less destructive and more efficient than mechanical assistance for lifting the logs from the steep slopes and two professional tree-clearing horses have been imported from Yorkshire to do most of the work. This will also protect visitors from the noise pollution of heavy machinery.

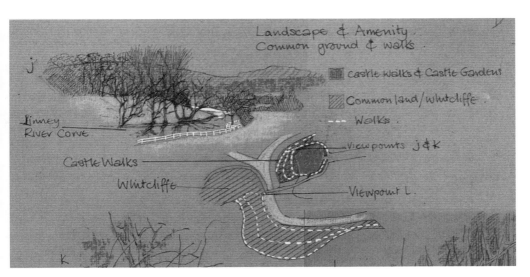

Landscape & Amenity.
Common ground & walks.

■ castle walks & Castle Gardens
▨ Common land / Whitcliffe.
--- Walks.

Linney
River Corve

Castle Walks

Whitcliffe

Viewpoints j & k

Viewpoint L.

j

k

L.

The landscape and public amenities.

k

Current practice is to bring 'greening' into the urban development and in Ludlow natural landscape exists on the perimeter of the town encircling the whole of the urban development. This could be used in the defining of suburban boundaries, to tease out urban villages from the city milieu by defining the boundary through landscape, thus providing public amenity, buffers for noise and cleaners for pollution.

Functional Needs: Summary

Initiative

Many modern cities have abandoned the physical master plan for the nonphysical infrastructure plan (Frampton 1983) which is concerned with institutional or economic logistical projections of changes in land use and with the augmentation of existing distribution systems. Consequently they have been unable to maintain good physical defined urban form. Ludlow emphasises the importance of a well-defined master plan that maximises the best use of site within clearly defined boundaries. This contains and guides development in terms of functional adaptability to socioeconomic growth or nongrowth and the appearance of the architectural conurbation. At Ludlow this is done through the design context of streets, plan units and burgage plots in relation to the relief of the site. Ludlow is now able to limit growth without stifling the adaptability and creative expression of civic life. By the same means it can also see that growth cannot extend beyond the latest physical boundary, the A49, without loss of focus.

Further Investigation

1. Through the master plan (streets, plan units and burgage plots) a sense of interconnectedness is stressed. Each element conditions the other's origins, physical relations and functional significance, not just in historical time but also in time present and time future. Future generations are saved from wasteful 'patch up' development. More research is needed on master plans and the city. In particular, do the expected high density and rapid growth of cities make the boundaries of concentric or grid master plans too restrictive?
    i. What is a sensible master plan for the control of unlimited growth?
    ii. With existing city master plans that have become exhausted is it possible to devise a system of plan units and allow more landscape separation?
    iii. By taking a number of case studies of towns or cities which have outgrown their master plans, is it possible to define the breaking points – encroachment, sprawling suburbs?
2. Adaptability and harmony in the architectural configuration, vertically and horizontally, have been achieved through the adherence to restrictive units of measurement – perch, burgage, bays.
    i. How useful is this concept as a design strategy, especially in relation to the need to reduce the spread of architectural configuration horizontally and the consequent increase in high density, high rise?
    ii. The box frame allowed successive generations to adapt facades to new functions and expressions of social aspirations. How important is an adaptable frame in view of adaptable building form for future climate change?
3. The hypothesis that geophysical infrastructure together with climate and building configuration have an important role to play in the thermal comfort of the town should be taken into simulation so that more accurate data may be made available.
4. Within the town walls all public space seems to be treated as transitional space – thermal comfort, psychological comfort, public function, division of activities – yet because of the cool climate there are few sitting-out spaces. Monitoring the use made of these spaces and the benefits they afford to inhabitants of the town may inform future design strategies.

Institutional requirements: Indicator matrix

Indicator	Positive	Negative	Comments
Economic base	/		Stable – agriculture and forestry. Little industry – declining, consequently Ludlow has set limits to growth.
Integration or reductionism	/		Positive interaction as regards the influence of people on each other.
Systems that reward efficiency and saving resources		/	Highly protective of visual amenities and historical architectural conurbation which indirectly act as a reward for saving resources and efficiency.
Incentive structures	/		Natural desire to be part of a beautiful environment, caring community; civic pride in architectural heritage.
Professional government: local; national; international	/		SSDC keenly aware of regional character and responsive to opinions and to problems of area – census to formulate local approach to sustainability.
		/	Negligible national interaction other than through mandates.
		/	Negligible international interaction other than town twinning.
Communication and infrastructure: local; national; international		/ / /	Poor communication infrastructure locally – population dependent on private transport – nationally and internationally.
Legislation: taxes; building regulations; conservation		/	With one main town and a sparsly populated rural area little revenue comes from taxes.
	/		Building regulations are strict and aimed at preserving regional character at the expense of creativity.
	/		Conservation is the main priority in landscape and architecture.
Pattern of conservation	/		Protection of visual amenity.
Welfare services: health; education; social services	/ / /		Services comparable with national average with the added advantage of extensive locally based charity organisations and strong community responsiveness.
Land tenure		/	Open to private speculation.
Opportunities		/	Limited possibilities for economic growth – tourism presents potential, if guided.
Public transport		/	Poor – roads and railway expensive and inefficient
Property speculation		/	Beautiful environment entices people from industrial areas where cost of living higher – this is causing rising property and land prices.
Population changes		/	High proportion of immigrant population is of retirement age, creating an imbalanced mix of working and not working.
Civic responsiveness: societies;	/		Many societies, such as civic and trade and commerce societies, act as enlightened intermedaries organisations between policy-makers and citizens.
	/		Receptive to local needs.
TOTALS	13	11	

Institutional requirements: Statement of assessment

Land Tenure

The speculative nature of landownership and the injustice associated with the private appropriation of the unearned value of land, or land rent, is an issue of sustainable development: rent, lease and ownership. Significantly, one of the biggest drains on state funds is paying the rent of those who are unable to pay. South Shropshire is no exception and housing benefit consumes almost a third of the district council's budget of £5,000,000 (SSDC 1997–8). Town or city councils who have little control over land tenure are unable to protect the vulnerable, as regards humane housing, from exploitation by speculators and provide a negative indicator for sustainable development.

In Ludlow it is possible to trace development from a time when land was plentiful and labour scarce, so land could be had for the asking, to a time when the demand to own land and property is causing a type of speculation that may have adverse effects on a healthy mixed population and equitable rights to live in the town.

Ludlow has very few industries or businesses to support a population that is of employment age. The South Shropshire District Council is the largest employer. Others such as SW McConnel, Agricultural Engineering and Wells of Tenbury Wells are relocating because of the inconvenient road and rail communication infrastructure or because better business incentives exist in other areas. The average hourly rate in Ludlow is £7.00 compared with £9.50 in Birmingham, 30 miles to the east (CSEA 1998). As an area of outstanding natural beauty and a town of great historical character, Ludlow is becoming a resort for wealthy, retirement-age

The grammar school.

people who, having earned their money and sold properties in areas where the cost of living is higher, are prepared and able to pay high prices for land and property. This is a negative indicator for sustainable development. In Ludlow it is possible to trace the development of land tenure to give an indication of how adverse situations arose.

The town's acquisition of land   At the beginning of the town's history all land was owned by the king. He apportioned it between his feudal lords for them to manage and some of it eventually passed into their ownership. They subsequently subdivided the land between their heirs. Management of the town's plots of land was passed to burgesses (citizens of a borough or town who later had the right to elect people to town government) who managed them for the lord (D Lloyd, private communication 1997–8).

'The Liberties'   As medieval towns had to produce most of their own food, control of the surrounding countryside was an economic necessity. In Ludlow the burgesses were given specified land rights over the neighbouring parishes, known as 'the liberties' (Lloyd 1997). Freemen (people who had practised their trade and lived within the town for a year and a day) had certain rights of pasture and cultivation within 'the liberties'.

Faraday gives more insight into the nature of the early town. It had a class of resident farmers who went out to the countryside to farm and at harvest time crops were stored in town barns or 'any empty building would do; in 1598 the town corn was "inned" in St Leonard's Chapel' (Faraday 1991). Several barns existed in Galdeford because it was near to town fields. We are told that most town agriculturists combined this activity with other trades and interests. Hay was essential. Horses provided transport and, in a town like Ludlow, might well have numbered 500 at any one time so grazing and hay close at hand would have been required. Faraday explains: 'The castle meadow, running below the castle along the Teme to its confluence with the Corve, was never part of the original borough but remained in the Stanton Lacy parish, still part of the lordship of Ludlow. Its exclusion may have been because it was once used for grazing the castle's horses. In practice, it was rented out as grazing to Ludlow residents by the bailiffs acting for the lords. After 1461, the rights were generally leased out by the Crown.'

At the time of the corporation survey book of 1579 'the liberties' totalled about three square miles or approximately 2000 acres (Lloyd 1997). By this time this land had passed to the corporation or town council, given in the charter of 1461 by the king as a reward for Ludlow's loyalty during the first decade of the Wars of the Roses. Lands and rent from lands had previously belonged to the lords of Stanton Lacy (Faraday 1997).

Demesne   Another large area of land acquired by the corporation was 'demesne' land. Initially this was land retained by the lord for his own use, and worked either by his own bailiff and servants or by tenants obliged to give free service. David Lloyd explains how this was transferred to the town:'The moiety of Ludlow (an approximate subdivision) held by Nicholas de Verdun at his death in 1271 contained 23 acres of arable land outside the Borough . . . while the other "moiety", held by Joan, the widow of Peter de Grenville in 1322, had 20 acres of arable . . . and a meadow.' This demesne land came to the corporation in 1461 and until 1592 was listed separately in the corporation rentals. It was described as 'demesne' land in the corporation register of leases as late as the 1660s (Lloyd 1997).

Whitcliffe Common   Another early acquisition was Whitcliffe Common which, although greatly reduced in size, remains common land today. This was obtained in the first half of the 13th century in exchange for the right of free trade within the town. Charges for entrance into the town, plus tolls and taxes on produce bought and sold, were very high and provided considerable revenue for the town (Faraday 1991).

About a third of the common came from the parish of Bromfield, by agreement with the abbot of Gloucester, who was lord of that manor and to whom the Benedictine priory at Bromfield was subject. The land was in exchange for rights of trade within the town plus a 'few pounds of wax yearly' to light the priory church. However, the monks retained access to 'their stone quarries in the afore said pastures' (Felton 1821). The remaining land came from the manor of Ludford, confirmed by Jordan of Ludford, 'to all the Burgesses of Ludlow my common of pasture on Whitcliffe' at a cost of 100s and with the right of his heirs and servants 'freely to buy and sell in Ludlow' (Weyman 1938). Pigs, cattle and sheep would have been taken from the town to graze on this common.

The Palmers' Guild   This signifies corporate ownership of land other than that belonging to the corporation or borough. The Palmers' Guild was a kind of local and national spiritual insurance company. People gave money, land and property in return for prayers for their souls. It became extremely wealthy and in turn sponsored other charities such as schools and hospitals and held office in town government (Lloyd 1997). By 1546–51 the guild held 152 tenements and 75 properties within the town and considerable lands in the surrounding parishes (Faraday 1991). Faraday comments on the transfer of this property at the time of the Reformation: 'In Ludlow, the Reformation was concerned with property as much as belief. The dissolution of conventional houses benefited a few speculators and local landed families who were quick to take advantage.' After the Charities Act of 1547, which dissolved religious guilds, the corporation and not the Crown took control of the Palmers' Guild endowments. Faraday writes, 'the Guild had a good case in law for their exemption, but political prudence suggested compromise that is, Corporation control of the Guild endowments at the price of the Guild's abolition; the Crown, for its part, was fearful that, if Ludlow won in open court, other towns would be encouraged similarly to resist, so in 1551, the Crown acceded to Ludlow's petitions and granted the Guild's possessions to the Corporation in return for an annual fee from rent of £8 13s 4d, payable into the Court of Augmentations and on condition that the corporation continued to maintain the almshouse, the grammar school and the organist and also maintained a preacher in the church.' So, after 500 years the town had acquired considerable land and property; but the usual form of tenure for the population was lease and rent and this does not change until the 'great lawsuit' and the aftermath of reform from 1838 to 1851.

The 'great lawsuit' and the aftermath of reform, 1838–51   This final stage in the history of Ludlow's land tenure brought corporation land into private ownership with adverse consequences for the wealth and sustainability of the town. By 1831, Ludlow's population was considerable – 5253 (Lloyd 1977) compared with 9011 in the 1991 census (SCC 1991). Faraday (1991) estimates that during the Middle Ages the population fluctuated at around 2000.

The Municipal Corporations Act of 1835 sealed the fate of the old system of town administration and a new borough council based on the election of four aldermen and 12 councillors was put in place in Ludlow. The Act ruled that all charity and municipal property should be separated and that the council would retain the latter. This is the first time national bureaucracy interfered with the administration of the town and precipitated an argument and legal entanglement that cost Ludlow Town Council almost all its accumulated wealth in land and property (Lloyd 1977).

The root of the problem, as David Lloyd explains, was that 'Demarcation of the lands and funds supporting the minor charities was not difficult but both the Borough Council and the Charity Trustees now represented that it was impossible to distinguish the former Palmers'

Guild estates from other Corporation property, particularly from the "demesne" lands granted by Edward IV in 1461.' A bitter legal battle – the great lawsuit – ensued, fuelled by antagonistic factions within the town. Stories of previous corruption and misappropriation of Palmers' Guild rents and leases added further confusion and antagonism.

A conclusion was reached that was by no means satisfactory but was designed to put an end to the escalating cost of the lawsuit. In 1845 the Lord Chancellor, Sir Rowland Hill, referred the case to the Master of the Rolls, suggesting that a compromise be accepted by both parties to prevent the expense of further litigation. The settlement to the trustees became law on 7 May 1846. They received land allocated in 16 parishes with an annual rent of £1500. The borough council was to give a further £4305 as a fund for repairs and also meet the lawsuit costs of £37,000. The council was obliged to auction nearly all its remaining Ludlow properties to discharge debts. This left the town not quite bankrupt but greatly impoverished, and started the process of private ownership within the town (Lloyd 1977).

A positive indicator for land tenure would be one which allowed for an equitable distribution of land and housing for a mix of population, and one that was not open to speculation and exploitation by external forces. It would seem that Ludlow relinquished this indicator in 1846.

Courting opportunity

Ludlow had otherwise had few periods of unsustainable development. It suffered the epidemic diseases and bad harvests of the 12th, 13th and 14th centuries as a result of which between a third and half of its population died. This must have provided the supreme test for local government to provide good policies and commercial incentives so that the town might revive. Quantitative evidence to estimate the incidence of epidemic disease for the early centuries is not available but Faraday has recorded from corporation minutes certain measures taken by the town in the 16th century (Faraday 1991):

1593: The digging of plague pits; in July, common carriers were barred from travelling to London for a month lest they bring back infection, while carriers and goods from outside were not allowed in the town, and the fair was suspended.

1594: In March a pesthouse was ordered to be built at public expense for lodging infected people; the town gates were guarded to bar entry to strangers.

The Civil War and its aftermath, from 1642 to 1660, also had a negative influence on development. During this period the town's population fell from about 2600 to about 1500 (Faraday 1991). Large parts of the suburbs were burnt by royalist defenders, and the decline in the population reduced the incentive to rebuild quickly. The royalist garrison wanted to clear arcs of fire for guns on the town walls and to deny Ludlow's Parliamentary besiegers cover for tunnelling and sapping. Therefore many houses close to the walls were demolished. After the capture of the town it became a military backwater under a series of Parliamentary military governors (Faraday 1991). 'Although the forms of government of Ludlow survived the war and Interregnum, economically, demographically and architecturally, the town suffered severely.' Despite rebuilding incentives by the corporation, the town took a long time to recover. Faraday continues: 'Even a century after the war the corporation was still not satisfied with the rate of rebuilding.' Leases from between 1730 and 1761 still had a building regulation governing the facades of properties fronting the streets in the eastern plan unit (Faraday 1991). This strongly suggests that Ludlow had become seriously impoverished. It seems not to take an active role in national events after this time.

Ludlow's history otherwise exemplifies the positive indicators of opportune incentives and political and religious tolerance.

Although agriculture is, and has been for 9000 years, the business that occupies most of its inhabitants directly or indirectly, this is not to say that its secondary role – the 'courting' of favourable consumer opportunities – has not been important. In the Middle Ages the kings and lords who held large courts at the castle encouraged the growth of consumer trades and support services as well as providing foreign connections for trade outlets. The wealthy Palmers' Guild with its national and local membership left charitable buildings such as the grammar school (1390s). The Council of the Marches, which resided in Ludlow from 1501 to 1661, brought a new type of sophisticated intelligentsia from London: lawyers and courtiers whose residence in the town brought architectural patronage which manifested in The Feathers hotel and the Readers House. County families of the 18th and 19th centuries, eager to build, refurbish or rent houses for the season left their mark in the Georgian character of Broad Street. The prestigious architecture within the town is an indicator of this heritage.

21st-century developments All Ludlow's institutions move cautiously and tolerantly into the 21st century. As a market town it depends on, and is integrated with, the economic potential of its hinterland. Two-thirds of the population of South Shropshire live in the country areas. The livestock market was moved in 1992 to a rural site approximately a mile south of the town. Having paid £1.5 million for the old site, the district council was eager to reclaim the expenditure by selling to the supermarket chain Tesco. Opposition came from traders in the town centre who feared this would reduce their business. A thriving produce-market takes place in Castle Square on Mondays, Wednesdays, Fridays and Saturdays, and will continue to do so even when proposals to enhance the square are carried out. Produce sold in the market is not exclusively from the locality.

Is a superstore a negative or positive indicator of sustainable development in small rural areas? After a five-year battle against civic resistance, and after enormous costs, political inquiries and numerous design proposals, Tesco secured a place within the town of Ludlow. The Minister for the Environment gave his approval for the store to go ahead. A public relations promotion and exhibition of the new plan proposals confirmed Tesco's intention.

The architects, MacCormac, Jamieson and Prichard, began by courting local approval with references to architectural heritage (*Ludlow Advertiser* 1998): 'The idea of the burgage plot is central to the new design for a Tesco store and means the design is "bespoke" for Ludlow.' Richard MacCormac said he thought it 'very important for the modern and commercial to be

Computer-generated image and photomontage of the proposed Tesco store (1998). The reality varies slightly in that the white tower on the right is square and not curved, and the trees are not in place.

able to be accommodated into a historical situation'. When others expressed some doubts about his version of this – the building is on the corner of a street where Georgian and medieval buildings predominate – he showed some lack of tolerance and ethical regard for cultural identity: 'If an architect listens to everyone, you end up with a ten-legged camel with fifteen humps.' So the people of Ludlow had the choice between a 10-legged camel or mediocrity. In the design's favour it may be said it respects the scale in height of other buildings in Corve Street. However, aesthetically it does not deserve to coexist, as an architectural statement, with such buildings as The Feathers a few hundred yards up the street.

The superstore is a very powerful national institution. At first it seems a positive indicator, an incentive towards wider communications and infrastructures. In Ludlow, people were told, Tesco would create 248 full- and part-time jobs, and provide everything under one roof – food hall, delicatessen, bakery, cafeteria, laundry, banking services, free parking and even outdoor seating areas. Seductively, the superstore enters small rural towns with something of the aura and monopolising capability of the medieval guild, only it is not taking money for the salvation of your soul. Rather, it is promising you the material status of the affluent worldly consumer. Has Ludlow's cautious move towards superstore status paid off?

Sustainable development is about considered growth, maintaining a certain equity for all people of a locality. Many local producers and farmers, especially to the west of the region, took a considerable drop in income between 1990 and 2000 – South Shropshire District Authority figures show a 44 per cent drop in the agricultural economy during 1997. Excellent meat, dairy and fruit and vegetable products, plus wines and ciders, are produced locally and within the region. Very little local produce ends up on the shelves of Tesco superstore. In areas like Ludlow a good indicator would be restrictions in favour of selling local products.

However, the superstore is up and functioning and, surprisingly, it has had a modest impact on local traders. There are a number of possible reasons for this. The services and products Tesco offers may be said to be scaled down in comparison with its general national image. Between 1998 and 2002 trade in Ludlow's central market area modified and adapted to what seems to be a suitable economic role within 21st-century market forces. Traders have focused on creating a reputation for quality, especially in respect of food products. The town of Ludlow has moved towards exclusivity, with many excellent eating-places and shops that sell quality organic and local produce. Tesco provides a back-up service by selling basic low-cost commodities that local establishments such as hotels, nursing homes and restaurants would otherwise have to purchase in bulk from Shrewsbury. Consequently, Ludlow is able to nurture a certain regional autonomy.

South Shropshire Structure Plan to 2006 The Ludlow observational study 6 (town plan to 2006) shows the limits to growth and new development for the Ludlow town plan, which is considered to be an optimum size for the town's development. The reasons are:

- Large-scale growth would necessitate the outward spread of the town which would start to breach serious environmental thresholds.
- The town sees itself as servicing a wider rural community with few opportunities for employment growth within the town. Sufficient land has been allocated for industry but has not been developed, probably because of the inaccessibility of area and national routes of communication and transportation.
- The underlying strategy is to strengthen the market town by ensuring there is an appropriate balance between jobs, dwellings and services that reinforces the high level of self-containment within the community.

Given Ludlow's economic base, lack of good rail and road links with national transport infrastructure, and the need to provide welfare support for the less well-off, limiting growth is a positive indicator.

The South Shropshire District Council discussion paper The district council discussion paper, *Sustainability and the Local Plan* (SSDC 1997), states: 'There is a widening gap between the rich and the poor with a significant poor minority living amongst a comparatively affluent majority'; 'Past research has shown that in the region of 25% of households in South Shropshire (3850) are living on the margins of poverty'; and: 'There continues to be much concern about the need for additional affordable housing aimed at retaining young people within their own rural communities.' Are these central issues of sustainable development?

So far as affordable housing is concerned, the council has allowed 100 new houses a year since 1985, a quota to be phased out by 2006 because of the limit set on town growth. The council estimates that there will be a shortfall of 1700 affordable dwellings by that date. Household details from the 1991 census for Ludlow showed that the local authority and housing association provided a total of 855 rentable dwellings for the poor on housing estates to the north and east of the old town. Of the 3806 households in Ludlow, 2619 were owner-occupied. Most of these were in the old town and represent to a great extent the wealthy retirement population, many of whom recently migrated there. The 1993 population survey for South Shropshire, which includes Ludlow and rural areas, shows that a disproportionately high percentage of the population is over 65 years of age – 66.26 per cent for Ludlow and 56.65 per cent for the district as a whole.

Civic Responsiveness

Within this group of retirement settlers are large numbers of wealthy and accomplished business and professional people. Their wealth enables the good maintenance of Ludlow's historical heritage in housing – none of the beautiful houses and gardens in Broad Street have been turned into flats or nursing homes. Their business and professional expertise are utilised and extended to fulfil institutional requirements, with their participation in associations, such as the town council and civic society, that are concerned with town government. This is an indicator that active interest is taken in town development, sustainable tourism, conservation and planning regulations. A relationship exists between these associations and the South Shropshire District Council (SSDC).

In compliance with the national government initiative, Agenda 21, the SSDC sent out questionnaires to assess public opinion as to an approach to sustainable development and reactions to the South Shropshire Structure Plan. This went to all district parishes and civic associations and the result was a discussion paper – *Sustainability and the Local Plan*. Organisations such as the Civic Society are part of local incentive structures which constitute an enlightened form of mediation and communication between local citizens and policy-makers, a positive indicator. Dr James Harris, who was a lecturer in architecture at Manchester University before retiring to Ludlow, replied on behalf of the Civic Society.

Apparent from this correspondence is the contrast between global objectives and the specific and particular response to sustainable development in locality. A framework of assessment, if it is to be a useful tool, must use indicators that have relevance when applied to varying places in differing global locations. The general indicators arising from this extract are: reducing the need to travel; energy issues; conserving and enhancing the rural environment; a sustainable rural economy; and social needs and housing, in particular improving the lives of the least advantaged. The use of the word 'rural', applied to two of the indicators, is a crucial reasoning and not as a particularity of locality.

Every town has an impact on, and is dependent on proportionally, an area of rural landscape whether for food, energy or amenity. Every urban area must take responsibility for what may be termed its 'ecological footprint'. The case of Ludlow suggests that there is an advantage in knowing the purpose of hinterland held in reciprocal relationship with urban configuration. Each of these indicators may demand a specific response within a particular locality. However, general principles which significantly affect sustainable development are also apparent. The communication of ideas, information, hopes, aspirations, likes and dislikes from all sectors of society is of crucial importance as a vehicle of change. This may be achieved through an efficient institutional infrastructure of private and public organisations exemplified here in the relationship between local district council management and the Civic Society. Psychological reaction to certain types of change has also to be sensitively taken into consideration. No matter how much analysis supports the viewpoint in favour of wind turbines, if a critical mass of the population perceives these as being incompatible with their visual amenity this has to be respected.

Institutional Requirements: Summary

Initiative
In South Shropshire a good communication infrastructure has been built up between all factions of the community and local government. This has been achieved through concensus from parish councils, town councils and local organisations among which the Civic Society is especially proactive in matters of the town environment and architectural conurbation and public amenity. The implication is that this is the most suitable way to produce local indicators towards sustainable development.

Further Investigation
1. Land tenure. A hypothesis may be made: economic logic requires that we maximise the use of land in urban areas, control development into rural areas and move away from the speculative and revenue-producing power of land, which has led to unethical distribution and unequitable systems of welfare and amenity for citizens of the town. Investigation needs to take place into how the land of the town may be cooperatively and equitably managed for the benefit of the town and all its citizens.
2. The interests of regional areas are not always served by national policy. Should more power be given to small towns and regions to take the best advantage of local opportunity?
3. A comparison of towns and cities with strong civic institutions should be made, to evaluate the impact of these institutions on sustainable development.
4. An investigation into the regional impact of the superstore:
   i. Changes in local economic activity.
   ii. Architectural suitability, especially in areas of historical interest.
   iii. Is the aquisition of land and planning permission within the ethical and equitable remit of civic responsibility?

Cultural identity: indicator matrix

Indicator	Positive	Negative	Comment
Equilibrium	/		Good interaction between people – problems resolved through the involvement of all.
Human scale	/		Urban conurbation and country housing of human scale.
Humane housing	/		Majority of the population has comfortable housing.
Individuality	/		Developed self-reliance of rural area and appreciation of the individual as opposed to the corporate identity of multinational.
Enlightened behaviour and attitudes	/		Population small – everyone in some way known by, and accountable to, their community.
	/		Generally responsible and caring towards people and environment – although example shows intolerance of needs of youth – enlightened interest in concerns of sustainable development.
Heritage: environmental; historical	/ /		Rich and diverse heritage in landscape and architecture.
Cultural stimulation		/	Stable, consistent and comfortable rather than stimulating.
Permanence of population	/		People come here to settle – this is not a temporary stopping-off place en route to settling down.
Regional character	/		Seldom compromised in landscape or architecture.
Sense of community	/		Traditionally developed sense of community able to accommodate a certain number of immigrants.
Religious and ethnic toleration	/		Not an area that is religiously or ethnically diverse – toleration exists between those who do live here.
Creativity: 'Creativity, if it has any meaningful boundary, lies within the moment when potential begins to emerge into reality.'	/		This place has the potential to become a role model for a well-sustained rural environment.
Human misery	/		There is probably nowhere where a degree of human misery does not exist – here it is sharply contrasted – but relatively, in proportion to the population, it is not a conspicuous factor.
Local particularity	/		Beautiful and diverse countryside and human-scale settlement – architecture of regional character built with the materials of the locality.
TOTALS	15	1	

Cultural identity: Statement of Assessment

Regional Character

Why are you not fishing on the lake?

Why are you not out fishing on the lake?

I caught a big haul yesterday which I sold and the money will last for three days. Why should I fish today?

Because, if you fish today, you can have more money than you have today!

True, but why should I have more money?

Because you can buy a motorised fishing boat.

True, but why should I buy a motorised fishing boat?

Because, then you can catch ten times more fish and earn ten times more money!

True, but why should I catch ten times more fish and earn ten times more money?

Because, you can then build a palatial house and swimming pool?

True, but why should I buy a palatial house and swimming pool?

Because, then you can enjoy life and lie lazily in the sun all day.

True, but that is what I am doing now, am I not?

(Anon)

Ludlow does not epitomise the fast-growth philosophy we have come to associate with our modern cities. It may be said that it uses material growth as a considered tool, not a perpetual mandate; it recognises its own limitations, such as lack of industry; and it has made arrangements accordingly, by setting the limits to growth.

'The growth of employment and services should relate principally to the local needs of the area, including needs arising from population movement in to the area. In each case the scale of development will take account of the town's ability to expand while retaining it's essential character, major environmental and investment thresholds and the rate of development of strategic growth locations' (SSLP 1995–2006).

Society is predominantly rural. Ludlow is the main market town and shopping centre. It is also the main administrative and service centre in South Shropshire. Services and facilities such as hospital, college and leisure centre serve a wide rural hinterland. Although significant architecturally as an outstanding example of a Norman planned town with listed buildings ranging over the centuries, the town is very close to the rural life which has so influenced its cultural identity.

Rural people are perceived as industrious and very efficient with resources and time. Having worked closely with the land and livestock they possess a special kind of timing. It is a prerequisite of their sustainability that they accept and develop a receptivity to sign-stimuli in nature. The ripening of the corn is not governed by a 3.00 pm deadline on 24 July but it is conditional on the weather. Sheep don't conveniently lamb without difficulty between 9.00 am and 5.00 pm. Periods of waiting are often thwarted by the anticipation of what might go wrong. Hence the people are rather stoical, cautious of change and not given to overindulgence.

Similarly, we do not find opulent or pretentious buildings. Describing Broad Street Alec Clifton-Taylor commented: 'As for the buildings themselves, apart from one rogue elephant, the Methodist Chapel, they all show regard for the two vital needs of a successful street: they show respect for the scale of their neighbours, and they use the right, which means to say the local, materials'. This applies generally to buildings in the whole of the area. Another important characteristic, probably connected to people's expectation that they will settle in the area for some considerable time, is that they are prepared to wait for the right time to build.

With two-thirds of South Shropshire designated as an area of outstanding natural beauty it is not surprising that the strongest aesthetic is felt through nature. AE Housman's 'A Shropshire Lad' is probably the closest artistic expression of that potential. It is about the changing nature of beauty and about man rearranging his inner clock in time with the seasons of nature. And having done that, proportionally man's time seems precious and he is able to prioritise the moment.

> Loveliest of trees, the cherry now
> Is hung with bloom along the bough,
> And stands about the woodland ride
> Wearing white for Eastertide.
>
> Now, of my threescore years and ten,
> Twenty will not come again,
> And take from seventy springs a score,
> It only leaves me fifty more.
>
> And since to look at things in bloom
> Fifty springs are little room,
> About the woodlands I will go
> To see the cherry hung with snow.
>   *A Shropshire Lad* II

Housman wrote most of *A Shropshire Lad* while working in London, but lived for many years in Bromsgrove just east of Clee Hill. He obviously had an intimate relationship with the area described in this chapter because he recognises and incorporates all the idiosyncrasies of its character objectively and subjectively.

The seventh poem in the cycle with its felt description of landscape, nature and mans relationship to both, is particularly apt in the context of our discussion. Details such as the still air in the windless valley area to the south of Ludlow that causes smoke to rise vertically; the humid conditions from excessive moisture rising from the river and landscape that produce characteristic mists; the long tradition of forestry and coppicing so essential to building and livelihood. 'Strode beside my team' suggests a positive purpose, but acceptance of interdependency of man and nature. The stoical nature of the area's people and their philosophy are felt particularly in the third and sixth stanzas, which convey an almost fatalistic philosophy of life. The frustration of that stone thrown with will. The wishing to end the story but the impossibility of it, so ingrained is it in the cultural identity. That stone is being thrown hard by the interests of youth in this area, so in need are young people of fostering and nurturing. What has this to do with architecture? Well, architecture has implications in the particular.

Sense of Community

Retaining young people   One of the biggest difficulties in this area is providing adequate affordable accommodation, transport, training, employment and recreational facilities for the young. The National Foyer Society helps set out initiatives for the integration of young people into employment and society. It gives support to less able 15- to 25-year-olds and helps them to find campus, training for employment, and social and leisure activities. It receives no funding and fund-raising had to be carried out locally to buy and renovate the Marston Warehouse as a 'Foyer project'. A committee to realise this objective was put in place with the support of the local authority. The national charity Stonham also keeps a hostel for homeless young people, run by a warden, where they may stay for up to six months. The social services in Ludlow provide a Housing Young People Service (HYPS).

> When smoke stood up from Ludlow,
> And mist blew off from Teme,

And blithe afield to ploughing
Against the morning beam
I strode beside my team,

The blackbird in the coppice
Looked out to see me stride,
And hearkened as I whistled
The trampling team beside,
And fluted and replied:

'Lie down, lie down, young yeoman;
What use to rise and rise?
Rise man a thousand mornings
Yet down at last he lies,
And then the man is wise.'

I heard the tune he sang me,
And spied his yellow bill;
I picked a stone and aimed it
And threw it with a will:
Then the bird was still.

Then my soul within me
Took up the blackbird's strain,
And still beside the horses
Along the dewy lane
It sang the song again:

'Lie down, lie down, young yeoman;
The sun moves always west;
The road one treads to labour
Will lead one home to rest,
And that will be the best.'

A Shropshire Lad VII

Young people without qualifications are more likely to face unemployment. And although many of the rural youth are able to obtain work in towns such as Ludlow, Leominster, Hereford and Shrewsbury, they are unable to reach it because of the lack of transport. Ludlow's local plan recognises this problem. An improved mainline railway from Hereford to Shrewsbury and small-scale road transport links to stations would be functional.

For the rural young social isolation further complicates the step from home to adult independence. Many of them are forced to stay in the parental home or move to culturally alienating urban environments. Parish council surveys that take into consideration the wishes of young people are being carried out. However, these do not identify the problems of the 18- to 25-year-olds – youth work stops at 17 years of age when young people move from groups such as scouts, guides and youth clubs.

Teme Valley Youth Group (TVYG) The social and cultural difficulties of the young are best related through a particular situation with all its social, cultural and environmental ramifications. This story involves an area within an 8-mile radius of Leintwardine which falls short of any towns.

In 1992 a young person working in Leintwardine let her difficulties become known to her employer. Young people of 18 to 25 had no place to meet to share interests and compare situations other than Leintwardine Bridge. The employer lent her kitchen as a temporary, once-a-week meeting place. The young people who met there went around the rural area interviewing their contemporaries and formed a matrix of what they wanted from their community. This was produced in the spring of 1994. High on the list was somewhere to meet; training, education, learning about job opportunities and, surprisingly, leisure facilities were not priorities.

Because it was youth led the movement caught the mood of the young within the area, and guidance and support came from sympathetic adult members of the community. It became an issue of raising money for a place, and linking with the community at large. In November 1994 a delegation of young people, accompanied by a much-respected representative of the community, attended a parish council meeting intending to explain their situation. They were not listened to; not even asked to speak. However, other initiatives had taken off. A building had been donated for weekly meetings and fund-raising had produced £2000 from the Christian Initiative Charity. The group, which called itself the Teme Valley Youth Group, was not affiliated to any religious organisation but the charity was reassured that the enterprise fell within their conditions. The need for affordable housing for many of these young people brought in the South Shropshire housing development officer and £150,000 for a Foyer-governed initiative.

By the autumn of 1994 the group was run by a youth committee, and had a steering committee of adult advisers and a body of trustees for fund-raising. Fund-raising was highly successful and a constitution was formulated. TVYG applied for charitable status. It had achieved results, except with the parish council and citizens of Leintwardine, who maintained a critical, even hostile attitude. A site for a building was located in Paytoe Lane, Leintwardine, but this was opposed. Attempts to connect with the local citizens were thwarted. Invitations to see a display of the proposed plans for the building in Paytoe Lane provoked vociferous opposition: 'We want no teenagers here!' Leintwardine's inhabitants, incensed by fear and anger, saw the initiative as threatening their community and envisaged that their village would become a rehabilitation centre for drug addicts, that the crime level would go up and that they would have to tolerate excessive noise and antisocial behaviour. The members of TVYG were not equipped to deal with the unprecedented misrepresentation and unpleasantness displayed through leaflets and public demonstration. Two hundred people turned up at a parish council meeting to discuss the proposed plans, and the meeting had to be adjourned to the church. A period of mediation occurred, but unpleasant opposition fuelled the outcome – a no-compromise situation. In October 1996 a referendum declared that 80 per cent of the population was against a TVYG building in Leintwardine.

The movement itself had taken off with 50 young people meeting for four to five sessions a week. The group was given charitable status and money was provided for community service volunteers and running costs. The Paul Getty Trust provided £40,000 to pay the salary of a trained youth worker, at £20,000 a year, for two years (this was subsequently taken over by the local authority). In the spring of 1996 the group received £360,000 of lottery money. Research carried out by TVYG with local young people established a list of the facilities they required; and from this a group of Birmingham architects drew up plans integrating facilities for training, employment and living. Leintwardine proved so bitterly opposed to a TVYG building that a new site was found in the nearby village of Wigmore. Planning application was obtained in 1998 and the project is ongoing.

Over the whole of the South Shropshire district an urgent need for appropriate housing was identified by South Shropshire Housing Association for sixty-five 14- to 25- year-olds. Of these, 26 were considered in immediate housing need; of those living at home, approximately two-thirds, only 17 were content with the arrangement and 15 wanted to move out; over half the respondents may qualify for housing benefit. A typical response from a young person asked to comment on the need for housing in the area was: 'It is very difficult to be able to stay in the area you are brought up in because everything is so expensive and you have to travel for employment. I feel that affordable houses are needed, especially in an area like this where not everyone can afford to buy.'

The catchment area of Ludlow represents the dispersed settlements that exist in the Marches region area of Shropshire and Herefordshire. The TVYG initiative is a small, low-key solution to address the current needs of young people. It is innovative, and a direct initiative by people familiar with their place, its economy, lifestyle and options. It is a unique and innovative form of development and may become a prototype for rural areas and an approach to sustainable development that becomes standard practice.

Human Misery

The 1991 census of South Shropshire indicates that this area has its share of poverty, with wages below the national average and difficulties of communication and providing transport in the rural areas. The visual indicators that would make people aware of this in the city are not readily noticeable here. Ludlow has areas such as the 'Sandpits' where high levels of unemployment, crime and poverty are reflected in the neglect and ugliness of urban form. However, rural poverty and misery are often imperceptible because they occur in isolation, on small-holdings in the west, in isolated cottages off the beaten track. Physical poverty, whether urban or rural, is in many ways quantifiable. We can calculate the water, food, clothing and shelter necessary for the sustenance of the human body. But human misery is not necessarily proportionate to material poverty or to a particular age group. Indications that there is a particular problem with isolation/loneliness have come from carers within the community.

Homestart is one such organisation, whose members are trained to deal with the specific problem of isolation. Each member makes a commitment to a few people who are alone and takes on the responsibility of bringing them back into social contact through whatever means is suitable. Members go to these people in their homes until they are able to acclimatise to social situations. The alone person might be a mother at home with small children or an elderly person whose partner has died. Trust and reassurance are built through a type of communication that is not particularly one of words but is more one of sensibility and cultural identification. The alone man or woman sees reflected in the other person, like a mirror image, confirmation that they are not alone in their experience and that the strength to overcome is not beyond them. Others have been there before, and what they are experiencing is a 'minor cultural landslide' common to the area. However, to the west of this region there is a high suicide rate in the local farming communities.

Sometimes creative works that have their stimulus in place value, and express the benign qualities of the local landscape, are enough to turn the mind from feeling unfortunate to fortunate. For those who have to move away, or for whom lifestyle necessitates long absence, nostalgia plays an important role in identification with the countryside.

In my own shire, when I was sad,
Homely comforters I had:
The earth, because my heart was sore,
Sorrowed for the son she bore;
And standing hills, long to remain,
Shared their short-lived comrade's pain.
And bound for the same bourn as I,
On every road I wandered by,
Trod beside me, close and dear,

The beautiful and death-struck year:
Whether in the woodland brown
I heard the beechnut rustle down,
And saw the purple crocus pale
Flower about the autumn dale;
Or littering far the fields of May
Lady-smocks a-bleaching lay,
And like a skylit water stood
The bluebells in the azured wood.

Yonder, lightening other loads,
The seasons range the country roads,
But here in London streets I ken
No such helpmates, only men;
And these are not in plight to bear,
If they would, another's care.
They have enough as 'tis: I see
In many an eye that measures me
The mortal sickness of a mind
Too unhappy to be kind.
Undone with misery, all they can
Is to hate their fellow man;
And till they drop they needs must still
Look at you and wish you ill.
                    A Shropshire Lad XLI

Housman, whose intimate sketches of this environment have led to its immortalisation, has in some senses encouraged a disadvantageous town-country culture divide. Understanding from both town and country people is necessary if we are to balance, through countryside, some of the harm caused by the city. It is, therefore, a negative indicator when city people see the countryside as some romantic place, full of overindulged people, which they may visit occasionally – rather than appreciating, as they should, that it is a well-managed and cared for working environment that has, over a prolonged length of time, maintained development which has been, and still is, sustainable.

Cultural Identity: Summary

Initiative
Creative solutions to particular local problems in the context of architecture and the environment. Suitable local caring institutions and charities to address human misery.

Further Investigation
1. Form a matrix of problems and possible solutions through consensus and monitoring of the cultural difficulties experienced in movement from urban to rural, or rural to urban, environments.
2. Investigate ways of promoting mutual understanding and appreciation between rural and urban communities so that less harm is caused to rural environments and communities as the population balance is tipped in favour of city concerns.
3. Investigate the need for local indicators for particularities of place that are not addressed in the present forms of quantitative analysis or consensus.

STAGE 3: CAPABILITY ASSESSMENT

The capability matrix quantifies positive and negative indicators, as well as giving the most significant incentive and problem for further investigation in each of the constituent parts. This enables an evaluation of sustainable development capability in terms of low, moderate and high.

CAPABILITY MATRIX

PHYSICAL CONDITIONS	FUNCTIONAL NEEDS
NO. OF INDICATORS PRESENT: 22 POSITIVE. 19. NEGATIVE. 3.	NO. OF INDICATORS PRESENT: 20 POSITIVE. 14. NEGATIVE. 6.
INITIATIVE: agriculture & forestry stress importance of enlightened management adaptation to changing need & renewing of natural resources. Present management: National Trust – hillfort sites; English Nature – special scientific interest; Forest Enterprises – forest areas; private farmers – agricultural land. Balance seems to work well, maintaining a richness of diversity & protection from exploitative forces.	INITIATIVE: Ludlow has maintained good physically defined urban form – maximising the best use of site within clearly defined boundaries – mainly as a consequence of well defined "master plan".
FURTHER INVESTIGATION: geologically rich & varied-area provides excellent opportunity to investigate how climate differs over the locality as a consequence of the relief of the land & physical conditions.	FURTHER INVESTIGATION: the hypothesis that the geophysical infrastructure together with the climate and building conurbation have an important role to play in the thermal comfort of the town should be taken into simulation so that more accurate data may be made available.
CAPABILITY OF: HIGH.	CAPABILITY OF: MODERATE/HIGH

INSTITUTIONAL REQUIREMENTS	CULTURAL IDENTITY
NO. OF INDICATORS PRESENT: 24 POSITIVE. 13. NEGATIVE. 11.	NO. OF INDICATORS PRESENT: 16 POSITIVE. 15. NEGATIVE. 1.
INITIATIVE: good human communication infrastructure – census – parish councils town council local societies & organisations – pro-active in matters of environment – Implication – this is the best way to produce local indicators for sustainable development.	INITIATIVE: creative solution to local problem of facilitating the needs of rural young people in the context of architecture & environment.
FURTHER INVESTIGATION: Land Tenure; how the land of the town may be protected against external speculation & equitably managed for all citizens.	FURTHER INVESTIGATION: address the need for local indicators for particularities of place that are not accounted for in present forms of quantitative analysis or consensus.
CAPABILITY OF: MODERATE.	CAPABILITY OF: HIGH

Summary Statement

Ludlow presents a moderate to high recording in each of the constituent parts of the assessment exemplifying the potential for a balanced and holistic approach to development. Many positive indicators under physical conditions are due to South Shropshire's ancient and consolidated geological formation together with centuries of good regenerative agricultural and land management methods. With this rich and varied landscape and an abundance of advantageous natural resources it is not surprising that the rural landscape surrounding the town of Ludlow enjoys a level of industry and productivity based upon agriculture, forestry and some tourism.

Natural resources are of sufficient quantity and quality to be used locally as building materials without resulting in serious depletion or exploitation of the supply. A renewable energy audit suggests a potential combination of energy crops, biomass and hydro-energy. The impact or ecological 'footprint' of the town of 9000 population is counteracted by the landscape immediately outside the town walls.

The hilly landscape and cool winter climate pose problems for human thermal comfort. Basin like glacial river valleys with little air flow hold excessive moisture in the atmosphere. An abundance of natural vegetation in the form of forest exacerbate these conditions, which are especially problematic between November and April when damp, mist and poor visibility are compounded by low temperatures and the low winter sun. During this period some north facing slopes remain in shade continuously, and this results in radiation frost and frost pockets. The slope on which the town is built faces south east and is therefore able to derive maximum benefit from the low winter sun. The contours of the terrain, the configuration of the town plan, and the use of local materials counteract climatic conditions: the hill-top site allows for better air flow, natural materials are able to absorb some of the moisture and cope with the expansion and contraction caused by alternating wet and dry periods. The town plan and architectural configuration are designed to maximize solar access.

Economically the town of Ludlow functions as an agricultural market town and increasingly as a centre representative of qualitative local products. It is also of considerable historical significance attracting a large number of tourists that occasionally over tax the car parks and road infrastructure of the walled town. Ludlow retains the structure of a grid master plan that was set out in the eleventh century the strong internal logic of which has adapted to meet the socio economic needs of successive generations including the present. Today the town acts as a mixed-use conurbation with a diversity of residencies catering for differing socioeconomic groups from the large houses and gardens of Broad Street to the more modest accommodation on bye lanes and burgage infill. Many of the very practical considerations that went into the planning of the town are pertinent to the present-day concern with sustainable development and efficient land-use. Almost all the land inside the town walls has been utilized. The predominance of enclosed building plans helps to ensure a clear distinction between public and private space. The town is of such a compact nature that very little public landscape is found within the walls, however a large tract of common ground is found just outside the walls on Whitcliffe and is easily accessible to residents and visitors.

The national trend for people of retirement age to leave industrial centres and seek homes in rural areas of natural beauty, if unchecked, could pose a threat to the diversity of population and cultural identity of this area. As a place of outstanding natural beauty, rich biodiversity, historical and cultural character it has become a focus for retirement age people from industrial centres. While this brings certain economic advantages that effect the upkeep and appearance of the town, it makes it difficult for the town to maintain a balanced, mixed age range, community. Sixty seven per cent of the population is over the age of sixty five. These people have usually sold homes in prosperous industrial centres and are prepared to pay highly for the amenity of living here. This has led to property speculation and greatly inflated house prices. The wages of local inhabitants is below the national average and there is a disincentive for industry and commerce to settle here because of poor connection to national road and rail infrastructure. Consequently Ludlow has experienced decline in a population of working age and an exodus of young people to the city. Unless a system of equitable housing is put in place and stimulating and productive occupations are created to encourage a residential community of employment age, it could become a large retirement centre. Its sense of purpose as a rural market town, with civic-conscious organizations and a sensible and informed local government able to plan for future development, affords some control over this problem as well as a possible solution. In contrast to the national trend for housing development, Ludlow has established limits to its growth. Land has been allocated for industrial use, and measures are being taken to provide housing and training for the youth of the area in an effort to retain a balanced population. Ludlow talks of developing sustainable tourism that will neither degrade the area nor monopolize its economy.

STAGE 4: DETERMINING

In terms of risk assessment, national policy and institutional requirements that should encourage equity and equality of opportunity for all citizens are ineffective and present the single most serious risk to sustainable development. The sustainable development of this area is dependent upon good links with national road and rail infrastructure, business and industry suitable for this area and legislative policy that provides realistic incentives for purposeful local occupations for a population of employment age. National and local government must look toward innovate policy and regeneration which supports and realizes the potential of such areas as South Shropshire rather than propitiate an irresponsible mandate of 'Diversification'. This area offers the potential for the study of many concerns of significance to the longevity of rural cultural and economic environments.

Chapter Seven
In Search of an Aesthetic

We use words like 'sustainability', 'environment', 'conservation', 'culture', 'green', 'community spirit', 'global society', themselves riddled with ambiguity, in debate over the confusing and controversial issues affecting the whole of our planet. Attitudes in the professions of architecture and landscape reflect this ambiguity. This means that the public's interest in its environment tends to be 'problem oriented' rather than secure, healthy and enjoyable. The depth of understanding and tolerance that is needed to achieve a balanced interaction of attitude on a global scale, which sustainability involves, may be considered an idealistic utopian dream.

Do we have a precedent in theoretical and philosophical thought on landscape and architecture that is universally applicable and relevant to our concern for sustainability? Does this have a visual validity? Does it suggest ways forward towards an aesthetic that is representative of the wholeness of landscape and architecture?

Aesthetic concerns in the 20th century were not so much about the symbiotic relationship between man and his environment, as perceived through landscape and architecture, as they were about man's dominance and control of all areas of his environment. Sustainability poses the question of whether there can be an environmental aesthetic, the general principles of which have human spiritual depths, and of whether this may be assimilated into a global consciousness of sustainability without devaluing the relevance of local identity.

This chapter looks at the writings of Leon Battista Alberti (*On The Art of Building in Ten Books*), Jay Appleton (*The Experience of Landscape*), Steven Bourassa (*The Aesthetics of Landscape*) and Roger Scruton (*The Aesthetics of Architecture*). Alberti, while not denying the importance of an aesthetic, writes about building, giving specific advice on capitalising on location and climatic conditions. This approach is important today with the need to reduce the use of artificial energy. Jay Appleton puts forward the idea that beauty is some sort of a reflection, or imitation, of an underlying order that cannot be perceived except in so far as it is manifest in perceptible things. Bourassa, Scruton and similar thinkers give the human and cultural response to landscape and architecture. Roger Scruton asks, what is architecture? Why is it important? How should one build? The conscious and subconscious connections between man and the environment, whether these are attributable to man or nature, are essential life forces.

20th-Century Background to Architecture
Encouraged by the rapid growth of industrialisation, the first half of the 20th century was characterised by a certain readiness to receive and experience rapid change. Circumstances were conducive to creative individuals making certain innovations, and the 'First World culture' was poised to embrace these innovations. With this readiness to see in a nontraditional manner an emphasis was placed on the architect as an individual creator. The architect has a building problem that has to be solved in the context of design and he designs a form that fits the purpose. The traditional aesthetic theories of Greece and Europe, classical versus Nature, were questioned and architecture faced an ambiguous future.

Modernism is characterised by an architecture of rationalism and functionalism with no place for idealisation or the imitation of nature, or for traditional criteria of style. It has posited a totalitarian solution to urban problems. By contrast, Post-Modernism presented a mixture of eclectic permissiveness, symbolism and contextualism. It has posited an incremental nature for urban problems.

It is interesting to note the political and economic conditions of post-modernity and modernity. Both these periods were characterised by the growth of capitalism, but in the 1970s a relatively rigid 'Fordist' mode of standardised mass production was replaced by a regime of 'flexible accumulation' characterised by considerable flexibility of both production processes and consumption patterns. In the 1980s globalisation of capital and financial markets set in. Whether this is a creative or destructive force on sustainability is open to argument, depending on the potential of universal equitable development. However, this force was too strong to be resisted significantly by local, regional or even national efforts.

20th-Century Background to Landscape

The modern concept and use of the word 'landscape' developed at the same time as the evolution from feudal to capitalist forms of land ownership. The intimate tie between land and user was severed with the development of capitalism. This put many people at a distance from open stretches of land and they began to view the countryside from afar and call it 'landscape'. As with many other interesting, but not quite palpable, categories of study originating in the 19th century, landscape has remained somewhat isolated. The profession of landscape architecture was established, which both gave importance to the study of landscape and isolated it from a possible development in conjunction with architecture.

There are signs of change. Given the present concern about overpopulation, the depletion of the world's natural resources and the high energy requirements of modern living, in cities in particular, benign landscaping is increasingly regarded as an ally in all concerns connected with the environment. If man wishes to sustain a quality of life for future generations there is every reason to start relating landscape and architecture in a kind of 'wholeness'.

In the interests of sustainable place we need to appreciate the benefits of maintaining healthy landscapes as well as developing appropriate building technologies for specific geographical locations, not only as a means of reducing high energy consumption but also as the human response to local and distinctive identity. There is a need for a common aesthetic to encompass both landscape (the human response to local and distinctive identity) and architecture (appropriate building technologies).

Aesthetic Sources   Consideration of the following questions provides part of the background for an aesthetic that is more appropriate to sustainability than to any style of architecture or landscape. Are there signs of an aesthetic that is universally applicable and relevant to our concern for sustainability? If we are to make a global impact on the influences that destroy sustainability it must be by accepting that all people can share similar aesthetic experiences in the perception of their visual surroundings. Only through a common aesthetic can all people feel that the pursuit of sustainable place is purposeful, recognisable, definable and therefore eventually rewarding within the quality of man's life. So the question is asked: 'Does sustainability have a visual validity that can be expressed as an aesthetic?' It is not the intention to posit such an aesthetic – only to present a case in its favour. This would provide evidence of interaction, of a relationship between landscape, man and architecture, and show that this could be met by common human response.

Leon Battista Alberti

Leon Battista Alberti wrote *On the Art of Building in Ten Books* in the middle of the 15th century, in Renaissance Italy (Alberti 1994). He was probably the first person to write on architecture since Vitruvius over a millennium earlier. He looked on the writings of Vitruvius as a challenge and in his own work makes constant comparisons with ancient Greece. However, unlike Vitruvius, who wrote retrospectively and recorded the works of individual architects, Alberti consciously sets out to prescribe how the buildings of the future were to be built. He wrote not just for architects but also for all who were interested – princes, merchants and patrons. He insisted that the ultimate criterion is neither written nor ruined examples, but nature.

His concept of nature has more in common with the Latin *natura* than present-day 'landscape'. His interpretation is similar to the natural philosophy of ancient Greek writers. A considerable part of the reasoning behind the *Ten Books* is concerned with the interaction between natural environment, climate and location, and building type. Much of the advice he gives on where, when, why, and how to build in respect of location and climate would satisfy present-day concerns about the environment and energy use, and bears similarities to what we may term environmental design or bioclimatic design. In Book Ten, 'Restoration of Buildings', he has this to say about cooling:

> Air is a more effective means of cooling than shade . . . in a building, when air reaches an open space, especially one exposed to the sun, it becomes warm; but if it passes through a more constrained and shady passage it comes out quicker and cooler . . . In order to make the shade cooler, it might be useful to protect the roof with a second roof, and the wall with a second wall; the greater the space between them, the cooler the shade will be. Anywhere sheltered and protected in this way will grow less warm. For the gap has almost the same effect as a solid wall of equal size, and it even has an advantage, in that whereas a wall would retain heat and be slower to absorb the cold, the air between the double walls that we have described will maintain an even temperature.

Does Alberti present us with an aesthetic that can be applied equally to landscape and architecture? Here, it is useful to remember that Alberti is challenging the work of Vitruvius. On the one hand he is telling us how much he respects the thought of the Greek philosophers, and on the other he seeks credit for himself as a knowledgeable person. Consequently, he sometimes describes the philosophies of the ancient Greeks in order to then present his own thought and thus gain acclaim for himself. So there is some confusion over what he is saying about the philosophy of architecture and nature. For example, in Book Nine he states: 'The great experts of antiquity . . . have instructed us that a building is very like an animal, and that Nature must be imitated when we delineate it.' He does not say this is his philosophy. 'A building is very like an animal' implies that a building has a biological process of functioning. Alberti writes about how buildings should be designed to interact with nature and maximise the potential benefits of location, site, climate, winds, sun and water – not that they produce those effects themselves. He does refer to parts of a building as if it were a body, with the use of words such as 'bones' and 'figure'. That 'Nature must be imitated when we delineate it' suggests that the actual outline of a building should look like forms in nature. However, he describes the representation of natural forms only as part of the detail of ornamentation. The likeness to a human figure is metaphorical: 'For every body consists entirely of parts that are fixed and individual; if these are removed, enlarged, reduced or transferred somewhere inappropriate, the very composition will be spoiled that gives the body its seemly appearance.' His work does stress the importance of the 'appropriateness' of building to location, and he strongly advocates the use of scaled models in this process. It must be remembered that before he wrote his 10 books he had set out the new method of constructing three-dimensional space on a two-dimensional plane – 'monocular perspective' – first formulated by Brunelleschi.

The nearest Alberti comes to explaining an aesthetic of his own is through the use of the word *concinnitas* (Latin = fitness). He tells us that *concinnitas* flourishes most in 'Nature herself' and calls it the 'spouse of the soul and of reason'. *Concinnitas*, which Jacob Burckhardt (1984) described as Alberti's 'most expressive term', is firstly an experience gained from the appearance of Nature, architecture or city, but also one that is gained through listening to music or reading poetry.

What does *concinnitas* involve? In Book Nine, where Alberti discusses the theory of beauty, he writes: 'From this we may conclude . . . that the three principal components of that whole theory into which we enquire are number, what we might call outline, and position. But arising from the composition and connection of these three is a further quality in which beauty shines full face: our term for this is *"concinnitas"*. . . It is the task and aim of *"concinnitas"* to compose parts that are quite separate from each other by their nature, according to some precise rule, so that they correspond to one another in appearance.' And: 'Beauty is a form of sympathy and consonance of the parts within a body, according to definite number, outline, and position, as dictated by *"concinnitas"*, the absolute and fundamental rule in Nature.'

It is interesting that he conceives of a oneness of aesthetic experience as an 'absolute and fundamental' law of nature which dictates the human design aspiration. He does not differentiate between aesthetic experience which originates in man-made design solutions, and aesthetic experience which originates in natural formations or occurrences. To make this clearer 'number' means quantity and also quality; 'outline' means more specifically, measured drawing or outline; and 'position' relates to the decisions that determine the arrangement of buildings, and a building, to a site.

What may we conclude about *concinnitas*? Firstly, it is an aesthetic experience gained through appearance in the case of landscape and architecture. Secondly, that in landscape it is present through a natural, not man-made, order and that in building it occurs when a specific combination of visual elements come together. Thirdly, the inference is that beauty is more likely to be achieved if these elements come together through an exactness of care and design. Does this mean that Alberti regards *concinnitas* as something experienced by an elitist group of visually trained people? Well, it would seem not, for in Book Two he writes: 'It is remarkable how some natural instinct allows each of us, learned and ignorant alike, to sense immediately what is right or wrong in the execution and design of a work. It is precisely with regard to such matters that sight shows itself the keenest of all the senses.' He then explains that whereas all may sense the visually inappropriate, it is only the few who have the ability to correct this.

Alberti gives us a design vocabulary that emphasises the interaction of climate, location, site and architecture. He expresses an aesthetic that satisfies the preliminary requirements of sustainability both globally and locally. Beauty is composed of the interaction of quite separate parts (a shared science); these are brought together by the exactness of technique and beauty is the result of this synthesis or consonance. Alberti's concept of an aesthetic has an underlying dependence on nature, if not the more inclusive relationship of man and nature being subject to the same universal laws of creativity. The order of this creativity has to do with appropriateness, and skill and care in execution. And finally, it has a universal appeal. Everyone is able to recognise the beauty in 'appropriateness' but not all are able to explain this or correct something that looks inappropriate.

Jay Appleton

In contrast to Alberti, Jay Appleton writes almost exclusively about landscape. He is in search of an aesthetic for it, and throughout *The Experience of Landscape* (1975) he asks: 'What is it we like about landscape and why?' Some of his reasoning may apply to both landscape and architecture, in respect of the questions asked earlier about whether there are signs of an aesthetic for sustainability, and whether sustainability has a visual validity.

Appleton takes into consideration the thoughts of philosophers such as Berlyne, who posits that aesthetic behaviour has emerged out of an evolutionary process; Lee, who believes the inspiration and uplift we derive from certain qualities in scenery can be attributed to conditioning, and that we could therefore learn to obtain aesthetic satisfaction from other conditions; and David Stea, who sees the liking for landscape as what he calls 'territorial behaviour' synonymous with a desire to take possession of place. The philosophy expressed by Brenda Colvin has already been mentioned: 'Humanity cannot exist independently and must cherish the relationships binding us to the rest of life. That relationship is expressed usually by the landscape in which we live'. All this begins to seek out and understand not only the inter-relationship between man and landscape, but also the dependence of man on nature.

This argument is developed in Appleton's Habitat Theory and Prospect-Refuge Theory (1975). The Habitat Theory proposes that aesthetic satisfaction from contemplation of landscape stems from spontaneously perceiving features that act as sign-stimuli indicating conditions in the environment which favour both biological and psychological survival, whether or not they really are favourable. This could apply equally to landscape and architecture. So the aesthetic experience is gained through looking attentively at place. The immediate visual sensation prompts a mental action related to the ascertainment of conditions favourable to survival both biological and psychological. But are we just concerned with life at the level of existence? Surely we need also to experience a reflection of human creative and intellectual qualities? How does Appleton explain the powerful aesthetic excitement experienced by perceiving such potentially dangerous and awesome sights as the Victoria Falls?

The Prospect-Refuge Theory postulates the following: because the ability to see without being seen is an intermediate step in the satisfaction of many of those biological and psychological needs, the capacity of an environment to ensure the achievement of this becomes an immediate source of aesthetic satisfaction. This goes back to the basic instincts of man. Early man needed to find a cave quickly to protect him from the dangers of a hostile environment. Exposure to the elements, or being in view of other animals, meant imminent danger or death. Therefore, the most advantageous position was one in which he himself was hidden from sight, but had the advantage of being able to survey the whole of his environment and assess potential dangers or difficulties. Although there are no longer such threatening conditions, psychologically man retains this instinct and has it built into his aesthetic appreciation of place. Hence Appleton is saying that landscape which affords both a good opportunity to see and a good opportunity to hide is aesthetically more satisfying than one which affords neither. However, there is no conclusive consensus that proves this a universal truth.

Perhaps Appleton is merely stating a philosophy that was fundamental to Plato over 2000 years ago: the idea of a physical object being, as it were, the manifestation or representation of some ideal equivalent. This concept has recurred in one form or another throughout the history of human thought. It has played a central role in all religions, because religion deals with areas of existence that can only be reached through symbols. Rather, Appleton is probably suggesting a much more instinctual interaction, common to all people. He proposes a relationship between man and the environment that is based on quite different, and much simpler, premises. Namely that man is descended from ancestors who, being at risk as soon as they were born into the world, reduced the danger of premature extinction proportionately in the only way they knew – by using the environment to further their chances of biological existence. This is instrumental in the concept of sustainable place. Are not people today, faced with so many forces that could destroy the environment, compelled to have a cognitive feel for landscape and architecture? Our senses, especially visually, are becoming attuned to the perception of certain benign or malign stimuli in the interaction of landscape and architecture.

Appleton's Prospect-Refuge Theory, although developed for landscape in particular, has implications in all spatial experiences. Grant Hildebrand (1994) has applied it to 33 of Frank Lloyd Wright's major houses. All are analysed in detail in terms of their spatial characteristics. His findings give weight to Appleton's aesthetic. 'Fire-places, seating, ceiling-form, glazing, terraces, and roof overhangs are seen to follow a repetitive organisation or pattern characterised by complementary juxtapositions of "prospect" (a condition in which one can see over considerable distance) and "refuge" (a place where one can hide).' Pleasure is derived from the lead

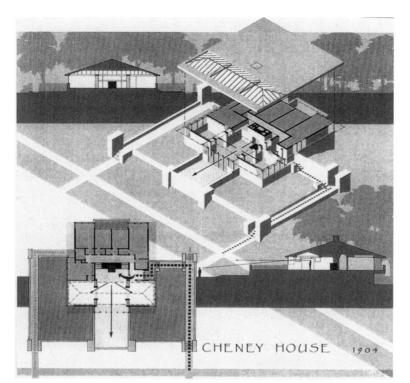

The Cheney House, Frank Lloyd Wright, 1904 (Hildebrand 1994).

The Palmer House, Frank Lloyd Wright, 1950–1 (Hildebrand, 1994).

into the house, an experience of refuge spaces, and the heart of the house, where the ability to see distances without being seen is afforded. Hildebrand does not suggest that prospect-refuge is not to be found in other architecture in an elemental way, but rather that with Wright this is a controlled design strategy. 'The thesis here is that the degree to which they are present in Wright's work appears to be unique. If Wright has a claim, and there is wide agreement that he does, to a quite extraordinary significance in architectural history especially that of the dwelling, this seems to me to be an essential part of its foundation.' He concludes: 'Beauty in a fundamental sense is related to characteristics of prospect and refuge.'

Everyone would probably agree that there is both excitement and comfort in viewing a potentially unknown, dangerous or constantly changing environment from the stability of a secure vantage point. This is a component in aesthetic satisfaction in landscape and architecture. Landscape is not synonymous with environment; it is the environment perceived, especially visually perceived. Kevin Lynch (1976) describes how we are culturally attuned to think of sensed form as a surface phenomenon: 'A lustre applied after the inner essence of something is formed.' He goes on to explain: 'But surfaces are connected to interiors. They play a key role in the functioning of the whole, since the surface is where any interchange goes on. All that we know and feel beyond our genetic inheritance comes to us from surfaces.'

Steven Bourassa and Roger Scruton

The 'culture'-based aesthetics of Bourassa and the 'architectural'-based aesthetic of Scruton present a case for the particular and localised. Steven Bourassa in *The Aesthetics of Landscape* (1991), and Roger Scruton in *The Aesthetics of Architecture* (1979), complement each other in that they are in agreement on a common aesthetic that would encompass both landscape and architecture.

Bourassa notes that landscape and architecture are similar because they are both aesthetic objects that function as settings for human activity. Scruton argues that one of the distinguishing features of architecture, as an aesthetic object, is that it is 'localised', therefore, in his terms, a good building reflects a well-developed 'sense of place' on the part of the architect. This localised feature of architecture suggests that a building's aesthetic value is very much dependent on the quality of its surroundings, and that the building itself has an impact on the aesthetic value of adjacent buildings and the whole scene. Consequently, the implications of the 'localised' nature of architecture lead to the conclusion that the aesthetic object of architecture should be the landscape rather than the individual building. As Scruton says: 'We expect an architect to build in accordance with a "sense of place", and not to design his building – as many a modern building is designed – so that it could be placed just anywhere.'

The distinction between landscape and architecture as aesthetic objects, noted by Bourassa, is that 'architecture implies modification by human agency while landscape does not'. Landscape and architecture share both functional and public qualities. In both we have a mixing of the aesthetic and the utilitarian. In both landscape and architecture it would be inappropriate to abstract aesthetic elements without considering their interrelations with functional qualities. The 'publicness' of both landscape and architecture suggests that one cannot study aesthetic qualities without reference to the values they symbolise. Architecture's public quality implies that it necessarily has political, social or moral implications. According to Scruton, 'A building may stand as the visible symbol of historical continuity, or equally as the enforced announcement of new-fangled demands ... Bourassa explains: 'Landscape is at least as public as architecture, and the values it displays are as inescapable as those of works of architecture.' Both are critical of the Modern Movement because it did not address the 'publicness' of architecture. For them, it tended instead to emphasise the idiosyncratic whims of the individual architect or the peculiar aesthetic tenets of Modernism rather than values that were meaningful to the public.

Scruton is especially critical of purely functional architecture: 'A merely functional building does not lend itself to the imposition of a public meaning. It stands in the world like an individualistic ego, pursuing its own aim in defiance of, or indifferent to, the aims of others. And that is how the observer will see and understand it – it has no more life or reality than the individual purposes which gave rise to it, and contains no intimation of any objective world of values beyond the pursuit of limited desires. In seeing it under that aspect – as a manifestation of architectural individualism – the observer will see the building as alien to himself. On the other hand, a building which answers to his aesthetic sense, which extends to him an invitation to understand and identify, such a building provides him at the same time with an intimation of public order, of a world responsive to objective values, a world in which the individual is realised and not merely gratified.'

From this we can deduce that Scruton considers aesthetic judgement an indispensable part of everyday life, that it is recognised at an individual level and that it has a public nature recognised by the common people as a collective value. Therefore the aesthetic, in landscape and architecture, should be part of the process of self-realisation, whereby man knows that the world is responding to his worth – and knows this through a sense of wellbeing and satisfaction gained from seeing and identifying with certain images in landscape and architecture. A component of aesthetic sensibility is the task of endowing the world with an order and meaning. In the appearance of landscape and architecture, humanity may be rebutted or confirmed. However, the difficulty here is that cultural and personal attitudes vary from region to region, nation to nation. An aesthetic that satisfies the universal objectives of sustainability must be transcultural and transpersonal yet allow for these regional expressions of identity to be nurtured. In this sense Appleton's Prospect-Refuge Theory is more appropriate, although limited.

Bourassa's 'critical regionalism' also takes a cultural stand. Here connections are made between Appleton's reasoning from biology and Scruton's 'sense of place'. To quote Bourassa: 'The critical regionalist's concern with the creation of meaningful places necessarily involves an emphasis on contained urban forms or enclaves and their boundaries . . . Some of the most satisfying spaces are enclaves open to prospects.' Cultural stability and identity are emphasised in the symbolic meanings of places or, more specifically, the creation of spaces for groups of people. 'Aesthetic value' is attached to places that afford symbols of cultural stability and identity. The critical regionalist wants to intensify cultural identity by increasing the 'cultural density of places'.

Within this theory of critical regionalism Bourassa also argues for creativity within local culture: 'A necessary condition for creativity is a thorough knowledge of the context of the problem to be solved . . . designing and planning necessarily occur within a context and inadequate attention to that context explains the failure of many design efforts.' Here he cites the example of Australia's new Parliament House in Canberra, by Romaldo Giurgola. Giurgola had not visited the site when the design solution was conceived. The vast rearrangement of the landscape, and the introduction of nonindigenous vegetation, showed an insensitive disregard for natural conditions. From a cultural standpoint it seems that Giurgola had worked from second-hand sources – films and publications – and was unable to grasp the Australian culture in any meaningful sense. Acknowledgement of culture was reduced to the decoration of the building with certain symbols of the natural environment devoid of local meaning, such as green marble columns in the foyer evoking eucalyptus trunks. An opportunity to bring about a culturally vitalising architectural solution has been lost. For his part, Bourassa emphasises the need for a creative and critical engagement with all dimensions of the environment.

Kenneth Frampton (1983) suggests that the restrictions imposed by consumerism and land speculation stifle the expression of regional identity. In architecture this means 'the practice of architecture seems to be increasingly polarised between on the one hand, a so-called "high-tech" approach predicated exclusively on production and, on the other, the provision of a "compensatory façade" to cover up the harsh realities of this universal system.' He regards a sustainable architecture as one that resists these processes and cultivates cultural identity, while at the same time optimising the use of advanced technologies without regression into nostalgic historicism. He defines the aim of critical regionalism as being 'to mediate the impact of universal civilisation with the elements derived indirectly from the peculiarities of a particular place.' Peculiarities range from the quality of local light to vernacular forms of construction. In essence, a global consciousness will not destroy local cultural identity.

This chapter has touched briefly on some interesting possibilities that indicate an aesthetic of sustainability – qualities that relate to man's needs within the context of his place, as manifested in landscape, architecture and their arrangement. With Alberti, beauty is seen as a very inclusive relationship with nature in that they essentially share one creative process. This is concerned with bringing together diverse essential elements of physical and biological dynamics, with regard for skill, expertise, technique and appropriateness, in such a way that they transcend the mundanity of their parts and become a thing of beauty. Both Alberti and Appleton attribute significant importance to human comfort as a component of the aesthetic. This is seen not only in terms of human comfort and biological security, but also in terms of psychological comfort, afforded especially by the creation of prospect and refuge spaces. Bourassa and Scruton, in their writings on critical regionalism, confirm the aesthetic value of enclave and prospect spaces as symbols of cultural and general stability. Frampton, on the other hand, puts forward the view that an aesthetic must strengthen cultural identity morally, socially and politically and is important to both the individual and the collective public of a place. This strengthening should occur without recourse to nostalgic historicism or a style representative of global anonymity.

The following chapter brings together contemporary examples of design methodologies that address the creation of places. Some of them express potential only, and have not yet reached a point of physical reality. As we are concerned with an aesthetic of being and moving in a three-dimensional plane it is only the varying phenomena of the reality of place that can test the aesthetic. In the words of Appleton: 'It is the expectation aroused by the deflection in the vista that causes aesthetic excitement, and that expectation is one phase in a comprehensive environmental experience.'

Chapter Eight
Coming Through

The following projects exemplify the evolution of design strategies and methodologies, in the context of place, that embrace some of the concerns of sustainability. The framework of assessment has not been applied to any of the places in these projects. The works represent design solutions from a diverse range of practices in response to a variety of client briefs. Discussion of the projects acknowledges that the conceptualisation and practical application of these design solutions are dependent not only on an informed and enlightened attitude towards sustainable development on the part of landscape, architecture and planning practitioners, but also on the state of sustainable development awareness of clients, connected institutions and policy-makers, the cultural receptivity of the inhabitants of specific environments, and the skills and expertise of those carrying out construction. However, the following examples do provide specific and particular solutions to some of the demands of sustainable development. They may be seen to have responded to considerations of climate change in the reduction of fossil-fuel and energy emissions; reduced resource use and encouraged biodiversity; worked with the physical conditions and ambient energy sources in satisfying certain functional needs and thermal comfort; adjusted to the institutional directives and policy pertinent to particular place; and to have respected and strengthened cultural and aesthetic qualities so that the new developments identify with place and are liked, bringing pleasure to their communities.

Port area, Colombo, Sri Lanka.

MILLENNIUM CONSORTIUM WINNING DESIGN COMPETITION ENTRY FOR REDEVELOPMENT OF THE FORT AREA OF COLOMBO, SRI LANKA (1996)

The following builds on a presentation by Mario Cucinella, of the Millennium Consortium, given at the second symposium on urban sustainability, held at the Architectural Association in London in March 1997. It involves the analysis of the winning design competition entry for the redevelopment of the Fort area of Colombo, Sri Lanka in October 1996. The Millennium Consortium is formed from three diverse practices based in Europe – Mario Cucinella Architects (MCA), Paris; Brian Ford Associates, UK; and Ove Arup and Partners, UK – plus planners, economists and architects based in Sri Lanka. Urban design and proposals for key sites were undertaken by MCA, Brian Ford Associates with consultant Mark Hewitt developed the energy guidelines, microclimate assessment and design building initiatives, and the Sri Lankan partners were linked into the process by contributing ideas in parallel. Ove Arup and Partners made the proposals for improving infrastructure, traffic flow and public transport. The competition, in part, arose out of the need to restore the Fort area of Colombo following bomb damage. However, the winning proposal takes an overview of urban planning, in consideration of the future projected expansion of container trade to the port area and local aspirations to attract global business concerns to the centre of the city.

The restoration of the Fort, which is the business area of Colombo, includes the redesigning of the Janadhipathi and Mawatha districts to incorporate high-rise office blocks and appropriate servicing facilities to accommodate potential expansion of business and commerce. This area is also the cultural heart of the city and therefore it is vital that development caters for an improved mix of activities to benefit both the local population and visitors. The development proposals suggest certain institutional and economic pressures on the urban planning side: the physical accommodation of a transport infrastructure necessitated by increased business and expansion; and uncertainty surrounding economic and service infrastructures especially because of the fragmented landownership that exists in this area. This would suggest the need for a design solution that will have a sustainable impact not only environmentally but also on the stability of the place, politically, economically and socially. Mario Cucinella, in his introduction to the project, emphasised that the search for equilibrium had been fundamental.

In considering the circumstances that gave rise to the need for development and how qualities of stability, equilibrium and consistency may be effected through good design strategies, significant a priori reasoning has gone into this project through an exploration and evaluation of the physical configuration and ecological infrastructure of the area, climate, environmental heritage, and the potential for demographic and economic development. In terms of the interconnectedness of landscape, architecture and master-planning in bringing thermal comfort to a particularly difficult city microclimate, the project is innovative and hopefully enlightening in respect of future design strategies. Urban design strategies are developed in response to historical and contemporary contexts, climate and the need for incremental development and social stability. This project is important to the concept of sustainable development in the use it makes of a master plan to initiate incremental development that is not dependent on sequential time and therefore allows for qualitative growth as need and resource dictate; and in the use made of climate and ambient energy sources through the interconnectedness of design strategies in landscape, architecture and master-planning, to satisfy functional needs and thermal and psychological comfort. Although the development as a whole was not intended to be dependent on time targets, immediate benefit to the inhabitants of this environment was to be felt through altering the streetscape, especially by landscaping, to modify the effects of an uncomfortable microclimate. This was to have been carried out without a great capital investment. This scheme was not built due to political instability at the time (civil war) and the consequent lack of inward investment. The recent resolution of this longstanding conflict will, one hopes, herald an era of stability in which such projects may be realised.

The significant contribution of the project to sustainable development is purposeful intent and not final design details. The presentation material states the aim of the design proposal: 'The final proposal will be the result of deep cognitive work and of a detailed programme responding to precise objectives.' The project is evaluated within the confines of these objectives. The objectives of the proposal became:

- accessibility
- distribution axes
- landscaping and zoning
- climatic response
- open spaces
- building.

Accessibility, Distribution Axes and Open Spaces
The master plan maintains the same grid pattern as the existing plan. **(Figures 18 and 19)** Strong emphasis and identity are given to the town centre through the accentuation of the east/west axis to create a dynamic curve with a number of focus points where north/south axes interject. This is probably to be further enhanced by landscape features – a 'greenfinger' to the east and the sea to the west. **(Figure 20)** The concept of a 'pinball' urban design strategy is used to link focus points that are aesthetically memorable – prospect views and a visual reference points – and aid legibility of access, presenting a clear image of the city. **(Figure 21)**

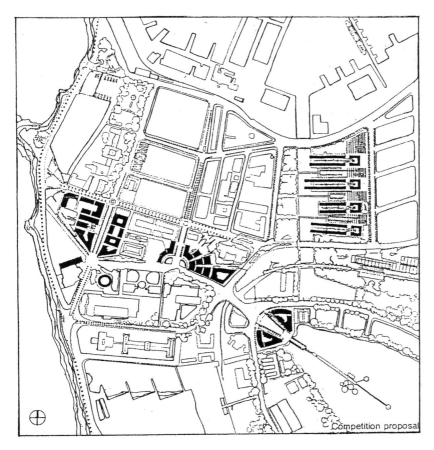

Figure 18:
Colombo master plan; Millennium Consortium competition proposal.

Figure 19: Colombo existing plan.

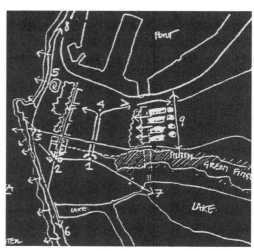

Figure 20: Landscape features.

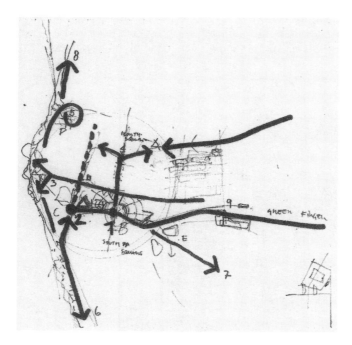

Figure 21: The 'pinball' urban design strategy.

The focus points are a mixture of framed views of the sea and city, squares, piazzas, green open spaces and heritage landmarks linked by boulevards and linear parks. Focus points are a strong element in the master plan. They are also referred to as nodal points, suggesting resting places, places of human interaction, meeting places where everyone of a particular place passes through at some moment in the day and stops to rest or talk. The focus points create the framework for future development. The pinball strategy means the approach to the centre of Colombo is marked by a series of focus points that underline the progressive increase of activity and urban density. These points provide a dynamic organisation of the space and create a clear system of visual references. **(Figure 22)** The physical creation of these focus points will mark the demarcation from analysis into objective. The growth of the master plan begins with these spaces and continues with the definition of volumes leading to the design of individual buildings. A model showing the position and scale of development on the distribution axis suggests space is considered horizontally and vertically. Space is created so that core buildings have a prospect view of the sea. In the development proposal a mutual compatibility between conservation and future development is presented which may aid cultural adjustment to change. It quotes Ashworth (1993), expressing the attitude that development within historic cities is neither 'preserving nor recreating a past city, but shaping a new city in which preserved forms and past associations play an important contemporary role'.

The master plan becomes the pivot, a still centre of equilibrium, around which all coexist – past and future, analysis and objective, beginning and end. Through an evolutionary and flexible process, rather than through a time sequence, the master plan is to encompass past, present and future. After an initial setting out of spaces, any part of the development may be carried out at any point in time, thus allowing for purposeful development as need, function and resource permit. Time becomes a qualitative factor, relative to need, function and resource. This is in contrast to the more typical approach of time used as a quantitative measurement to determine stages of development. A qualitative approach is maintained throughout this project. The consortium looks to existing elements of quality within the locality and climate, and begins, in the truth of these, an evolutionary process of change and development. Aesthetic is not dictated by style.

Significant in terms of sustainable development is the sensitive and purposeful preparation of a master plan that through incremental phasing to accommodate change aids, by evolutionary process, transitions in the life and form of the city that could otherwise have instigated disruption and instability. These are: conservation, protection and enhancement of certain existing features which stabilise and strengthen local identity; the intention to give immediate gratification to local inhabitants through creating spaces and landscape features to offset disturbances that may occur through the evolutionary development over an indefinite period of time; and, through their scope to define and control future development, reassurance about the form of future growth with none of the restrictions connected with sequential time. Transport infrastructure includes pedestrianising, or allowing only limited access to, the whole of the Fort area. This area would then be served by a tram-loop system connected to a wider network of trains and buses. Increased through-traffic as a result of the expansion of the port was to have been diverted away from the city centre by the building of a new bridge.

Figure 22:
Definition of the
volumes of core
buildings.

Landscaping and Zoning, Climate Responsivity and Building

This project is a particularly good example of the combined integration and interaction of design strategies in landscape, architecture and master-planning to utilise the ambient forces inherent within an environment in order to both bring human thermal comfort and reduce energy needs and emissions. Therefore it is important to describe what is known of the climate and existing contemporary and past development.

Sri Lanka is situated at 6° to 9.5° north and 80° to 81.5° east. This location has a very warm humid, monsoon climate. The concepts of passive cooling for this project are based on typical local ambient temperatures for the monsoon period, December to May, of between 25° and 32°C. On average there is a 3°C swing between day temperatures and night-time cooling. Relative humidity for this period is high, 75 to 95 per cent. Wind speed varies between 0.5 mph to 1.5 mph at ground level. Design strategies here are based on wind speeds at a height of 10 metres, which average 3mph. In the monsoon period rainfall can be excessive, up to 250 to 300 millimetres a day. In a study by Ratnaweera and Hastnes (1996) the climate is termed outside the threshold of human thermal comfort and cooling is a critical issue. However, it provides fecund condition for plants and trees. The same study states that modern office buildings and dwellings are designed on the assumption that electrical air-conditioning systems will be used to cope with the country's high humidity and warm climate, but that old traditional buildings seemed to preserve indoor comfort better without these systems. So, working within sustainable development objectives, it would be an advantage to reduce the high energy needs of electrical air-conditioning systems while providing for human thermal comfort in both internal and external environments.

Physical conditions and landscaping play an important part in the design methodology, acknowledged in the aim: 'To create a "park" as a coherent place where different activities are organised, over time, together with the open spaces and the natural elements.' An abundance of vegetation will cool the ambient city temperature and improve air quality and public amenities. However, in a place where high relative humidity is a problem cooling by plant transpiration alone may exacerbate thermal discomfort if adequate attention is not given to air movement, absorbent surfaces and spaces. Here the introduction of natural vegetation is to play a significant role in localised cooling. The external spaces, ground elevation and roof surfaces are shaded through varying levels and types of landscaping. In the outdoor environment thermal comfort is further improved through considerations of the permeability of urban form and its effect on street-level air speed, and radiant exchanges off elevations and large tarmac surfaces. Design solutions are put forward that would respectively increase wind speeds and air movement, and convective cooling, and reduce the effects of solar gains and reflectance reradiating off surfaces through the use of shade and vegetation.

The prevailing north-east and south-west wind direction is utilised to give maximum penetration of available breeze at street level in both north-south and east-west streets. **(Figure 23)** This is done through avoiding street-level obstruction; using clean-stemmed vegetation with a horizontal canopy, such as the royal palm; and proposing that gaps are left in the north-south streets so that the breeze can pass through. It is also suggested that roof levels could provide particularly comfortable outdoor spaces because airflows are less obstructed. The east-west streets have the sun directly overhead for most of the day and the tarmac surface of the street is therefore in need of shading. Here it is suggested that stages of horizontal shade canopy, such as palms and pergolas, over a central pedestrian park running the length of the street would prove effective. Tree canopy will absorb heat to be released in the cooler temperature of night-time rather than reflecting heat on to elevations. In the north-south streets elevations are subject to high solar gains for part of the day. **(Figure 24)** We are told that these streets pose a microclimatic problem. Air movement is strongly influenced by the height/width ratio. Because of their width – over 40 metres, and the reflectance and reradiation off nonabsorbent

ORIENTATION OF STREETS

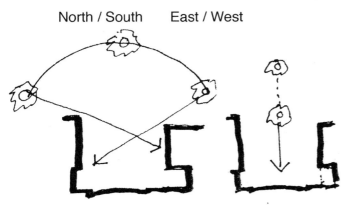

North / South   East / West

Janadhipathi	Church Street
York Street	Mundalice
Duke Street	Chatham Street
Bristol Street	(Lotus rd)
(Lotus rd)	

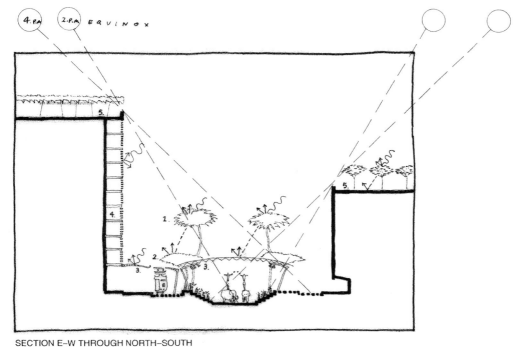

SECTION E–W THROUGH NORTH–SOUTH

Figure 24: North-south oriented street.

surfaces, they could act as 'sun bowls'. Again, to prevent or offset this, linear parks with varying stages of horizontal canopy are introduced at the centre of each street, while building canopy or first-floor projections provide protection and shade for pedestrian walkways close to buildings. As a further building design strategy, double-skin facades, moving the glazing back from the perimeter of the building, will give shade and make breezeways. Planting on the roof tops will reduce the impact of solar radiation on the building as well as providing the amenity of new pleasant outdoor spaces.

The core building block uses design strategies responsive to climate and the reduction of energy use. The objective was to realise the potential of what is termed Low Energy High Rise. The customary high-rise office block, which houses extravagant energy-consuming plant for maintaining adequate conditions for human thermal comfort, uses 260 kilowatt hours per square metre per annum. Here it is estimated that Low Energy High Rise would reduce this to 135 kilowatt hours without detriment to the servicing and facilities of the building or the quality of the internal environment. This not only has advantages in terms of environmental sustainability but also reduces the amount of economic investment needed on the part of the client.

Detailed plans were not produced for this project. However, Figure 25 illustrates an amalgamation of passive and low-energy strategies in relation to new core buildings. As mentioned, the double-skin facade will create a breezeway, protecting the interior of the building not only from the extremes of high temperatures and high relative humidity, but also from the effects of noise pollution. The volume between the inner and outer skin acts as a 'chimney stack'. With vents open, increased airflow in the volume created around the inner skin would keep the building cool. During less humid and cooler periods, windows in the inner skin may be opened onto the transparent vent so that stale air is drawn out of the building. Figure 25 shows this system working with a building which incorporates an atrium. The atrium floor is higher than street level; this presents another possibility of convection cooling. Air movement will be created through air being sucked from the lower street level through the narrow opening and drawn up to the top of the atrium void. Transpiration from internal vegetation would further aid cooling. The directions of the arrows suggest a system of cross-ventilation is also operating between the atrium and void of the double-skin facade. At roof-terrace level a breezeway is created by the increase in air speed at the higher altitude and there is protection from solar gains through the use of a pergola. A system of shades, deflectors and reflectors is also apparent on the exterior of the buildings and the interior walls of the atrium. Given the obvious energy disadvantages of the typical high-rise office building, the lack of space and the disinclination to use that space horizontally for building development within city centres, low Energy High Rise becomes a blueprint for the future.

With this intelligent, holistic approach to sustainable development comes the need for intelligent user awareness. Whereas a couple of centuries ago a cognitive feel for conditions of thermal comfort made an intuitive understanding of when and when not to obstruct spaces or open or close windows and vents a necessity, modern societies have grown accustomed to automated systems. In the interest of sustainability, energy reductions have to be made, so buildings dependent on large energy-consuming plant for automated functions and user services will no longer be a sensible investment. Many of the design strategies discussed here draw the occupants of place into natural interactions with their environment. However, users will want to maximise what energy is available for essential electrical services. No one would wish to climb 50 flights of stairs to reach their office or go without an efficient public transport system. Suggestions are made to capitalise on the locality's potential to supply alternative forms of energy, such as a waste power-generating station and the use of wind turbines sited on the southwest breakwater. The consortium also gives alternatives for a sewage system that would prevent pollution of the sea, an efficient water-management programme that takes advantage of rainwater collection and an adequate drainage solution for the monsoon season.

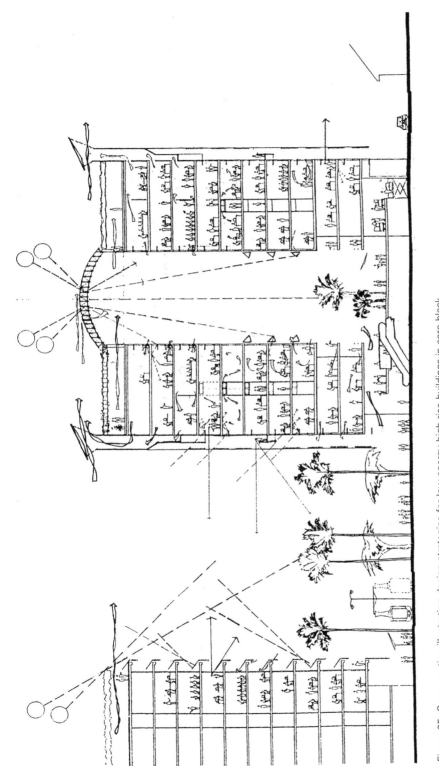

Figure 25: Cross section illustrating design strategies for low-energy high-rise buildings in core block.

MASTER PLAN, CANON'S MARSH, BRISTOL HARBOURSIDE, UNITED KINGDOM: EDWARD CULLINAN ARCHITECTS

Edward Cullinan Architects' master-plan design for a 16-acre piece of land known as Canon's Marsh, on Bristol Harbourside, makes a significant contribution to sustainable development in relation to the urban regeneration of a brownfield site close to a city centre. This case study appraises the plan that was given outline planning permission in October 2001. Further detailed design development has followed since then. Potentially, this design proposal will set the form and character of future development for an area that is likely to grow in strategic importance in its interconnection with the city and wider communications. Here there is the unique opportunity to guide and initiate the formation of an environment that has a particular cultural identity arising out of its harbourside location. Initially, two dominant physical conditions had to be addressed: the decontamination of the site and design strategies to minimise the threat to human thermal comfort of a windy harbourside location where wind speeds, direction and frequency may pose a problem.

Institutional factors governed the design of the master plan. The Harbourside planning brief was approved as Supplementary Planning Guidance to the Bristol Local Plan in July 1998. Consequently landowners involved with the site undertook a commitment to cover the cost of decontamination and site clearance in preparation for development, under the Landowners Joint Dispersal Agreement. The cost included the remediation of a gasworks site and contribution to a road infrastructure. In return they were given the incentive of a commercial return from the new development. This is a development for profit scheme.

A detailed public consultation process, to involve the local population in consensus and establish public criteria for the development of the site, began, overseen by a panel of key stakeholders known as the Canon's Marsh Consultative Group. As a result the brief given to the master-planning team by the developers, Crest Nicholson Properties Ltd, sets out a range of various types of space provision for this mixed use development in order to achieve the threshold of return required. The approximate proportions are: 40 per cent residential of mixed tenure (of which 10 per cent is affordable housing); 40 per cent commercial and public sector; and 20 per cent leisure and retail. It was considered advantageous to limit the last type to specific locations within the site so that it did not interfere with the character of place as a whole. Institutional policy defining both the cost and quantity of affordable housing on new development is vague. The government expectation is that 30 per cent of a residential development is affordable housing; however, this is not as yet a legal requirement and should be measured against other benefits the development brings to the community.

Of the issues which are of interest to sustainable development, two are appraised here. How far can good urban design and form facilitate the process of emerging cultural identity? To what extent is the careful consideration of landscape, architectural form and master-planning able to influence the discomfort factor of a prevalent ambient force such as wind?

Cultural Identity

The site is of strategic importance not just to the city of Bristol and the harbour area, but also to a much wider environment through its convenient position for transport communications. However, at present it is a predominantly derelict and contaminated site with a history of isolation from the city to the north, and a cultural heritage of 19th- and 20th-century industrial development of gasworks, timber yards, a railway depot and tobacco bonds. To the north, Anchor Road, which is part of the busy A4 that feeds the city centre, divides Canon's Marsh from the city. Therefore there must be a strong connection across this road to make integration with the city possible. The floating harbour, an environment of intrinsic character and pleasant acoustic quality from the sounds of maritime activities and sea birds, occupies the southern boundary. This area has the potential to form a nucleus of cultural quality and density. In effect the new development is to form a satellite development, strongly linked to the city but having its own nucleus and idiosyncratic particularities. **(Figure 26)**

Figure 26: Canon's Marsh, Bristol Harbourside. The boundary to the site development is outlined in white.

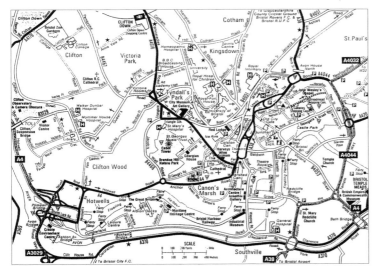

Figure 27: The site of the redevelopment is shown within its immediate urban context.

Boundary

Figure 27 shows the development within its immediate urban context and suggests a larger local boundary. Given that main highways form barriers influencing the movement of all species, the larger pragmatic boundary for the locality is likely to be formed by two main roads: the A4 along Hotwell Road and Anchor Road to the north, and the A370 along Coronation Road to the south, vertical intersections formed by continuations of the A3029 and A38 close the boundary to the west and east. The master plan should take into consideration future sustainable development of the two distinctive horizontal landscape features – the floating harbour and River Avon – by allowing for greater emphasis and flexibility of access. It would be unreasonable to ignore these two dominant features which, in terms of cultural identity, amenity and the potential to generate purposeful occupational and economic activity, are significant in future sustainable development.

The immediate sustainable objective is to secure and strengthen dependence with the city, and for this to happen in physical terms a powerful and dominant link across the A4 boundary is essential. However, within the local boundary as a whole there is the possibility of diversity and a degree of localised autonomy. The population of this area will have convenient access to communication infrastructure without recourse to the city centre. The roads that form the bound-ary lead conveniently to the M5 and Clifton Suspension Bridge, opening up communication links with the southwest, Wales, the Midlands and the north. To the east of the site Bristol Temple Meads railway station gives communication links with London and the southeast. The master-plan design report stipulates considerable car-parking facilities, approximately 1200 spaces, which may prove a convenient asset for new businesses. Some of this parking will be placed inconspicuously below ground level. As part of the remediation of the gasworks site, the voids formed by the removal of the contaminated material will, where convenient, form basement parking.

An architectural perspective of the proposed development by Richard Carman, enables an assessment of its quality through contained urban form. **(Figure 28)** The defining of urban form, which may be seen clearly in the skyline from a distance, helps to establish a strong image and identity for the place. The visual impact of this development, within its wider urban setting, has been considered carefully from both inside and outside the boundary area. This prevents the new development from becoming part of a confused urban sprawl. Figure 29 shows the important views across the site. These are points at which the visual identity of the place will either prove credible from an objective distance or provide a point of inclusive refuge from which to view the prospect of a wider city environment. The perspective view suggests the marrying and completion of dynamic rhythms and forms, old to new. From the master-plan design report, some of the important considerations were the completion of a harbourside walkway through to Hotwell Road; the completion of the Brunel Mile from Temple Mead station to SS *Great Britain*; links across the floating harbour; the enclosure of Millennium Square; and the balancing and integration of existing dominant buildings, such as the strong convex form of Lloyds TSB seen on the right of the perspective, by new forms within the proposed development, to give a harmonious appearance.

Figure 28: An architectural perspective of the proposed development from the south.

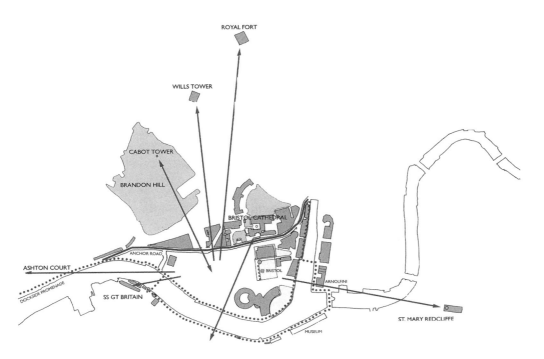

Figure 29: Important views from and across the site.

Axis, Spaces, Building Type and Form

The main axis of the site connects positively across Anchor Road with the green public spaces of College Square and College Green, Bristol's largest civic space. **(Figures 30 and 31)** The cathedral becomes the dominant landmark in this connection, overlooking the old and the new. The pivotal point of the new development occurs a third of the way down the main axis at Millennium Square. From here secondary axes fan out towards the harbour area. The intention of the designers of this master plan is to give visual pleasure from outside and inside the site. From the cathedral, the eye is led out along a tree-lined boulevard, to be known as Cathedral Walk, along the diagonal axis to the floating harbour and beyond. From the harbour the view up Cathedral Walk is effectively closed by the commanding presence of the cathedral. From Millennium Square we see both down Cathedral Walk and Millennium Promenade towards the harbour inlet. The latter presents the prospect vista of SS *Great Britain* on the south side of the floating harbour. So, after a short distance along the axis, the transition from the old to the new is made positively through a clear identity with place. Giving an established landmark like the cathedral such dominance will have significant cultural advantages and help in sustaining equilibrium and stability as the proposed development emerges into reality. The cathedral is symbolic of cultural heritage, incremental growth and longevity, a reassuring and stabilising presence. By association, the occupants of the new development will wish to connect with these qualities as part of a larger identity that is representative of their city. Later, as public

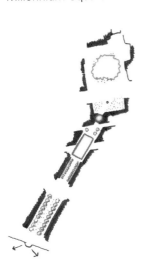

Figure 30: Spaces along the main axis.

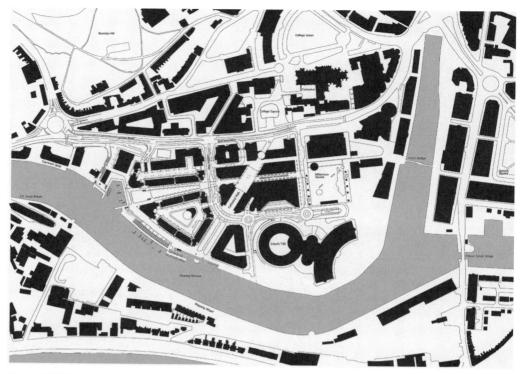

Figure 31: The master plan of Canon's Marsh site within Bristol's urban context.

attitude adjusts to the new forms of the development and functional patterns of behaviour are established in relation to these forms and spaces, the image of old looking over the new will give a sense of equilibrium. The clear logic to the main axis is to lead from the old to the new, and the way it fans out towards the harbourside not only presents direction towards the new urban nucleus but also extends the potential of future development across stretches of harbour.

Public consensus has requested that the spaces along this main axis are predominately green, again linking into the large green space of College Green in the city. In terms of landscape heritage little will remain from the old site of Canon's Marsh. In the decontamination process it must be cleared and replaced with new soil and vegetation. Some of the planting of trees will be containerised to allow for the underground parking facilities. However, the desire to bring pleasure through establishing what is in effect a green finger into the city is part of the aesthetic of environmental sustainability. It is regarded as benign. The site generally has extensive planting of trees. If this place cannot as yet be said to be of great significance to biodiversity, the new landscaping will undoubtedly take up some of the impact of city energy emissions and pollution as well as providing a public amenity.

Amenity, surprise and visual stimulation are predominant characteristics of this master plan, and make possible the experience of large prospect vistas and intimate inclusive views. Cathedral Walk leads to the Harbourside Walk where many small vistas of the floating harbour are to be experienced, framed through an avenue of trees. Corners of buildings are defined by towers and give framed views of a space beyond. The continuity from old to new, and of traditional city form leading out to a new urban nucleus, can also be seen in the harmonious and sympathetic use of space and form. From the master plan within the urban context, it can be seen that the shape, size and directional flow of spaces and building plan knit together. The new may be described as the completion of the missing pieces of a jigsaw puzzle. The more public

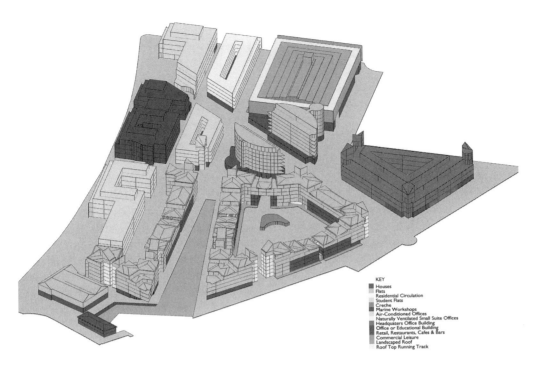

KEY
Houses
Flats
Residential Circulation
Student Flats
Creche
Marine Workshops
Air-Conditioned Offices
Naturally Ventilated Small Suite Offices
Headquaters Office Building
Office or Educational Building
Retail, Restaurants, Cafes & Bars
Commercial Leisure
Landscaped Roof
Roof Top Running Track

Figure 32: An axonometric of the proposed building blocks.

and commercial buildings have been arranged at the periphery of the site, to the north and east.
(Figure 32) The scale and function of these buildings are compatible with similar existing development along Anchor Road and balance the large convex form of Lloyds TSB. Thus the urban residential nucleus is afforded protection, buffered from the noise and activities of the city by the
scale, type and form of commercial buildings and facing the more private harbour environment.
The whole of the development has a 24-hour occupancy use and safety considerations.

Houses, flats and residential circulation routes are protected from main city functions and
noise, and occupants are able to enjoy the more private views and intimate sounds of the harbour environment. However, an interesting factor of the residential quarter, and the master plan
in general, is the lack of completely private outdoor space. All space is either public or transitional.
This may be an uncomfortable prerequisite of sustainable development in British cities, where
land scarcity and the numbers of homes required necessitate compact areas of human habitata-
tion so that scarce natural resources such as countryside are not compromised by development.
The design of the residential properties is based on the proportions of the traditional terrace building within the Bristol area: three storeys in height with a 3.9-metre frontage and a simple strong
order of single 2-metre square openings on each floor. Residential buildings are enclosed around
a semiprivate court or in mews form. **(Figure 33)** Many of the dwellings will have the semiprivate outdoor space of an elevated balcony and at eye level it will be possible to look out from this
over the heads of passers-by. **(Figure 34)** In effect these transitional spaces will give some psychological comfort in that they provide 'prospect' views while affording some degree of protection and 'refuge'. However, they would not be adequate as safe, functional, outdoor playing
spaces for children, or suitable for private human relaxation or the propagation of gardens.
They do give an indication of the expected lifestyle of the city dwellers who will occupy this
site. Further incentives to encourage a certain quality of community are suggested through the

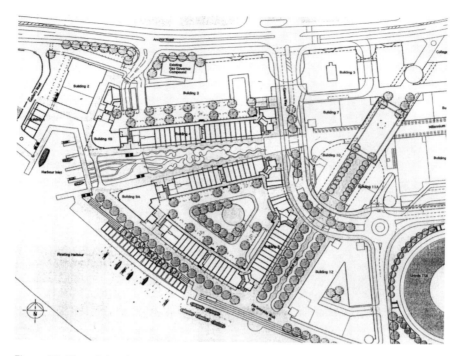

Figure 33: Plan of the site showing buildings and landscaping.

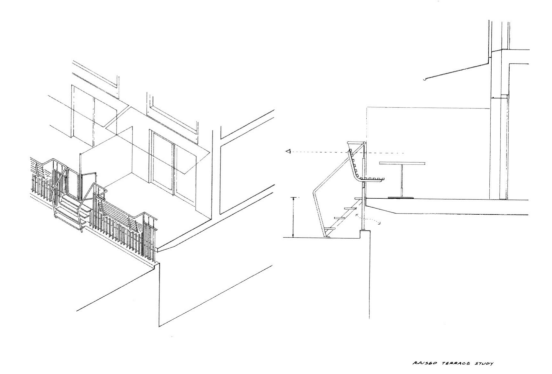

Figure 34: The eye level from the balcony gives the comfort of the refuge-and-prospect position.

provision of craftsmen workshops in the harbour inlet area. In other areas of the harbourside it is hoped that the provision of small retail and eating premises will encourage local entrepreneurs.

The proposal suggests areas of incidental character that project a more detailed identity. Residences will be painted in various muted hues, and the corner framing towers in a stronger shade. The conservation of the purifier house and the refurbishing of the walls and paving of Gasferry Road will emphasise the Victorian past. It will also add the interest in the colour and texture of grey Pennant stone in the harbour inlet vicinity. It is planned, where possible, to recycle materials from the existing site into the walls and paving of the new development. The following summarises the designers' vision of what it will be like to enter the new place: 'The glittering glass facades of the leisure building overlooking Millennium Square, the university, the office buildings along Anchor Road will create a shell through which you pass through red brick gateways to a progressively "softer" world.'

Designing for a Windy Harbourside Urban Location

The most significant physical condition on the site of Canon's Marsh, which could pose a threat to human thermal comfort, is exposure to strong, frequent, prevailing southwesterly winds. Yet a stated objective of the brief to the architects is that this site should be enjoyed in all kinds of weather. This section appraises how the detrimental effects of wind may be mitigated through careful design consideration of landscaping and architectural form. This is an area where design should be informed by accurate meteorological data and take advantage of available scientific simulation processes such as wind-tunnel tests. However, this scheme is at a proposal level and therefore possible solutions are investigated below. In terms of national legislation, which requires all local authorities to identify renewable energy resources by 2006, wind should not be dismissed as a strong ambient energy source. Large-scale wind turbines would not be visually acceptable, but unobtrusive, small-scale wind generators, in keeping with the character of the development, could prove an interesting challenge for sustainable engineering.

A desktop study of the site's envisaged exposure to wind, and the likely effects of wind on the proposed architectural conurbation, has been carried out by the University of Bristol Flowcentre in the Department of Aerospace Engineering. The study is based on the architectural configuration represented in Figure 32. The most prevailing and strongest winds come from the southwest and are likely to be warm and moist. The site is protected from a colder and less frequent, secondary wind from the northeast by high land to the north and the mass of high buildings on the boundary of the site at Anchor Road. The report concludes that conditions for pedestrians should be tolerable, highlights problem areas for the development and, where possible, suggests remedial action.

The master plan and architectural conurbation will affect wind- and airflow around the site. In some areas wind nuisance will be mitigated while in others it will be accentuated. The wind from the southwest approaches the buildings on the northern embankment of the Harbourside at approximately right angles. If unprotected, these bear the initial brunt of the wind force. Figure 35 suggests the likely effects of wind shear on the residential block facing the harbour. The building is likely to experience wind 'nuisance factors' at the corners where there are maximum suction regions. At ground level, downward-flowing air is decelerated by the presence of the ground and turns into the oncoming windflow to form a vortex that is drawn out to the high suction areas at the corners. Wind turbulence is likely to affect both the outdoor thermal comfort of the residents of the building and pedestrians passing around the corners of the block. The corners are especially subject to high pedestrian-level wind. The wind encounters freeway when it reaches the openings of Cathedral Walk and Millennium Promenade and is likely to accelerate. Dependent on the height of buildings to the width of street canyons, the wind will be either channelled through the site or dispersed vertically out of the street canyons. The main axes from the harbour into the site will render the place vulnerable to wind disturbance. The configuration of

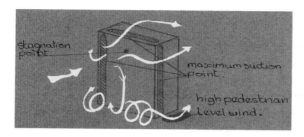

Figure 35: The effect of wind shear on a tall building.

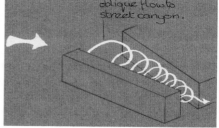

Figure 36: Wind forming a vortex up a street canyon.

spaces and buildings at the intersection of Cathedral Walk and Millennium Promenade, around Millennium Square, is likely to produce unique patterns of wind turbulence. From the master plan it is apparent that wind speeds will be uninterrupted along the centre of Cathedral Walk. **(Figure 31)** There is also a rise in land level from the Harbourside to Lower College Crescent, which may even cause some acceleration of wind speed. The wide street canyon of 30 metres may possibly mitigate this. Along Millennium Promenade, from the widest (30 metres) and windiest opening at the harbour inlet, the wind is effectively funnelled towards a narrowing of street canyon (17.5 metres) just before entry into the vicinity of Millennium Square where it intersects with the airflow travelling up Cathedral Walk. It is possible that either the large space of the square or the speed of the airflow up Cathedral Walk, or both, will draw the airflow through the narrow section of Millennium Promenade so that it is accelerated on entering the vicinity of the square therefore creating a turbulent force. This is known as the Venturi effect. Wind will approach Millennium Promenade at an oblique angle and will probably form a vortex, with a similar effect on buildings to that illustrated in Figure 36. The report by Bristol University suggests certain remedial actions to compensate for possible wind nuisance, such as landscaping and the provision of vertical screens to balconies to provide shelter, and the provision of a horizontal canopy running along the Promenade at first-floor level. It is to be remembered that this street places importance on the provision of outdoor patio spaces for residents.

Landscaping

The appraisal of how to alleviate wind disturbances on the Canon's Marsh site is based on considerations of the proposed architectural conurbation. Landscaping, which can be equally, if not more, effective at diffusing wind speed and energy, needs to be considered in correlation with this report. Architecture and landscape need to be considered together, as landscaping will not only act as a diffuser of wind but can also redirect it so that points of turbulence may vary from those in the Bristol University report. The site is to be effectively cleared of all existing vegetation as part of the decontamination process and then replanted with trees and shrubs. **(Figure 33)** The main street planting is to be selected from London plane, silver lime, English oak, gingko, honey locust and crab apple. All these deciduous trees have moderately dense foliage and branch systems. The growing rates and maximum mature heights of the trees vary. Lime and plane mature fairly quickly, in 30 years. Some such as oak take longer to mature but will provide extensive opportunity for biodiversity. However, in terms of wind control the difference between landscape design solutions and those applied through architectural form is one of permeability.

Taking the areas that were discussed above – the Harbourside residences, Cathedral Walk, the harbour inlet and Millennium Promenade – the presence of landscaping greatly changes the scenarios. Consideration of the line of residential buildings fronting the harbour, at a right angle to the southwesterly winds, provides a reasonable scenario of what will happen when the wind meets an impermeable surface such as a building. **(Figure 37)** The force of the wind is directed over the top of the building and quickly resumes its unhindered progress. Vigorous turbulence is likely to occur leeward of the building, which in this case will be the northeastern part of the courtyard. A contrasting scenario is what happens when wind meets a permeable surface such as a shelterbelt of trees, which is proposed by this development. **(Figure 38)** The wind is filtered and much of its energy is absorbed, so it emerges on the leeward side at a slower speed. This prevents the wind forced over the top from sweeping down to the ground, and resuming its normal pattern and speed, until it is some considerable distance downwind. Poplar trees probably form the most effective shelterbelts. However, of the trees described, above lime and plane would also serve this purpose. A moderately dense line of trees provides useful shelter for two to four times its height upwind and as much as 15 to 20 times its height downwind. This therefore becomes the scenario for these residential buildings when landscape has developed. **(Figure 39)** Corners are still going to be points of wind turbulence, especially for pedestrians. However, slightly extending the tree alignment to that of the building, together with allowing wider spacing of trees towards the entrances to the harbour inlet and Cathedral Walk, will gradually open up the permeability of the shelterbelt so that its effect on wind is tapered off laterally and vertically, thus reducing the wind velocity on the corners. The shelterbelt will be further effective if there is some density of vegetation at ground level. Here again along the Harbourside Walk this seems to be the intention of the landscape proposal, which shows shrubs and floating reedbeds. **(Figure 40)**

The avenue of trees along Cathedral Walk will also have a diffusing effect on wind, and strong wind will tend to travel through the centre of the avenue. The wide opening at the harbour inlet and consequent funnelling of wind up the street canyon towards Millennium Square still remains a problem and no tree planting is envisaged for this area. Millennium Promenade will be significantly exposed to southwesterly winds. Lack of trees and unprotected patios suggest that the outdoor thermal comfort of residents and pedestrians is likely to be threatened by winds as strong as 14 metres per second. It is an objective of the master plan to capitalise on the prospect views from the centre of the site and it therefore becomes a priority to give uninterrupted vision from Millennium Square through the harbour inlet towards the SS *Great Britain* on the opposite side of the harbour. A solution may possibly be found through consideration of a shelterbelt on the southern embankment of the floating harbour. As wind passes over water it has a tendency to drop down and gather speed, which here will contribute to the speed and velocity of wind entering the harbour inlet at ground level. A shelterbelt, even at a distance, will greatly reduce the risk of this happening.

In conclusion, this promises to be a development of strong visual identity with beautiful prospect views that will afford visitors and occupants considerable aesthetic pleasure. It is an excellent example of how a master plan may integrate the old with the new and set the potential for the formation of a new urban nucleus with a particular cultural identity. The opportunity to give cultural definition to an emerging residential quarter with its own unique qualities has been taken. Ideas for workshops and small businesses for local entrepreneurs, which would give the Harbourside further cultural identity, will be dependent on incentive structures. It is likely that windy physical conditions will cause some discomfort in particular areas of the development. However, with the high degree of psychological comfort afforded occupants by the pleasant visual environment, the toleration threshold of thermal discomfort is likely to be high.

COFFEE CREEK CENTER, CHESTERTON, INDIANA, USA: WILLIAM MCDONOUGH AND PARTNERS

The architectural practice of William McDonough and Partners of Charlottesville, Virginia, acted as design team leaders to a group of firms and individuals in the master-planning of a 'new town' development: Coffee Creek Center, Chesterton, Indiana. This provides a prototype for sustainable development in respect of the integration of landscape, architecture and master-planning. It has been recognised by the Urban Land Institute, the US Environmental Protection Agency and the US Department of Energy as a role model for future development. Environmental sustainability objectives are strongly linked to good business incentives and the stimulation of new markets for innovative products and ideas. This section appraises the valuable contribution to environmental sustainability of this rural town development on a 640-acre greenfield site adjacent to the town of Chesterton and within commuting distance of Chicago. **(Figure 41)** In 1995 the

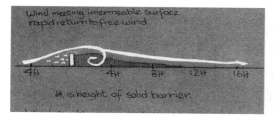

Figure 37: Wind meeting an impermeable surface.

Figure 38: Wind meeting a permeable surface.

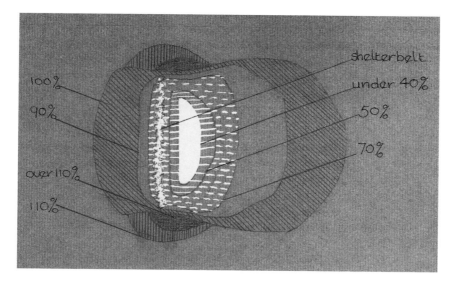

Above: Figure 39: The effect of the shelterbelt on upwind and downwind reduction of wind speed.

Figure 40: Landscaping of the Harbourside Walk.

site, predominantly farmland divided by a riparian corridor, was acquired by the developer Lake Erie Land. The master plan outlines the distribution of land to meet the needs of a polycentred urban conurbation, community-planned mixed-use development. **(Figure 42)** This incorporates residential, retail and office buildings, with a system of streets and spaces oriented towards pedestrian use. The master plan has a dynamic and particular local identity through the approach it takes to restore and utilise the central riparian corridor as common landscape space linking a development of mixed-use neighbourhoods. **(Figure 43)** This appraisal refers to the Coffee Creek Center design report by the architectural practice of William McDonough and Partners.

Underlying the conceptualisation of the master plan is a specific philosophical approach by William McDonough and Michael Braungart (McDonough & Braungart 1998) that equates sustainability to the environment, equity and economy. This acknowledges sustainability as involving the interconnection of environmental health, social health and economic health. The virgin site, with its exceptional landscape feature, becomes the perfect component for the realisation of such ideas and objectives. The process is largely unencumbered by considerations of unalterable layers of incremental building development, overpopulation or compact high-density conurbations. The design of Coffee Creek makes certain assumptions about, and has expectations of, what a sustainable society should be like and how it should function within the context of this place. At the root of this is the belief in a partnership, for their mutual benefit, of man and nature. The coexistence of man and nature is essential in a positive concept of the world. By living in kinship with nature man can work with natural systems such as climate, geology and ecology, in mutually beneficial and regenerative ways. Nature is similarly benefited, by the elimination of practices that would deplete natural resources and cause degradation such as monoculture, soil erosion, pollution and excessive energy emissions. Consequently, design strategies work in harmony with the local physical conditions of this prairie site – climate, geology and ecology – setting a framework for a symbiotic relationship between man and nature. However, this is a 'for profit only scheme' and sustainability is used as a sales mantra. It is good business economically, based on the growing concern over health, pollution, energy and amenities. People who move to Coffee Creek are buying into this. Investors are investing because they see that a potential exists for profit on these terms.

Ecological Restoration

A significant contribution towards sustainable development, not only in terms of environmental health but also of cultural identity, is the ecological restoration of the watershed. The master plan has addressed man's need to understand his cultural heritage through conservation of remnants of ancient landscape. It illustrates an intelligent consciousness of his responsibility to restore the ecology of a region where previously his presence and activities have degraded the quality of the environment of the watershed, almost to a point of deadness exemplified in states of erosion and the depletion of biodiversity. Directly prior to this development, the land had been used as what is described as 'farm field'. **(Figure 44)** The Coffee Creek design report suggests that patterns of agriculture and industrial technology, together with a lack of good management, have resulted in the degradation of the natural ecosystems. One of the objectives of the master plan is the integration of people and natural systems, explicitly through the design of the communities. Building sites, parks and gardens have been designed with water-management, native plant communities and soil structure in mind. On areas of remnant lands **(Figure 45)** ancient systems of control are exercised, with the controlled use of fire to remove dead or overgrown vegetation, activating space and light for new life to grow. The riparian corridor becomes the central artery of this master plan. This, the Coffee Creek watershed, is part of the Great Lakes Basin. Therefore any ecological restoration that affects the supply or cleansing of water here will directly affect the quality and flow of water through farmland and settlement on its course ultimately to Lake Michigan. Consequently many people, plants and animals are affected by the environmental health of this

Coffee Creek Centre: landscape restoration in progress (top); eroded banks stream banks prior to restoration (left); and a stream bank undergoing restoration (right).

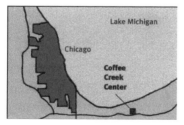

Figure 41: The geographical position of Coffee Creek Center, Chesterton, Indiana.

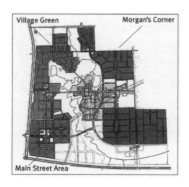

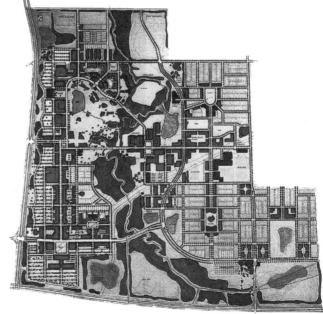

Figure 42: Master plan of Coffee Creek Center.

Figure 43: The relationship of neighbourhood units and the riparian corridor.

watershed. Likewise, the settlement and ecosystems of Coffee Creek will be affected by development upstream. No indication is given in the design report of any institutional requirement or regional programme that may assess the whole of this water-catchment area.

The master plan takes inspiration from the restoration of this dynamic, sensory curve of landscape that cuts the site in two, and in contrast sets the tone of order and formality. **(Figure 42)** It becomes the reason behind the relationship of built form and natural landscape. It is possible to envisage how this natural environment is to work in terms of facilitating human need, for health, amenites and psychological comfort, and biological functioning while protecting biodiversity. **(Figure 45)** This dynamic curve, running through built development, is neither a 'leave alone' strip of wilderness nor a nostalgic romantic return to nature. It is a pragmatic approach towards natural environments in the enlightened knowledge of the significant threshold of 21st-century concerns of pollution, energy requirements and emissions, and the need for human psychological comfort. This aims to be a positive working environment.

The landscape of Coffee Creek has been divided into three land area components: new native landscape which encompasses most of the common open spaces of the site, including areas adjacent to the creek corridor, where indigenous plants will replicate the nature of remnant land; cultural landscape where, again, native species will be planted but will be designed for the more developed area of the site around buildings, roads, parking areas and village greens; and remnant lands, small tracts of ancient landscape where heritage and particular habitat need to be conserved.

Further functional objectives of the Coffee Creek landscape design are described in the report. Landscape designs are used which facilitate the infiltration of precipitation where it falls. This is to reduce the need for storm-water infrastructure, such as land drains, and reduce the risk of local flooding. Certain plants such as swale will be used to filter, slow down and absorb storm water. Attention is given to the biodiversity of the prairie, savannah ecology with the planting of native plants, which are not only most likely to thrive better here without high maintenance involving irrigation and chemicals, but will also benefit soil enrichment and attract native wildlife. Over time native plants will restore the original structure and composition of soils. Of course, a most significant effect of this ecological restoration will be the unique aesthetic attributes of appearance and the sense of cultural identity this will foster.

A further dimension of the riparian corridor is watershed protection and wastewater management. **(Figure 46)** The designers describe this as: 'Ecologically intelligent infrastructure', which 'strives to weave the systems that sustain human settlement into the cycles, rhythms, and systems of the existing site. At Coffee Creek Center, cost effective storm water and wastewater systems are designed to complement rather than bypass natural systems.' Whereas

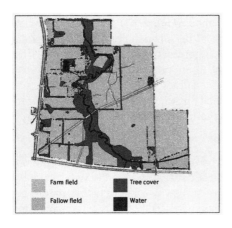

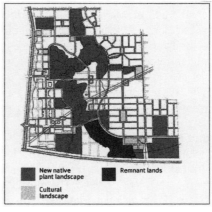

Far left: Figure 44: The Coffee Creek site prior to development.

Left: Figure 45: Types of landscape.

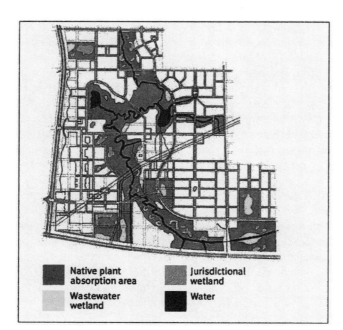

**Native plant
absorption area**

**Jurisdictional
wetland**

**Wastewater
wetland**

Water

conventional systems of storm-water management are designed to treat water as a waste product, with associated problems especially flooding, at Coffee Creek water filters directly into the soil. Here it either transpires into the atmosphere or becomes part of the ground-water system. Therefore all impervious surfaces over the site are minimised. The process of cleansing, slowing down and retaining water is effected through a number of design strategies, such as roof-top retention, green roofs, swales planted with native water-retaining vegetation, dry wells, cisterns, continuous tree-planting trenches, constructed wetlands, gravel trenches, engineered soils, perforated pipes and level spreaders. The effectiveness of these is monitored over time for water quality and quantity.

Wastewater Management
This scheme shows a real desire to integrate man into the wider picture of biodiversity, even though this is often through ingenuity rather than natural process. The wastewater manage-ment at Coffee Creek Center is dependent on the capacity of plants, soils and consequential bacteria to nurture the appropriate microclimate for the breakdown of wastes. This is achieved through the construction of wastewater-treatment wetlands. **(Figure 47)** These are artificially constructed environments, within the natural landscape of the riparian corridor but separated from the water and native plant absorption areas by impermeable liners. This process has obvious advantages over conventional indoor biological treatment systems. It reduces long-term operational and maintenance costs, may provide sediment and flood control and is an odour-free wildlife habitat. However, the project is an ambitious one and the designers concede that more conventional treatment systems may also have to be used.

Master Plan and Neighbourhoods
The designers take a traditional and logical approach to urban planning and focus on the grid form of master plan. What is inspirational in terms of sustainable development is the way this grid is interrelated with the landscape nucleus. The message is of inclusivity – nature within, nature per-meating throughout. Town planning principles are based on early 19th-century gridded commu-

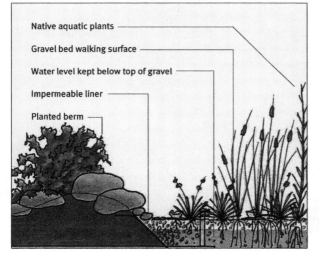

Figure 47: Details of constructed wastewater-treatment wetlands.

Wastewater-treatment wetlands.

nities. It is stated in the design report that most of the United States west of the Appalachian mountains was historically subdivided into a grid of square-mile areas, known as sections. This formed the fundamental structure that gave the region continuity and cohesiveness in the pattern of streets and property arrangements. Likewise, the designers wish to give the inhabitants of Coffee Creek Center a sense of stability and equilibrium through the acceptable forms of narrow interconnected streets, continuity of urban fabric and the potential for expansion through the extension of the grid. The master plan shows a grid of interconnected streets and their relationship to a central landscape nucleus and main highways. **(Figure 48)** No major highway forms a divisive intrusion with the site. The development is cradled within the right angle of two major highways and access to these, to the left, opens up wider communications. Otherwise development within the site is inclusive. The emphasis is on environmental sustainability; the grid system has been shaped to accommodate and protect natural features.

The urban development covers a large area and, to prevent this disintegrating into urban sprawl or anonymity, the site has been divided into a network of small community neighbourhood boundaries. **(Figure 43)** Each neighbourhood has its own particular identity. All have access to the core central corridor. The concept of these neighbourhoods is not new but reminiscent of Ebenezer Howard's garden cities or the more philanthropic Bournville or Wedgwood estates of 19th-century England. Possibly, it is futuristic in that it envisages the city as polycentred, an agglomeration of urban nuclei. However, they are designed to function within 21st-century market forces. The emphasis of these neighbourhoods is very much on the celebration of community and away from the specialisation of financial, technical, production and cultural zoning of the more global cities.

Each of the neighbourhoods is semiautonomous and may function without dependency on energy-intensive transportation infrastructure. **(Figure 43)** Jobs, housing and shopping facilities interconnect to form mixed-use urban units that are oriented towards pedestrians and encourage community interaction. Residential properties satisfy a varied mix of social and economic requirements within each housing location. It is believed that mixed income neighbourhoods promote informal social interaction between people of different cultural and socioeconomic backgrounds, and that this promotes a vital sense of social order and behaviour. As in Britain, the American dream is to continue the tradition of home ownership that is

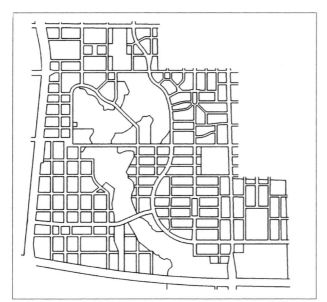

Figure 48: Master plan showing the
grid of interconnected
streets in relation to the
central landscape nucleus
and main highways.

now thwarted by the need for affordable housing in a marketplace of escalating property prices and an increase in demand for single- or couple-occupancy residences. Therefore a variety of house styles and sizes is incorporated in each neighbourhood. Great human psychological comfort and amenity are afforded all residents through an abundance of cultural landscape, public spaces and private gardens. **(Figure 49)**

Sustainable Development and Building Design
Whereas the appearance of the architecture borders on the traditional and acceptable rather than the innovative, awareness of sustainable development issues does not. Design strategies in respect of human thermal comfort and health are the result of careful considerations of the interactive and interconnected effects of relationships between landscape, architecture, new technologies and climate. The report states that buildings are designed to respect the specific prairie climate in which they exist, and are adapted to different sites and different orientations. Through a combination of advantageous orientation, correct placement of windows, and well-insulated walls and ceilings conditions for human thermal comfort, such as good levels of cooling, heating, daylighting and ventilation, need minimum backup from conventional energy supply. This passive and low-energy approach reduces artificial energy demand with a consequent reduction in energy emissions. Care has been taken to make use of ambient energy sources throughout the development. Every building site has a store of renewable energy that can be tapped for use.

The report does not give the percentage of energy supplied to this area by renewable sources. However, an interesting approach of partnership between local occupiers and local energy suppliers seems to be working in ways that make photovoltaics, wind generation and geothermal energy systems viable on a small scale. For example, local energy suppliers provide low-cost, clean power to building owners in exchange for the right to use roofs for the installation of photovoltaics. Various efficiency technologies are also used throughout the development to reduce energy consumption.

Careful consideration has gone into the selection of the materials used in buildings, without detriment to visual appearance. Development at Coffee Creek Center is very much designed to have an optimal environmental impact. Materials which have certain properties – such as a

Figure 49: Mixed-use development cultural landscape.

Below: A variety of housing around the village green.

high proportion of the product coming from a reused or recycled base – are preferred; natural resources such as timber must come from sustainable sources; substances such as volatile organic compounds which give off toxic emissions that could adversely affect human health are not used; materials that contain low amounts of embodied energy, are suitable for reuse and have been fabricated using low-impact manufacturing techniques are chosen.

The interest here has been in the symbiotic relationship of landscape, architecture and master-planning within the design of Coffee Creek Center. However, the multidisciplinary team has courageously sought the potential for sustainable development at many layers of symbiosis – social, economic, ecological – as well as addressing energy concerns and emissions. They have established the reality of a working environment, a place of sustainable development. The progress of sustaining the level of interaction, between man and environment, will be dependent not least on the enlightened attitude of the Coffee Creek Center inhabitants. This is to be monitored. With sustainability the symbiosis is between man and the planet he lives on. This association must essentially work to the benefit of both partners for mutual survival. In the recent past the land on which Coffee Creek Center is built has been abused or exploited so that it has become ecologically degraded. The ecological restoration described in the report is primarily for urban man. It is suggested that the land has been exploited for food production. Those who live on this site will now fundamentally be looking at food as an external dependency. The aesthetic excitement is the surprise created by the contrast of the sensory landscape core and the formal lines of urban development. However, this is part of a comprehensive approach to sustainable development; this place attempts to interact with nature so that it makes a positive environmental impact.

Conclusion

Sustainable Place has focused on the roles of landscape, architecture and master-planning in the sustainable development process. Based on the hypothesis: in a place, the quality and condition of landscape and architecture are indicative of the state of sustainability; of man's coming to terms with and responding to the physical conditions, his psychological and functional needs, cultural identity, and institutional requirements in a particular environment. The framework of assessment in Chapter Four makes it possible for the capability of sustainable development within the boundary of place to be assessed. The methodology allows for the characteristic feature of sustainability: the symbiotic relationship of parts – parts that are interconnected and constantly flexible, holding and pulling each other into a state of balance that acts for the mutual benefit of the whole. Sustainable development within the confines of place is similar to a state of homeostasis; the tendency for the many active cells of which a place is composed to maintain a constant and benign internal environment regardless of varying external conditions. The changes that external conditions, of necessity, activate are controlled from within. The framework of assessment is significant at a time when the impact of all development needs careful consideration environmentally, economically, socially, politically and culturally. Assessment forms a vital and necessary prerequisite in preventing costly mistakes in terms of both quantity and quality of development.

The lack of clearly defined mandates and the need to approach sustainable development issues as a dialectical argument frustrate measurement of progress, both locally and globally. Throughout this book examples have been cited that highlight developments in connection with environment and energy concerns, whether these be through new clean efficient technologies or passive systems that utilise ambient energy sources that are present in a place. However, in November 2001 the United Nations Environment Programme (UNEP) estimated that greenhouse-gas emissions were rising and that the Kyoto targets for the reduction of energy emissions by 2010 are unlikely to be met. The adverse effects of climate change – a main driver for change in concerns over environment and energy – are already evident, and natural disasters are more frequent and more devastating.

The World Summit on Sustainable Development held in Johannesburg in September 2002, which reaffirmed a global commitment to sustainable development, leant towards a qualitative approach and stressed that a determined effort, by all countries, was needed to produce a practical and visible plan for human development and the eradication of poverty. Apart from reassurances of commitments to the principles of Agenda 21 and environmental protection, little action was taken. The success of sustainable development has to be measured in terms of the persistence and endurance of certain ideals and ideas, and the readiness to act on them. In the years since Habitat I significant progress has lain not in determining action but rather in achieving a global consensus that consumption and production patterns must change, and that the protection and management of natural resources is essential for economic and social development, globally and locally.

Awareness of common aesthetic values in connection with the movement towards sustainable development has to do with the ambience of the times, considerations of what governs perceptions of beauty and pleasure, and with cultural identity. The resurgence of the last of these considerations is today being expressed in settlements of all sizes, coupled with a growing number of people who feel comfortable in all the megacities of the world and of whom it may be said that they belong to a truly global society. *Sustainable Place* has focused specifically on the design-orientated professions of landscape, architecture and master-planning whose practitioners inevitably aim to bring aesthetic qualities into the lives of inhabitants of place. Here the source of aesthetic interest is directed towards the enhancement of environment and design that is energy effective and efficient. Green seems to be the colour that all aspire to.

In this book the concept of sustainability has emphasised a kind of 'scarcity value' of natural landscape features, in both quality and quantity. Sustainability is not about a particular architectural style. Rather it is about the treasuring and appreciation of such qualities as light, spaces, clean air and thermal comfort in a way that is stimulating and pleasurable but which is, quite obviously, not achieved through any process that endangers the planet's capabilities of regeneration. Designers are showing a willingness to look into the psychology of place, what makes for individual and civic pleasure, comfort, dignity and ease of function; and to translate this into the landscapes, spaces and physical form that go to make places.

References

Alberti, LB [c1485] 1994. *On the Art of Building in Ten Books*, trans J Rykert, N Leach and R Tavernor, MIT Press (Cambridge, Mass.).

Alexander, C 1965. *The City Is Not a Tree*, Kaufmann International Design Award, Architectural Forum.

Anderson, B 1990. 'Solar Building Architecture', MIT Press (Cambridge Mass.).

Appleton, J 1975. *The Experience of Landscape*, John Wiley & Sons Ltd (Chichester), revised edition 1996.

Ashworth, GJ 1993. 'Heritage planning: conservation (an approach to managing historic cities)' in Z Zuziak *et al* (eds), *Managing Historic Cities*, International Cultural Centre (Krakow).

Barry, RG and Chorley, RJ 1992. *Atmosphere Weather and Climate*, Routledge (London).

Bateson, G 1980. *Mind and Nature (A Necessary Unity)*, Fontana (London).

Bateson, M 1900. 'The laws of Breteuil', *English Historical Review*, vol 15.

Bayliss, DG 1958. 'The lordship of Wigmore in the fourteenth century', cited in JM Hodgson, 'Soils of the Ludlow District', Rothamsted Experimental Station, Harpenden, Hertfordshire, 1972.

Beresford, M 1999. *New Towns of the Middle Ages*, Sandpiper Books.

Bole, D 1997. Private communication from David Bole, head forester, Mortimer Forest, Forest Enterprises, Ludlow, Shropshire.

Bole, D 1998. Private communication.

Border Oak 1998. Promotion pamphlet, Border Oak Design and Construction Ltd, Kingsland, Herefordshire.

Bourassa, SC 1991. *The Aesthetics of Landscape*, Belhaven Press (London).

Brown, CP 1997. 'Where Eagles Dare', *Guardian* (Society; Environment), 31 December 1997.

Brundtland, GH 1992. Cited in AJ Day (ed), *The Annual Register 1992. A Record of World Events*, Longman (London).

Buchanan, KM 1944. 'Worcestershire' in *The Land of Britain. Reports of the Land Utilization Survey of Britain*, part 68, Geographical Publications (London).

Burckhardt, J 1984. *The Architecture of the Renaissance in Italy*, Secker and Warburg (London), 1984

Chitty, LF 1963. 'The Clun–Clee Ridgeway' in IL Foster (ed), *Culture and the Environment*, Routledge & Kegan Paul (London).

Clark, J 1794. 'General view of the agriculture of the county of Herefordshire, cited in JM Hodgson, 'Soils of the Ludlow District', Rothamsted Experimental Station, Harpenden, Hertfordshire, 1972.

Clifford, S 1990. 'Turn yourself not the world upside down', *Common Ground*, The Council of Christian and Jews (London).

Clifford, S 1992. 'On buildings', *Common Ground*, The Council of Christian and Jews (London).

Colquhoun, A 1989. '"Newness" and "age value" in Alios Riegl', in *Modernity and the Classical Tradition*, MIT Press (Cambridge, Mass), cited in Mohsen Mostafavi and David Leatherbarrow, *On Weathering*, MIT Press, 1993.

Colvin, B 1948. *Land and Landscape*, Murray (London), second edition 1970.

Conzen, MRG 1966. 'The use of town plan in the study of urban history' in HJ Dyos (ed), *The Study of Urban History*, Edward Arnold (London).

Conzen, MRG 1988. 'Morphogenesis; morphological regions and secular and human agency in the historic townscape, as exemplified by Ludlow' in D Denecke and G Shaw (eds) *Urban Historical Geography. Recent Progress in Britain and Germany*, Cambridge University Press (Cambridge).

CPRE (Council for the Protection of Rural England) 1997. 'Time to Get Tough on Traffic and Sprawl'. Press release 17 April 1997. Research by Llewelyn Davies, the Bartlett School of Architecture and JMP Consultants, London.

CSEA 1998. County of Shropshire Employment Agency, Shrewsbury.

Daly, HE 1997. *Beyond Growth*, Beacon Press (Boston MA).

Department of the Environment 1992. 'Climate Change. A Discussion Document'.

Domestic Energy Fact File 1992. LD Shorrock, G Henderson and JHF Bown, BRE Report BR220, Building Research Establishment, Watford, Hertfordshire.

Eclipse Research Consultants 1997. Lecture given at Architectural Association, London, by Ian Cooper on behalf of Eclipse Research Consultants. Based on 1995 Survey of Current Practices – Environmental Initiatives in the UK Construction Industry.

Faraday, M 1991. *Ludlow 1085–1660 (A Social, Economic and Political History)*, Phillimore (Chichester).

Ford, B 1996, 'Passive Downdraught Evaporative Cooling', JOULE research project 1996–98. Lecture given at Sustainability Symposium 1, Architectural Association (London) 1996.

Frampton, K 1983. 'Toward A Critical Regionalism', PLEA (Passive and Low Energy Architecture) conference papers, Venice 1985, Sergio Los (ed). Published by Grafiche Muzzio (Padua), 1990.

Gardner, EG 1913. *The Story of Siena and San Gimignano*, Dent (London).

Gelling, PS 1996. 'Excavations at Caynham Camp Near Ludlow' (transcript), Shropshire Archaeological and Natural History Society, Shrewsbury, Shropshire.

Georgescu-Roegen, N 1971. *The Entropy Law and the Economic Process*, Harvard University Press (Cambridge, MA).

Gould, SJ 1991. 'Unenchanted evening', *Natural History* (September 1991).

Hams, A 1997. Lecture on Local Agenda 21 given to the Worcester Civic Society, February 1997, on behalf of the Local Government Management Board. Based on Local Agenda 21 Survey 1996. Compiled for the Local Government Management Board by Ben Tuxworth and Elwyn Thomas, Environmental Resource and Information Centre, University of Westminster.

Haught, JF 1993. *Promise of Nature. Ecology and Cosmic Purpose*, Paulist Press (New York).

Hawkes, D 1996a. 'Towards a sustainable city' in *The Environmental Tradition (Studies in the Architecture of Environment)*, Spon (London).

Hawkes, D 1996b. 'The Cambridge school and the environmental tradition' in *The Environmental Tradition*.

Hawkes, D 1996c. 'Building shape and energy use' in *The Environmental Tradition*.

Hildebrand, G 1994. *The Wright Space*, University of Washington Press (Seattle).

Hodgson, JM 1972. 'Soils of the Ludlow District', Rothamsted Experimental Station, Harpenden, Hertfordshire.

Hough, M 1995. *Cities and Natural Process*, Routledge (London).

Howard, NP 1996. 'The Design Challenge'. Lecture given at Sustainability Symposium 1, Architectural Association (London).

ICPD (International Conference on Population and Development) 1994. Cited in Von Weizsacker *et al* 1997. *Factor Four (Doubling Wealth Halving Resource Use)*, Earthscan Publications (London).

IPCC (Intergovernment Panel on Climate Change) 1995.

Jones, EL 1961. 'Agricultural Conditions and Changes in Herefordshire 1660–1815' (transcript), Woolhope Natural Field Club, Hereford County Records Office, Hereford.

Kuln, T 1962. *The Structure of Scientific Revolutions*, second edition, University of Chicago Press (Chicago).

Kurokawa, K 1997a. *Philosophy of Symbiosis*, Kodansha International (Tokyo).

Kurokawa, K 1997b. 'Eco-Media City 2020, Malaysia' in *Philosophy of Symbiosis*.

Lean G, 1997. 'Why My Wife Chained Up the Vicar'. *Independent*, 20 July 1997.

Lloyd, D 1977. *County Grammar School*. Private publication sponsored by Ludlow Grammar School, Ludlow.

Lloyd, D 1979. 'Broad Street (Its Houses and Residents Through Eight Centuries)', Ludlow Research Paper no 3, Studio Press (Birmingham).

Lloyd, D 1997. Private communication.

Lloyd, D and Klein, P 1984. *Ludlow. A Historic Town In Words And Pictures*, Phillimore (Chichester).

Lloyd, D, Howell, P and Richards, M 1986. 'The Feathers', Ludlow Research Paper, Studio Press (Birmingham).

Local Government Management Board, 1997. See Hams 1997, *op cit*.

Ludlow Advertiser 1998. *Ludlow Advertiser*, May 1998.

Lynch, K 1976. 'Managing the sense of Region', MIT Press, Cambridge, Mass.

McDonough, W and Braungart, M 1998. *Cradle to Cradle: Remaking the Way We Make Things*, North Point Press (New York).

Meadows DH, Meadows DL, Randers J and Behrens CW 1972. *The Limits To Growth*, Pan Books (London). Report for the Club of Rome's project on 'The Predicament of Mankind'.

Meadows, DH, Meadows, DL and Randers, J 1992. *Beyond The Limits (Global Collapse or a Sustainable Future)*, Earthscan Publications (London).

Ministry of Agriculture 1996. Local data taken from South Shropshire District Council June census returns, 1996.

Mumford, L 1961. *The City in History*, Penguin Books (Harmondsworth, London).

Murray, K and McDonald, S 1997. Transcript of 'The City', BBC Radio 4, 1997.

Phillips, C 1997. 'Sustainable City' (London and Globalisation), Environment and Energy Department, Architectural Association, London.

PiU (Performance and Innovation Unit), November 2001.

Ratnaweera, C and Hastnes, AG 1996. 'Enhanced cooling in typical Sri Lankan dwellings', *Energy & Buildings*, no 23.

Sassen, S 1991. *The Global City*, Princeton University Press (Princeton, NJ).

Scruton, R 1979. *The Aesthetics of Architecture*, Methuen (London).

Simons, LM 1998. 'Indonesia's plague of fire', *National Geographic*, vol 194, no 2 (August 1998).

Soddy F, 1926. *Wealth, Virtual Wealth and Debt*, Omni Publications (Hawthorne, CA), reprinted 1961.

Soddy, F 1922. *Cartesian Economics: The Bearing of Physical Science upon State Stewardship*, Hendersons (London).

Soddy, F 1933. *Money versus Man*, Hendersons (New York).

Speight, ME 1989. 'The Great House (no 112 Corve Street 1270–1980)', Ludlow Research Paper, Studio Press (Birmingham).

SRO (Shropshire Records Office) 1997. Paper no. 356, box 321. Shrewsbury, Shropshire.

SSDC (South Shropshire District Council) 1997–8. Discussion paper and questionnaire: 'Sustainability and the Local Plan', SSDC Offices, Ludlow, Shropshire.

SSLP (South Shropshire Local Plan) 1996–2006. South Shropshire District Council, Ludlow, Shropshire.

Stanford, SC 1967. 'Croft Ambrey Hillfort'(transcript), Woolhope Natural Field Club, Hereford County Records Office, Hereford.

Sustainability Symposium, Architectural Association 1997. AA Files nos 32, 34, Architectural Association (London).

Szokolay, SV 1996. *Solar Geometry*, University of Queensland Press (St Lucia).

Taylor, D 1996. 'The Design Challenge'. Lecture given at Sustainability Symposium 1, Architectural Association (London).

Von Thunen, JH.'The Isolated State'. Taken from: Hawkes, D 1996 'The Environmental Tradition', Spon London.

Von Weizsacker E, Lovins, AB and Lovins, LH 1997. *Factor Four (Doubling Wealth Halving Resource Use)*, Earthscan Publications (London).

Voysey, B 1972. 'Forestry', cited in Hodgson 1972, *op cit.*

Wakeham, O 1892. 'Some leaves from the records of the court quarter sessions for the county of Salop', cited in Hodgson 1972, *op cit.*

Watson, M and Musson, C 1993. *Shropshire from the Air*, Shropshire Books (Shrewsbury).

Wilson, DR 1982. *Air Photography Interpretation for Archaeologists*, Batsford (London).

Worldwatch Institute, 1990. Cited in Von Weiszacker *et al* 1997.

Yannas, S 1996. 'The demise of brute force engineering', AA Files no 32, Architectural Association (London).

Yannas, S 1998. 'Living with the city. Urban design and environmental sustainability' in *Environmentally Friendly Cities*, James and James (London). Proceedings of PLEA (Passive and Low Energy Architecture) international conference 1998.

Acknowledgements

The research for this book has brought me great enjoyment through contact with many people and organizations of which there are but a few listed here.

I would like to thank Simos Yannas and Brian Ford for the inspiration they gave during the research period of my PhD in the Environment and Energy Department at the Architectural Association. Their work has been instrumental in my thinking and approach to considerations of environment and energy. I am grateful to Peter Halls, GIS Advisor at York University, who patiently discussed matters of Sustainability and the Natural World and never let me forget the need to appropriately balance the scientific with the human response.

In both case studies I was fortunate to gain specific local knowledge through communication with the following people and organizations. In San Gimignano and locality: Pietro Toeska, art historian and philosopher; Dr. Giovani Flores, geologist; Stefano Bartalesi, geologist; Marco Magni, architect; Padre Vittorio Benucci, Convento Capuccini, Poggio Al Vento, Observationi, Siena, meteorological information; Professor Mario Serchi, translation of early manuscripts of San Gimignano; Comune di San Gimignano, Amministrazione Provinciale, Ufficio del Turismo and Ufficio dell'Agricoltura; and Stefano Stampa who often acted as translator. In Ludlow and locality: David Lloyd, architectural historian; David Bole of Forest Enterprises; Mr. D Small, local meteorological information; Ludlow Civic Society; and South Shropshire District Council.

I am grateful to the architectural practices, The Millennium Consortium, Edward Cullinan, Architects and William McDonough and Partners for their cooperation and supply of information regarding some of their current projects in Chapter Eight. The Society of Authors kindly gave permission for the use of poems taken from A E Housman's 'A Shropshire Lad'; and The University of Washington Press for permission to use two diagrams, which first appeared in 'The Wright Space' by Grant Hildebrand.

I would like to thank my own publisher, John Wiley and Sons Ltd, especially my editors Maggie Toy, Mariangela Palazzi-Williams and Abigail Grater for seeing this book through to completion.

In researching and writing this book I have met many new people whose friendship and interest has made the experience particularly pleasurable. I would like to thank wholeheartedly, Gulliana and Pietro Maddelena, and Alan and Rosemary Laurie for giving me a sense of place.

And finally, and most significantly, I would like to thank those members of my family and close friends who have given unfailingly of their love and support.

PHOTO CREDITS

Every effort has been made to contact and credit all copyright holders, but in case of any errors or omissions, our apologies are extended.

All photos and drawings courtesy of the author or the architects featured, with the exception of the following: fig 1 IPCC; fig 2,3 and 4 reproduced courtesy of Kogan Page from Earnst von Weizsacker, Amory B Lovins and L Hunter Lovins, *Factor Four*, 1997, Earthscan; fig 5a and 5b © Kisho Kurokawa Architect & Associates reproduced with permission from Kurokawa, *Each One an Hero*, 1997; fig 13 and 14 © S V Szokolay, from S V Szokolay, *Solar Geometry*, 1996, University of Queensland Press; fig 16 reproduced by kind permission from Michael Faraday, *Ludlow 1085-1660*, 1991, Phillimore & Co Ltd, Shopwyke Manor Barn, Chichester, West Sussex, PO20 2BG; page 158 photograph reproduced courtesy of The Ludlow Advertiser; page 178 diagrams from Grant Hildebrand, *The Wright Space*, University of Washington Press, 1991, reprinted with permission of the University of Washington Press

1789 137